Unleashed:

The Story Of

TOOL

Joel McIver

This book is dedicated to future headbangers Max Hogben, Amelia Bradbury and Alex Cooper, born in 2008.

Unleashed: The Story Of TOOL

JOEL McIVER

OMNIBUS PRESS

LONDON / NEW YORK / PARIS / SYDNEY / COPENHAGEN / BERLIN / MADRID / TOKYO

Exclusive Distributors
Music Sales Limited,
14/15 Berners Street,
London, W1T 3LJ.

Music Sales Corporation,
257 Park Avenue South,
New York, NY 10010, USA.

Macmillan Distribution Services,
56 Parkwest Drive
Derrimut, Vic 3030,
Australia.

Every effort has been made to trace the copyright holders of the photographs in this book but one or
two were unreachable. We would be grateful if the photographers concerned would contact us.

Typeset by: Phoenix Photosetting, Chatham, Kent
Printed by: Gutenberg Press Ltd, Malta

A catalogue record for this book is available from the British Library.

Visit Omnibus Press on the web at www.omnibuspress.com

Contents

Introduction

Things really shouldn't have worked out for Tool, but against all the odds, they did. Here's why.

Popular music is called 'popular' for a reason: because a lot of people like it. People usually enjoy it because it's friendly, or warm, or moving, or thought-provoking. The greatest popular musicians of the six decades of pop so far have all known one simple truth: that to make popular music, you have to have an audience, and to have an audience, you have to connect with people. Connections are most easily formed through music when the message or emotion contained in a song is simple, direct and easily understood.

There is nothing simple, direct or easily understood about the American rock quartet Tool, but they've sold close to 10 million albums over a two-decade career that shows no sign of slowing down, won a fistful of Grammy awards from a panel of industry experts who should really hate them, topped charts all over the world and still stayed on their own resolutely individual path. There was nothing easy about their rise to worldwide prominence, which is, of course, why you're holding a 100,000-word book that goes into rather more detail than the opening sentence of this introduction.

"Most people think, 'What are you guys about? Explain yourselves, your music, your videos,'" complained Tool's guitarist Adam Jones in 1997, adding "Why do we have to explain everything?" He had a point, and one that is made repeatedly throughout this book. The eye of the beholder is everything, say Tool, who refuse to publish their lyrics in their CD booklets, go too deeply into the meanings of their songs (apart from a few notable exceptions, as you'll see), appear in their videos or perform many interviews. Disassociating their identities from their music, they believe, frees their songs to mean whatever the listener chooses, unshackled by the parameters of conventional thought. Deep stuff for a band that started out as just another pack of Los Angeles head-bangers...

It's time for a Tool biography for two important reasons. First, the band are at the pinnacle of their career, issuing albums every four or five years as they see fit and redefining the face of rock music every time they do so. They may have started out on the club circuit, struggling to get their message across to every punk fanzine that would talk to them, but these days Tool are practically rock royalty, issuing edicts from on high when the whim takes them. Secondly, times have changed in rock music: the emergence of the progressive metal genre reveals that there is a market for music that is traditionally regarded as 'difficult' – music that only reveals its rich inner complexity after significant investment by the listener. Spin a Tool album a few times, especially one of their more recent releases, and the journey you'll take will be long, rich, psychedelic, heart-stoppingly beautiful and not a little terrifying. This vibrant intricacy has been a key element of progressive rock by Yes, ELP, Caravan, King Crimson and others since the Seventies, but a new wave of bands such as Opeth and Meshuggah have accompanied Tool on the second leg of the progressive journey, supported by millions of fans. The times, they are a-changing – again.

This book shows you how Tool fit into this haze of evolution. A couple of decades will be needed to reveal where they really fit into the pantheon of music, but until then, let these words show you the way.

Joel McIver, 2009
www.joelmciver.co.uk
joel@joelmciver.co.uk

Acknowledgements

Writers: Mark Brend, Steffan Chirazi, Ian Christe, Neil Daniels, Bernard Doe, Malcolm Dome, John Doran, Rob Dwyer, Murray Engleheart, Ian Fletcher, Gillian Gaar, Ian Glasper, Ross Halfin, Bill Irwin, Jake Kennedy, Christof Leim, Dave Ling, Joe Matera, Metalion, Greg Moffitt, Martin Popoff, Greg Prato, Steven Rosen, Joe Shooman, Tommy Udo, Jonathan Wingate, Henry Yates

Editorial staff: Adrian Ashton (*Bass Guitar*), Scott Rowley, Sian Llewellyn, Ian Fortnam, Geoff Barton (*Classic Rock*), Albert Mudrian (*Decibel*), Paul Brannigan, Nick Ruskell (*Kerrang!*), Alex Milas, Alex Burrows, James Gill, Caren Gibson, Jonathan Selzer (*Metal Hammer*), Alan Lewis, Jason Draper, Spencer Grady, Tim Jones, Ian Shirley (*Record Collector*), Phil Ascott, Chris Barnes (*Rhythm*), Steve Lawson, Claire Davies, Nick Cracknell, Lucy Rice (*Total Guitar*)

Industry personnel: Mike Exley (AFM), Darren Toms (Candlelight), Sarah Lees (Century Media), Joolz Bosson (Cooking Vinyl), Ron Veltkamp (Displeased), Talita Jenman, Dan Tobin (Earache), Sarah Vincent, Debra Geddes, William Luff, Tom Wegg-Prosser (EMI), Lars Chriss (Escapi), Andy Turner, Will Palmer, Andreas Reissnauer (Metal

Blade), Zoe Miller (Mute), Jaap Wagemaker (Nuclear Blast), Matt Vickerstaff (Peaceville), Richard Dawes (Polydor), Michelle Kerr, Kirsten Lane (Roadrunner), Scott Bartlett (Scream), Alex Herron (Scuzz TV), Sabiene Goudriaan (Season Of Mist), Andy Lewis, Chas Chandler (Union Square), Daryl Easlea (Universal), Phoebe Sinclair, Ben Hopkins (Warners), Chris Charlesworth, Helen Donlon, Sarah Bacon, Michael Ohst (Omnibus Press and Bosworth), Laurence Baker, Dave Clarke, Tina Korhonen, Gary Levermore, Kas Mercer, Jarrod McMaugh, Ravi and Kim Parsan, Marc Riley, Clint Weiler, Ian Whent

'Part Of Me': Emma, Alice and Tom above all, Robin and Kate, Dad, John and Jen, Naomi, the brothers Freed, the Corky Nips, Physt, Voon, Carlos Anaia, Bret Devooght, Jo Herbert, Tim Jolliffe, Jonathon Kardasz, Frank Livadaros, Billy Pilhatsch, Ian Salsbury, Louise Sugrue, Dora Wednesday, Elton Wheeler, the families Barnes, Bhardwaj, Bird, Cadette, Carr, Clark, Cooper, Edwards, Ellis, Eschapasse-Carr, Everitt-Bossmann, Foster, Gunn, Harrington, Hoare, Hogben, Houston-Miller, Johnston, Knight, Lamond, Legerton, Leim, Maynard, Miles, Parr, Sendall, Sorger, Tominey, Tozer and Woollard.

Chapter 1

Before 1989

"Progressive" means never having to stick to one point of view.
Here's an example. Danny Carey, future drummer for the most
unsettling rock band of them all, was born on 10 May, 1961. Then again,
he might argue that the true story of Tool had actually begun several
millennia before that, when the consciousness of mankind first took true
shape. What's the truth?

Born close to the dead centre of the USA in Lawrence, Kansas, Carey
enjoyed a secure upbringing, but not one that offered much chance to
deviate from the usual path. As he recalled, "I grew up in a very typical,
middle-class American house. My dad was manager for a large insurance
company and my mom was a school teacher. I have one older brother
and one younger brother, and we were raised to value education. My dad
is really into music, though, and my earliest musical memory was when
he took me into the music library at the University of Kansas and played
The Planets by Gustav Holst. That just blew my mind. I was only a little
kid at the time, but it made such an impression on me that, from then
on, I think I was musically aware."

As he later recalled, "I guess I was around 10 when I got my first snare
drum; it was at that age that I started playing with the school band. It was

the first time my parents were willing to sacrifice their peace and quiet, I think. I guess up to that point, I was just listening to Beatles records, The Who, and my older brother's records. That was kind of what got me into music. My dad was somewhat musical, he played saxophone and he always had music playing around the house, mostly classical and big band… He'd buy us records once in a while when we bugged him enough, which was pretty cool."

Like so many others of his generation, Carey was inspired by stadium rock, saying: "I guess one of the most inspiring things was probably the first time I went to see a full-on concert, I went and saw Lynyrd Skynyrd play… It blew me away, and from that point, I knew I really wanted to try and do something like that. The biggest force I had pushing me was my desire not to have a boss – I was never into working for somebody who seemed like a nitwit, or having a regular type of job or anything. It always made more sense to me to keep on going to school and keep pursuing music. I started getting more and more into the artists and reading about them and looking to take it to another place and start building bridges."

In 1964, James Herbert Keenan was born four states to the east of Carey, in the town of Ravenna, Ohio. While Danny's middle-class family stifled him with convention, Keenan's upbringing was almost diametrically opposed: his parents divorced when he was four and his father moved to Michigan, the start of a decade of insecurity that saw Keenan switch homes and schools on a regular basis. He has described this period of flux in some detail, both in allegorical form in his songs and more explicitly in interviews. His mother, Judith's, remarriage and the introduction of a stepfather into the young James' life (he only adopted the forename 'Maynard' in his late teens) only exacerbated the insecurity of his youth. Understandably, a certain cynicism informed later statements such as "I think most of us grew up in a pretty sterile environment, [where] everything is pretty much peaches and cream and flowers. Everything's nice, ignore all the bad stuff. And the world's just not like that, and I think that the sooner people get to the point that the ugly stuff is just as real as the beautiful stuff, that it goes hand in hand, then we can go on evolving."

In contrast, not much is known about Adam Jones' early life. He was born in 1965 in Libertyville, Illinois, and played the violin as a child in elementary school. However, he has said that music was part of his life from an early stage: "We always had a guitar sitting in our house. My dad was self-taught, and he showed me some chords. Then my brother and I would jam together and make really bad music."

Like Carey – but not Keenan, whose interest in music was sparked a few years later – Adam seems to have been committed to music from his earliest years, recalling in later interviews that the first LP he ever bought was Michael Jackson's *Ben*, released in 1972 when he was seven years old. He recalled, "I played violin when I was a kid, and I can't tell you how many times someone tried to kick my ass while I was walking home from school. My violin case usually prevented my head from smacking really hard against the pavement! But I didn't let that stop me, because I really liked playing, and I had a good teacher. He played Monty Python music for me, and did these really absurd things. He made me appreciate that music could be serious and fun. One time, we had a recital for the parents, and just before we went on, he gave us all toy guns, and said, 'OK, at this particular point, I want you to stand up and start shooting at the other side of the orchestra'."

In 1967, Paul D'Amour was born in Spokane, Washington – a town which he sarcastically referred to as the "home of *America's Most Wanted*". Like Danny and Adam, he was a musician from a young age, with an added passion for films that focused his attentions on Los Angeles, south of his home state.

By the mid-Seventies all four boys were showing a serious interest in music and the arts. Carey in particular was the first to notice the difference between his own ambitions as a musician, having discovered a love of the drums at an early age, and those of his parents. As he said, "My dad also played saxophone a little bit, but he wasn't at all into playing like I was into drumming, and I think it took my parents aback a little when I started getting into drums. They came from an era of that hard-core work ethic, and they didn't necessarily see music and drumming as the most responsible way to go through life." Despite this, Danny had begun playing the snare drum in his high school's marching band in 1972 and graduated to a full drum kit two years later. "I was lucky to have some really good teachers who had open minds and were passionate about music without being strict disciplinarians about doing things in certain ways," he recalled – an invaluable aid for the free-thinking approach he later honed.

In 1975 Keenan's mother suffered a stroke that left her partly paralysed. Two years later – on his mother's suggestion – the now 13-year-old boy went to live with his father in Michigan, one of six states in which he lived as a child. An undesired constant was his family's Christian belief: as he later noted, "I was raised a Southern Baptist. I witnessed first-hand the hypocrisy of this particular form of Christianity." The fundamental difficulties of Keenan's upbringing – a staunchly traditional religion, plus a lack of any permanent physical grounding – seem to lie at the heart of his unorthodox path later in life. After graduating from high school in 1980, he made a truly strange career choice, as we'll see.

Meanwhile, by the end of the Seventies Adam was playing guitar, bass guitar and upright bass as well as the violin. Attending Libertyville High School, he formed a garage band called Electric Sheep (not, it has been stated, named after the Philip K Dick book *Do Androids Dream Of Electric Sheep?*) with another student, Tom Morello, as well as singer Chris George, drummer Ward Wilson and keyboard player Randy Cotton. Jones played bass in this band, formed in 1980 simply for fun. As Morello later recalled, the group formed haphazardly: "One day, outside our drama club, we formed a band. Adam wasn't in the original line-up. There was this one guy who was sort of the principal player in the band – he was the only one in the group with any working knowledge of music – but he quit because he thought that he was far above us. Adam was his replacement. He was playing bass at the time. I was playing guitar."

Jones added: "Well, I played stand-up bass in the orchestra and I'd play bass with my brother, too. He'd play the guitar parts, and I'd play all the bass parts to Police songs or Fleetwood Mac or Chicago or whatever he was into at the time. I was just so excited to officially be in a band. Of course, I had to borrow a bass because I didn't have one of my own."

The songs Electric Sheep wrote were semi-punkish and lightweight (typical titles were 'Oh Jackie O' and 'She Eats Razors'), although Morello – who found fame a decade later with the über-political band Rage Against The Machine – did nail his colours to the mast with

'Salvador Death Squad Blues'. The band didn't last long, although they did contribute a cover of 'Born To Be Wild' by Steppenwolf to the 1982 live LP of a Libertyville High School talent show. There's also a video of the band contributing spoof interviews and a live performance from a gig called The Electric Sheep Farewell Tour Of The Americas.

As Electric Sheep came to the end of their brief and unpopular existence, across the country James Keenan had made a startling decision. On graduating from high school, he elected to join the US Army. "It was basically, 'Let me do the most ridiculous, illogical thing I can think of,'" he later said. "'And after that, if it's not right, I'll know it's not right.'" He added that he knew it wasn't the right decision for him "as soon as the bus pulled out of the parking lot. Realising I just... fucked... up."

Serving a period as an observer before embarking on a course of study in New Jersey at the United States Military Academy Preparatory School (known informally as West Point Prep School), Keenan added the name 'Maynard' to his forename and worked on his physical fitness, running in the school's cross-country team and planning for a future course of study at the famous West Point itself – the United States Military Academy in upstate New York – where America's most notable military officers have trained. This didn't come to pass, inevitably: the famously left-field elements of Keenan's character may not have been as fully developed as they are today, but he knew enough about dissension and the horrors of conformity to break away from the army before any long-term commitment. "It was a learning experience," he explained. "You can really learn a lot about human nature, because for the best part you're dealing with the worst parts of every walk of life – predominantly fucking ignorant people and followers. You can learn a lot about others, and in particular about yourself."

The military life also taught Keenan something about tolerance, or the lack of it. Although he was heterosexual, his fellow army recruits' attitudes to the many gay members of the academy disgusted him deeply. "I'll tell you something," he once observed. "I was in the army, and half of the people I knew were gay, and they were the ones that were running the fucking thing, running it better than the other idiots who were drinking cases of beer a night. What the fuck is the surprise here? You know... 'We don't want no fags in our military'. Bullshit! They're

5

already there, and they're doing a better job than you are! Go work on
your Camaro, and let them take care of it. Just because they have a different sexual motivation than you doesn't mean they can't shoot a gun
or defend our country or do a good job with what they're doing. We
need to get on evolving to the next step, whatever the next step is; most
of us have our thumbs.

"You'd think that integration would end up breaking down barriers,"
he went on, "but all it does is strengthen them. It's pretty sad. Then again,
the people put in the room together are pretty much poisoned before
they get there, so then they see a stereotype, and they hate that guy even
more now... But [homosexuals] are humans and being gay is just the way
they are. As soon as we figure out that [homosexuality] is a part of some
humans and has been an integral part of our society as long as we've
been in existence, the sooner we can accept that and get on to evolving."

A career in art seemed much more appropriate to him, and although
he was offered a place at West Point, he bailed out for a place at the
Kendall College Of Art And Design in Grand Rapids, Michigan – a
place opposed in every conceivable way to the strict regimen of his previous alma mater. Even in his earliest years, Keenan knew that he wanted
to do something artistic, as he explained: "Remember in elementary
school, at the end of the year you have that thing – who your best friend
was, and what you did, and what you learned, and what you wanted to
be when you grow up? I always had the 'Artist' box checked. And I
wasn't really sure what that meant. I have a beautiful photo of me on my
living room rug, and I have this big plastic rifle and I'm aiming it at my
little sister's little stuffed rabbit on the ground, I've got the classic velour
shirt on. To the left of me, on the ground, is Ted Nugent's *Cat Scratch
Fever* [LP]… I've always been one of those people who likes the balance,
so it seems like if you're going to sit down with your family and say,
'Look, I'm going to put on a tie-dye shirt to pursue an artistic career,'
and they say, 'But...', I can say, 'Hey, I was in the army and I didn't like it'.
I've seen that point of view, and although I can relate to it, it's not what
I want to do. I didn't necessarily fit in, as in blend in. It's definitely a
chauvinistic situation. No matter how you look at it, in the military
there are two orientations; you're a dyke or a whore. There's no escaping
it. You're pegged so hard. Ninety per cent of my friends in the military

6

were either gays or lesbians. Most of them kept getting called in and interrogated. I actually had a contract marriage with a lesbian so she could maintain her status."

At Kendall, Keenan was able to exercise his musical talents freely, joining a band in 1986 called Tex & The Anti-Nazi Squad, usually abbreviated to Tex A.N.S. and pronounced simply 'Texans'. The band, in which he played bass, existed for a year or so and recorded one demo, *Live At Sons And Daughters Hall*, which featured a cover version of Alice Cooper's 'Is It My Body?'. Along with singer Tex Porker, guitarist Kevin Horning, drummer Tom Geluso and keyboardist Mike Meengs, Keenan played a brand of humorous alternative rock that didn't make much of an impact, although internet videos of him singing "Suck my ass!" behind Porker's lead vocal are surreally entertaining. A more impressive band was Children Of The Anachronistic Dynasty, another Grand Rapids band that Keenan and Horning worked on after Tex A.N.S. folded: while Horning played guitar, Maynard expanded his remit by programming a drum machine as well as singing and playing bass. CAD's best-known recording was a demo called *Fingernails,* although a later EP called *Dog.House* is sought-after because of its scarcity.

Despite all these primitive efforts at music-making, Keenan seemed destined for a different career, and his awareness of visual arts expanded. As graduation from Kendall approached in 1988, he pondered his future – and like Carey and Jones, he looked westward for his next move.

Meanwhile, Danny Carey had completed a degree at the prestigious Conservatory Of Music in Kansas City. As he said: "Even when I was in high school, from my first concert experience of watching Lynyrd Skynyrd, I had the dream of, 'Wow! This is what I want to do'. I didn't know how realistic it was, and it took me a while to make that commitment. I had a scholarship to go to the Conservatory Of Music, so I did that. It was mainly oriented in classical music, although they did have a jazz band I played in. I'd read some charts in high school and did more of it in college."

So much of Carey's drumming style was honed at this college that he continued to refer to it even several years later, enthusing: "They have a pretty good-sized Conservatory Of Music there, and a big performing arts centre that had just been built a few years before I graduated. It was great!… It was dance and theatre and music and art and everything all close together… There was all the legit music there, orchestras and all that, and also there were jazz programmes and percussion ensembles. It was a really good environment."

Carey's love of the drums was almost matched by his talent for basketball, a sport at which he excelled, being six feet five inches tall. "I always did have a love of basketball," he said. "I even had a couple of offers to play at small colleges. But I knew I wasn't good enough to play major college basketball or to go pro. I also didn't have the desire to go that far with it… music was always my main interest. The coach at my school asked me to play, but I didn't want to sacrifice what I had going on with music in bands and at the Conservatory just to play ball… The thing about music was I never really had to work very hard at it. I took lessons and I practised, but things just sort of happened for me. I'm a person who really just goes with the flow and doesn't try to force anything. I think most Americans have a hard work ethic and they just want to achieve things for the sake of money, power and ego."

Carey, the oldest of the four musicians, was the first to move to Los Angeles from the American interior. More driven than Keenan, Jones or D'Amour by his musical instincts (the other three all had parallel interests in film and the other visual arts), he knew that the traditional hub of the West Coast music industry would offer him the most opportunities. Although it took him a while to find his niche, he landed on his feet in spectacular fashion, scoring studio gigs with Carole King and live sessions with Pigmy Love Circus and Green Jelly. LA was a revelation for him compared with his home town, of which he said: "Where I grew up, it was like a *River's Edge* type of thing. Everyone just smoked dope all the time. There was no emotional value in anything we did – it seriously was about that grim – people would die or whatever, and you were just like, 'You know, just burnouts'. It's great for me to find something that has feeling or emotional value. That's my goal."

Pondering his decision to move to LA, Danny said: "I played in bands during college and stuff in Kansas City, and I felt like I had finally gotten about as far as I could go, we were packing out clubs, but it didn't seem like there was any potential of taking it to the next level… We'd do original things, but never made any money. So I'd have to play in cover bands at the same time. That was kind of dull, nothing too interesting usually, but it was better than stacking dishes or something like that. I did that til I saved up enough money and made the move. I just bailed out to LA, I got a day job for a while and just started going through the wanted ads out there, 'Bands looking for drummer' and all that. I didn't know anyone there. It took a while to develop a circle of friends that I felt I had something in common with. A lot of times I'd go in to auditions, and usually they'd want me to play with them. But usually there'd [only] be one person there that seemed worthwhile."

He went on: "So I'd go to maybe three or four of these things and then kinda pick out the best players I thought were there and give them a call, and say, 'Hey, come and jam at this rehearsal space', and see if something worked out. I put together a couple of bands like that. Then after a while you just meet enough people and start falling into some studio gigs, playing for sitcoms, doing the changeovers when they're moving their cameras for the live audience, and stuff like that. I ended up meeting some of the guys from Carole King's band and then I ended up getting to play with her a little bit – it all kinda snowballed from that."

Despite his success as a session musician, Carey felt that his real talents lay elsewhere: "I'd been out here a good three or four years before things started really happening for me. Like anybody else who comes out to LA, you're totally lost, so you start looking in [newspapers] like *Recycler* and *Music Connection* for auditions that are worthwhile. And you end up wading through a lot of crap before you find something that might be promising. It's an experience everybody should go through... it wasn't until after I was 25 [in 1986] and after I moved out to LA... that I decided to take every project I could get my hands on and make it a do-or-die situation. Otherwise, I was just going to let it be a hobby. I learned pretty quickly in LA that even if you're in a hot band, things might not happen for you. So I figured the more irons I had in the fire, the better my chances were. I liked playing in all kinds of musical situations, but I never had any aspirations of being a session player. I always wanted to be in a band environment."

A similar career arc lay in wait for Jones, who, on leaving high school was offered a place at film school in Illinois, having decided to pursue a career in movie arts. However, he too chose to move to LA, signing up at the Hollywood Make-up Academy and then landing a job at Rick Lazzarini's Character Shop, a well-known supplier of special effects for the film industry. Life in LA was tough at first. "When I first moved here," recalled Jones, "I lived down on Normandie [one of the streets worst affected by the LA riots of April 1992], and you'd hear gunfire every night. I was trying to get into school, get a job, thinking, 'LA sucks'. My motorcycle was hit twice while it was parked. All this bad stuff was happening."

Jones' speciality was creating lifelike props for action and horror films: his work can be seen in *Ghostbusters 2* (for which he created a zombie head affixed to a spike), a skull for the famous scene in *Predator 2* where a collection of skeletal trophies is seen attached to a wall, and items for other blockbusters such as *Terminator 2: Judgment Day* and *Jurassic Park*. In the light of his later, more famous work, it's interesting to note that he was responsible for the design of a repellent Freddy Krueger *in utero*, seen in *A Nightmare on Elm Street 5: The Dream Child*. Not bad for a kid from the sticks, you'll agree.

Although Carey and Jones soon found their place in the crazed, plastic world of Eighties Los Angeles, it didn't work out quite so quickly for Paul D'Amour and Maynard James Keenan – who, like Jones, came to LA to pursue a career in film. Keenan found himself working at a pet store, one of a chain called Petland, where he specialised in interior design while attempting to branch out into stand-up comedy alongside performers such as Bob Odenkirk. While film work eluded him, he did have time to add guest vocals to a song by Carey's occasional band Green Jelly (who called themselves Green Jello at first, before being sued by the owners of the Jello foodstuff), which became a bona fide indie hit – a song called 'Three Little Pigs'. Carey recalled this unlikely success, saying: "I met some of the bands that were playing around in Hollywood and I ended up playing with the Green Jello guys... [who were] a cabaret type thing... lots of costumes, it wasn't all heavy metal, it was more pop and disco, just all sorts of styles, it was really a wide variety of things going on and it was more about the show, really, than the music. They ended up getting a record deal and they even had a hit for a while called 'Three Little Pigs', that got played quite a bit."

By 1989 Carey, Jones, Keenan and D'Amour were all resident in Los Angeles, struggling to get by without letting go of their respective ambitions – which, apart from Danny, didn't include major success as musicians. Many of the most dedicated musicians in the world, who strive for their every waking moment to make it in the music industry, fail to achieve anything despite their best efforts. What chance, then, did this disparate foursome from the wilds of hick-town America have, when they didn't even want to be in a successful band?

Chapter 2

1989–1992

Unlike many music biographies, this book won't dwell too long on the roots of its subject. Tool came together with almost serendipitous ease, and there's a lot of incredibly detailed and surreal music to discuss in later chapters – so we'll be brief here.

Los Angeles is equally loved and hated by the thousands of musicians who live there, whether they're already successful or trying to make it a step further up the greasy pole – but they go there anyway. The chances of anyone making a living by playing a musical instrument are slim wherever you live, but if your plan is to meet like-minded people to play together, you need to be as close to the industry as you can. This was the case with the future members of Tool, who landed radically differing gigs on their arrival in the city.

Maynard James Keenan, now some years clear of the army and a fully-fledged visual artist, could do a bit of everything – stand-up comedy, singing, playing guitar and bass, drawing – as well as his unexpected skills at pet-store design. Jones had his job as a special effects designer in the movie business. Carey was the first to find himself a genuinely important role, with his three gigs with Carole King, Pigmy Love Circus and Green Jelly gaining him some exposure to the great and the good of the music

13

business. He also scooped a role as the drummer in the in-house band on a TV sitcom titled *Sibs*, a short-lived ABC series that ran until 1992. The last of these roles suited him best, as he recalled: "They were all great gigs, especially the TV show, because I got to play James Brown and Sly & The Family Stone material. I'd never been hip on the Sixties music because it was before my time. I was more into the Seventies-era bands, like Led Zeppelin, so I learned a lot from that. And I was also playing in a country band with the bass player from Carole's band. So it was rehearsals or gigs every night… I was also working a day gig. I was literally sleeping three to four hours a night and playing the rest of the day. It got to be too much."

Coincidentally, Keenan lived in a room above Carey's apartment, and the two men got to know each other simply from inhabiting the same building. Green Jelly, the comedy act, was Carey's longest-standing gig. The band, who played heavy rock with an anarchic edge, featured several vocalists – prominent among them Bill 'Moronic Dictator' Manspeaker – and had signed an unlikely deal with BMG subsidiary label Zoo after six years of club-level success and a series of indie releases. Pitching themselves as a video-only band – a concept that might just fly in the pre-internet era – Green Jelly convinced the label to offer them $50,000 for the production of a video album, a series of promo clips on a VHS tape. This later appeared as the *Cereal Killer* album, whose most memorable song was 'Three Little Pigs', a minor radio hit notable for its claymation video and backing vocals (the falsetto "Not by the hairs on my chinny chin-chin!") from Keenan – the first time that two of the future Tool members had collaborated on a recording. The video is a distinctly recognisable blend of black humour and wacky cartoon homages, with a slightly sinister tone that hints directly at what was to come.

Here's the thing. Green Jelly's considerable body of work may look as cutting-edge today as Ugly Kid Joe or any of the other lightweight comedy-rock acts of the early Nineties, but they laid down more of the foundations of Tool than many observers might think. *Cereal Killer* was produced by the veteran Sylvia Massy, who was influential in shaping Tool's early sound; the album consisted partly of Claymation promo clips; and it combined humour and malevolence, as well as being pushed along musically by Carey.

"Green Jello [the band's former name] was how I met Maynard," recalled Carey later. "He actually moved in to the loft next door with the Green Jello guys... He would come out and do different things, I don't know if you'd really call it singing, a lot of it was more like acting or comedy or something like that, it was pretty much of a big variety show."

Things started to move quickly, and in 1990 Keenan – who had decided to form a band of his own – began looking for musicians to jam with. Carey offered Maynard the use of his practice room, and one of the first musicians whom the latter invited over to jam there was Adam Jones, who knew Keenan because he was a friend of a girl the singer was dating at the time. Although most of his creative energy went into his day job, Jones was also interested in starting a band, as he said: "I had been jamming with a bunch of different bands at the time, but none of them were really working out. Then one day, Maynard played me a tape of some joke band he was in [Green Jelly]. I just thought, 'Fuck, you can sing!' He really blew my mind. From that point on, I bugged him until he finally gave in and joined me."

The singer and guitarist cast around for a bassist and drummer, inviting several LA musicians to come over and play at their practice space. However, the as-yet-unnamed band couldn't find anyone reliable, as Carey laughed: "I had the rehearsal space right next door at that point, where I could play 24 hours a day if I wanted to, we could make all the noise we wanted. First [Maynard and Adam were] trying out things, [they] just wanted to use my space, but so many of the drummers in Hollywood are just flakes; a lot of times if they don't think it's a paying gig, they don't want to move their drum sets. My drums were there and when a guy would flake out I kinda felt sorry for them, and went ahead and jammed with them."

The first time this happened, a certain musical telepathy between the three musicians was evident, leading Danny to consider that perhaps this line-up could go further. This feeling was reinforced when Jones brought along bassist Paul D'Amour, whom he knew from his work in the film industry. Paul – who had qualified as a film technician – had ended up working in art departments on TV advertisements and rock videos (or, as he later put it, "jacking off the director... whatever it took").

15

"The second time, when it was the actual line-up, with Paul D'Amour and Adam and Maynard," recalled Danny, "there was definitely chemistry in the air! I knew it was something special so we continued doing it, kinda on a weekly schedule, and it kept going." Jones added: "I kept bugging [Keenan] to start a band on the side with me – just for fun. Danny lived downstairs from Maynard, and he didn't want to play with us. Then we had a practice session, and the guy who was supposed to drum for us didn't show up. So Danny felt sorry for us, and agreed to play. He said, 'Well, I'll sit in on the sessions, but that's it'. And he sat in and went, 'Wow, we should jam again'. We started rehearsing a couple of times a week, and pretty soon [we] became an actual band."

Not that any of them were immediately convinced of the band's long-term prospects. Carey had a lot going on at the time, as he explained: "I was playing for a TV show, I was playing with Carole [King], and I was playing with the Pigmy Love Circus, which was one of the biggest bands in Hollywood. They were packing out clubs too. I had so many things going on…" Most interestingly, he was also jamming with the young Jeff Buckley, son of the Sixties folk troubadour Tim Buckley, who had yet to make his landmark debut album *Grace* and – after his untimely death in 1997 – take his place in the pantheon of cult musicians who died too young.

"Jeff was an amazing musician," said Carey. "I felt lucky that I got to know him… he had gotten tired of the LA scene, and decided to move to New York. It wasn't long after that that he ended up making his *Grace* record. I remember some of the songs, I still have weird old demo tapes that he gave me of some of those songs that ended up on that record."

Adam Jones felt the same ambivalence as Carey about committing to a band seriously, as he had a full-time job – and their group was conceived merely as a hobby. However, when they started playing original songs, the net result sounded too good to pass up. Within weeks Jones and Carey's band were asked to play shows, requiring them to choose a name for themselves.

Their choice was impossible to ignore. To this day, no one knows whether to laugh when they hear that there's a globally successful rock band called Tool. Yes, Tool as in penis. Watch people's brows furrow as they wonder if there's a deeper meaning that they're missing – and in typical fashion, the band don't let anyone have a clear answer one way or the other. Maynard once famously put it, "Tool is exactly what it sounds like: it's a big dick. It's a wrench. It's also what it sounds like: it's a verb, it's a digging factor. It's an active process of searching, as in use us, we are a shovel, we are the match, we're the blotter of acid, your tool; use us as a catalyst in your process of finding out whatever it is you need to find out, or whatever it is you're trying to achieve."

He sort-of clarified: "A lot of times when people are listening to what we're doing, they see this really intense young band, Tool, and they think of this big, heavy wrench phallic thing. It's like we're gonna cut through everything like a wedge, like a missile, like some kind of cock-strong rock band, but there's totally this sense of humour and the other side, the serious approach to the world around us."

With a new name, a new line-up, new songs and a fresh attitude to heavy music in comparison with the established rock heavyweights of the day, Tool began to plan their next move. Live shows were obviously essential, and the band played a brief series of gigs in LA in May of 1991. Short, raw and devoid of the opulent light show that would characterise later Tool performances, these dates were poorly attended at first, although word of mouth soon ensured that a crowd grew.

"We started out playing in this little place in LA called the Gaslight, which later turned into a club called the Opium Den," remembered Carey. "The first time we played there, there would've been six or eight people – then next time those guys would show up and they'd bring all their friends, and it just kept snowballing like that. By the time we had done five or six shows at different little clubs, like the Coconut Teaser [and] the Central, all these places around Hollywood started packing out."

In late 1991 Tool cut a demo cassette, adorning it with an image designed by artist and friend of the band Cam de Leon of a wrench ('spanner' for UK readers) shaped like a phallus and scrotum. Said to have been recorded in order to attract record company attention (which is unlikely, given the band's lack of interest in the industry), the tape – known as *Tool, Toolshed* or the *72826* demo, depending on where you go for your information – contained three songs on each side. The raw, four-track versions of 'Cold And Ugly', 'Hush', 'Part Of Me', 'Crawl

Away', 'Sober' and 'Jerk-Off' are easily available through the internet and demonstrate clearly that Tool had raised their game spectacularly in the few months since they formed. Although the songs lack the scintillating clarity or the thunderous heaviness of the versions that appeared later, the unorthodox tone, left-field arrangements and the unnerving themes of sex and misery sounded decidedly different to those few music fans who heard them. The first of several dozen enduring Tool myths sprang up when someone pointed out that *72826*, tapped out on an alphanumeric phone keypad, equates to the word 'Satan'...

Among those few listeners, crucially, were a handful of record company reps, who snapped up the demo and passed it to their superiors in the corridors of power. Suddenly, it seemed that Tool was being taken seriously as a rock band; the musicians themselves were surprised by the reaction to their work. As Danny said, "Once the word spreads in LA, the record companies are like sharks: they start circling, looking for a piece of the action. They don't want something to get away from them. By the time we had done our seventh gig out in the clubs, they were there, inviting us to come and have meetings with them and wanting to sign us. But we were just laughing at them at first, because we weren't really looking to do that, it was really more like we were doing it just for our own sake. It wasn't like we were out looking for a deal."

Jones reinforced this *laissez-faire* attitude, adding: "We began playing out and had done about three or four gigs before being approached by A&R people. By our tenth gig, we had a bunch of record companies chasing us around... At first we all thought it was stupid. We didn't think we were any good. We didn't want to be musicians for a living; we already had jobs."

Carey laughed: "I mean, you can only imagine how strange it was for us when these record companies started making offers. There are a million bands out there banging their heads against the wall. They all want to get signed and we really didn't care. We all had our own lives. I was working with Green Jelly and that was in full swing. Adam was doing his special effects stuff with movies. We didn't need a record company to allow us to continue doing what we do. Tool was not the centre of our lives."

However, Keenan and D'Amour were less entrenched in their daily lives than the established professionals Jones and Carey, and were correspondingly more interested in the industry's approaches. The band began to take the offers seriously, and in due course were ready to sign a deal. Jones shrugged: "It [the band] was certainly something we all enjoyed. And making a living with it – what could be better? As long as we could do things our way as much as possible… Even though we all had steady jobs, when we got signed we said, 'OK, well, let's give this a try'. That's how I look at life. It's like you're surfing – you grab a wave and try to ride it as long as you can. And if you fall off, you can try to grab the same wave or go catch a different one. It was a little frustrating to have my parents going, 'What are you thinking?' But I loved music, and I wanted to give this an honest shot. I'm glad we did."

Carey was also persuaded to come on board, saying: "I'd been in Green Jelly for three years at that point, and Tool had only been together eight or nine months. But it wasn't a tough decision for me where to go, because Green Jelly was never a situation that any of us took seriously on a musical level. We were great fans and it was a lot of fun, which is why I think we became successful."

In the end it was Zoo Records, the BMG affiliate that had released Green Jelly's *Cereal Killer* video album, who secured the collective Tool signature. This was the label most prepared to concede artistic control to the band, in return for agreeing to a deal involving less money, as Carey explained: "We took our time to make sure we had complete control, from artwork and videos to advertising and content of music. It worked to our advantage not to be star-struck and greedy because we did get that complete control… We did not play the bidding game that some record companies wanted to play with us. It took a while after the initial interest for us to sign with Zoo. They were the first label to show interest in us. There is this thing in LA that once a label thinks you're good, they all think you're good. They all want a piece of the action and are afraid they might be missing something."

Keenan, Jones, D'Amour and Carey duly signed with Zoo and committed themselves full-time to the project. Of the four, Adam had the most to lose, having built a secure future for himself in movie special effects. As he said on quitting his job, "I worked for a make-up effects house, and everyone was convinced I'd be back in a month… To tell you the truth, I was pretty scared. I was worried that they might be right!"

Zoo's first move was to schedule the recording of an EP to introduce Tool to the music-buying public, with a single and video clip to be released to the media. Finishing 1991 with a New Year's Eve show at which songs were recorded for inclusion on the EP – projected for release in summer 1992 – Tool focused their energies on songwriting sessions. Right from the off, it was readily apparent that this was no ordinary band, with song lyrics that alternated between morbid introspection and venomous protest. Or at least, that was what people thought: Maynard James Keenan's abstract, often obscure words meant all things to all men, and he was often reluctant to share their meanings with his public. The rest of the band were privy to his thoughts, however – as Danny once said, "Oh, Maynard's willing to share it all with us. We have conversations about what the songs mean. I have a lot of respect for how much of his soul he's always willing to bear to everyone… it takes a lot of courage to do what he's done and continues to do. Maynard to me is the best singer out there. Let alone his persona and the way he can just pull it off… He's very conscious of making [his lyrics] able to be interpreted on a lot of different levels, and I'm sure he has his own interpretation that's probably far different to even to the one he shares with us."

Carey himself was far from the average rock drummer, bringing a fascination with the occult so deeply to the band that it had a permanent effect on the look of everything they did, right down to the set-up of Tool's rehearsal room. On the surface a tall, basketball-playing jock, Danny surprised many interviewers with the frank descriptions he gave of his songwriting process and gear setup. Some of what he has said over the years should be taken with a pinch of salt, however: as the official Tool website biography has it, after he sets up his drums ("utilising the circle and square of the New Jerusalem") he utters "a short prayer relating to the principles of the ace of swords from the book of Thoth", and he has "summoned a daemon he has contained within 'the Lodge' that has been delivering short parables similar to passages within the Book of Lies".

This kind of fascinating red-herring approach has always run through Tool: a constant strand that only the wisest can follow correctly. Note that Maynard has subtly warned that there is much sly wit inside the band, saying: "That's what people are kinda missing. There's humour sewn in to all the songs. Even if it comes down to something that a friend said that we thought was really funny and we completely write an entire verse surrounding this one statement that this person said. But then among this poetic dissertation… on the other side, there's also some real ugly things taken straight from nightmares in there, too."

While some of Danny's bio is bound to be sarcastic nonsense, Carey seems more serious when he discusses the setup of his drum kit: "My toms are set up in a harmonic fashion, to where all my energy flows uninterrupted. There's a symmetry to the way my toms are set up, and it's significant that I have five toms, a number that represents masculinity. Then I've got six six-sided [electronic] drums, which represent the female side. It just has to do with balance. I've studied some ancient geometry, and I feel this doesn't make as big a difference musically as it does for me personally. But that's why I try to bring a lot of these ideas into my natural environment, with all the geometric shapes and paint-ings on the walls and ceiling. It's all about setting my drums up so that I don't get in the way of the music, so I'm just a channel for the music." A large board with Enochian magic symbols is situated behind his kit in the rehearsal space, too, "so we could try to set up the proper mental and spiritual environment to record and create in".

Whatever the truth behind Tool's spiritual side – and it remains mys-terious to this day – it's apparent that things were working out well for them. In early 1992 the first Tool single was released, a song called 'Hush' from the *Tool* demo of the previous year. Read from a piece of paper, the lyrics look hilarious: the chorus runs, "I can't say what I want to, even if I'm not serious / Things like 'Fuck yourself, kill your-self, you piece of shit…' Just kidding!" However, under the overblown profanity lies a serious anti-censorship message: Maynard intones, "People tell me what to say, what to think and what to play", a theme that has been a mainstay of Tool's message for almost two decades. "Use us to achieve what you want to achieve," said Keenan when the band first chose their name, and an opening of the mind, an expansion of the ego, is clearly one of the achievements that they had in mind when they wrote 'Hush'.

The message of 'Hush' was hammered home even more clearly by its video clip, an understated black-and-white arthouse piece directed with devastating simplicity by Ken Andrews of the band Failure. The song starts with a funky, slightly distorted bass guitar riff from D'Amour, accompanied by a shot of two naked feet, one of which is tapping to the beat. The camera pans up the naked body of D'Amour (for it is he), stopping on a card that covers his crotch area and bears the Parental Advisory logo that has been affixed to so many CD cases since the Eighties, with the words 'Explicit Lyrics' replaced by 'Explicit Parts'. The song's main riff drops in, a heavy groove featuring a prominent rhythm section and introduced by Keenan's shriek of "Fuck you!" Meanwhile, D'Amour turns and walks away from the camera, revealing another Parental Advisory card covering his backside, towards the other three men, also naked except for the same cards obscuring the non-MTV-appropriate body parts. All four men have a black X of gaffer tape covering their mouths: the message is clear enough. A white, saliva-like goo starts to seep from each man's mouth; they rip off the gaffer tape and let it dribble down their chins; and as the video enters its final seconds, Carey and Keenan (the former a giant next to the diminutive singer, who is wearing a black hat) start to smirk knowingly.

In content, 'Hush' made perfect sense. After all, anyone listening to new American rock music from 1990 to 1992 will recall how strange that period was. In March 1992, when Tool released their first professional recording, music listeners were coming to the end of a couple of turbulent years: a sea-change had occurred in that brief time, thanks to three multimillion-selling records, each of which had paved the way for the huge wave of alternative rock that followed with Tool and certain other bands at its head. Understanding this process is key to understanding why Tool have been so popular in the years since then.

In 1990, when the four Tool musicians first met, heavy metal as we used to know it was coming to the end of an era of exceptional popularity. The Eighties had been an extremely fertile decade for metal worldwide, with the New Wave Of British Heavy Metal movement giving Iron Maiden and Def Leppard world-class status by 1982, Venom pioneering thrash metal and giving it to Metallica and Slayer to run with, black metal coming out of Norway, death metal emerging from Florida and Sweden and glam-metal erupting from the LA clubs to dominate the charts. The last of these bands were the closest to real contemporaries that Tool had, but their time was limited. Three albums ensured the defection of the hair-metal bands' fanbase, and thus their almost complete extinction for most of the Nineties.

The first of these albums came from Metallica. In summer 1991, that band released their fifth, self-titled album, a behemoth that went on to sell over 15 million units in the USA alone, let alone in the rest of the world. Endless amounts of text have been written about this record (for further Metallica information, the reader is politely directed to the author's 2004 book *Justice For All: The Truth About Metallica*, also published by Omnibus), but suffice it to say here that it didn't reject any of heavy metal's core values – it elevated and celebrated them. The riffs were bigger; the drums were heavier; and the lyrics stripped metal's preoccupation with death, violence and existential horror down to the bone. People loved it because it redefined heavy metal.

Simultaneously, the format of songs with big guitars was changed forever by Nirvana's *Nevermind*, released within weeks of *Metallica*. With none of the mature, stately confidence that infused the Metallica album but with a white-hot flame of hurt running through it, *Nevermind* showed the rock-buying public that you could write pop songs with hooks, fill them with lyrics about the corruption at society's heart and the basic agony of the human condition and still sound edgy.

Finally, just as Tool's EP was released in early 1992, the Red Hot Chili Peppers issued *Blood Sugar Sex Magik*, a funk/pop record that elevated them to the commercial stratosphere. The songs, which dealt with love, sex and drug abuse, were received with mighty acclaim by press and public, completing an expansion of the boundaries of rock that endured for the rest of the decade. The new-found emotional openness in metal (Metallica's James Hetfield bewailing his childhood in 'The Unforgiven'; Kurt Cobain of Nirvana framing his frustrations in 'Smells Like Teen Spirit'; the Chilis' Anthony Kiedis recounting how he injected heroin in 'Under The Bridge') led directly to grunge and – a little later – alternative rock bands such as Tool taking over the music scene for the next few years.

The importance of the timing of Tool's debut cannot be overstated. Five years before 1992, they would have been freaks, condemned to cult obscurity like Mr Bungle or Green Jelly; five years later and they would have been dismissed as bandwagon-jumpers. Heavy music's Year Zero, 1991, did the music-buying public a favour in more ways than one.

Chapter 3

1992-1993

"You're never sure what a major label is going to do with an album," said Paul D'Amour, "whether they're going to exploit every possible aspect and throw you out there and try to make you this big, hyped thing. So you kind of cripple them by giving them an EP they can't work with..."

When the six-track *Opiate* EP was released on 10 March 1992, no one – press, metal fans, label, anyone – knew what to do with it. The songs required too much investment by the listener to be instant hits; the artwork was disturbing; and there was far too much aggression in the music for radio to give it much airtime. The video for 'Hush' gave Tool some exposure, but the whole package was too relentless for mainstream success. This was, it seems, the band's intention, as D'Amour added: "[This] way you take it nice and slow and make a natural progression, rather than letting [the record company] do what they do best, which is interfere. Our label's cool, but there are a couple of people who aren't very creative, and they try to stereotype us because they don't get us."

Stereotyping seems to have been one of Tool's major bugbears from the very start of their career, specifically the way that they were immediately shoehorned into the heavy metal category thanks to the riff-weight of their songs. The metal elements of their sound were obvious, but the band applied certain aesthetic filters that took the songs up and beyond the usual expectations of the heavy metal fanbase – too far, in fact, for many. Tom Morello of Rage Against The Machine, whose own band debuted at about the same time, put it well when he said: "Their music has an intensity and heaviness that takes the absolute best elements of hard rock/heavy metal and drains all the bullshit out of it."

"When we were signed," commented Adam Jones, "we kept telling our label, 'Don't push us on all the metal stations. Don't push us with other metal bands'. But they did, because that's the only way they could see us. And that's what happened with the EP *Opiate*. We thought at the time that we should release the heaviest songs we had because those would make the most impact, but all it really did was force us into this little category. Which was ridiculous. Think about the metal bands that were around in '92: they were all glam bands. We didn't want to have anything to do with that."

He had a point. In 1992 the hair-metal scene was on its last legs, made obsolete by the big three rock/metal albums of that and the previous year by Metallica, Nirvana and the Red Hot Chili Peppers. The latter half of the Eighties had been dominated in heavy metal terms by bands who wore spandex pants, back-combed their hair into huge bouffant manes (held erect by entire cans of hairspray) and daubed their faces in panstick make-up. The glam-rock wave of the Seventies, spearheaded by David Bowie, Marc Bolan and The Sweet, which led directly to such excesses, was an adventurous piece of androgynous experimentation compared with the nauseatingly plastic version peddled by Poison, Warrant, Cinderella, Stryper, Faster Pussycat, Britny Fox, Ratt, Pretty Boy Floyd and a whole raft of other lipsticked goons. Only a few bands emerged from the hairspray scene with any credibility intact – Guns N'Roses, Motley Crüe and to some extent Twisted Sister – but even they were old news by the mid-Nineties.

Tool were disgusted by the glam-metal acts they saw around them in LA, and didn't hide their feelings on the subject. "We just went through some dark years in hard rock," said Carey. "I was losing faith in humanity. I could never understand how such theatrical stuff could have done anything for anyone. It never meant much to me, and it never inspired me to play. We play music we feel. If those guys feel what they play, I really feel sorry for them. There's always going to be lame music and it's made for the lowest denominator of people. Music is meant to bring people's level of consciousness up, not to drag it down to the masses."

Keenan was a little more charitable, musing: "The only thing I draw the line at is if they claim to be musicians and they're not sitting down and playing music. I think a majority of hair bands are businessmen, not musicians. If that's what they want – a lot of money, fast cars, fake-titted blonde women – if that's their goal, then they're being true to their goal. If they're musicians trying to make good music that's timeless and all that other stuff is secondary, then be musicians. First of all, it's all a matter of what they want, what they claim they want and what they get. And second, who am I to judge what they want or to evaluate who they are?"

Opiate was almost diametrically opposed, in mood and message, to the lightweight, hedonistic trash performed by the glam bands. Its cold, unfriendly tone was intimidating from the EP's opening seconds: the first song, 'Sweat', is a flurry of dark riffs in a decidedly radio-inappropriate time signature, with more melody heard from Paul D'Amour's treble-heavy bass than the more conventional guitars. Danny Carey plays a threatening double kick-drum pattern in line with a staccato guitar part at the song's midsection, and Keenan's vocals – a world away from the whine or bellow of the standard heavy metal singer – were plain weird, an almost sensitive soprano.

'Hush', with its almost funk-bass intro, the line 'Fuck yourself, kill yourself' and the droned central riff, is still an unusual song to this day – so imagine how it must have sounded back in 1992. 'Part Of Me' is even less digestible, with a slick intro that leads to a quiet/loud/quiet structure in another odd tempo that is more than a little unnerving. Keenan intones threateningly, "'I know you better than I know myself…" and the song changes direction completely, with a simple, four-note solo that completely goes against the grain of the shredding template of the day. "I know you best – better than one might wish!" snarls Keenan, building his vocal to a malevolent shout and the sudden end of the song.

Three live songs finish the EP, recorded the previous New Year's Eve. The title of 'Cold And Ugly' sums up the nature of the song perfectly, with the heaving riff from Jones and D'Amour perfectly mixed to complement Keenan's seething vocal. "I am frightened!" he wails, treading new ground in heavy metal terms – a path that eventually mutated into the full-on confessional lyrics of the emo and nu-metal scenes, to the disgust of many a true metal fan. D'Amour in particular is on amazing form in this brief live set, breaking down into a monstrous, slightly overdriven riff that leads to a dexterous guitar solo.

"There used to be a bunch of assholes that lived in this building right here," explains Keenan in his strangely high-pitched, dispassionate tone between the final three live songs, adding "but we systematically removed them, like you would with any kind of termite or roach." An appropriate introduction for the enraged 'Jerk-Off', which pulls off the rare feat of being both a discussion of the nature of right and wrong and a hate song, threatening: "Maybe it's just bullshit and I should play God, and shoot you myself". Building towards a frantic crescendo of Carey's drums and Keenan's scream of "Die!", the song is as violent a composition as Tool have ever committed to record, although it should be noted that Maynard hasn't sung the line about shooting for some years. He has replaced the gun references with sexual alternatives, usually singing, "Maybe I should fuck you in the fuckin' ass" – a line that somehow fits better with Tool's thematic blend of sex and body horror.

Received rapturously by the crowd, 'Jerk-Off' is succeeded by the EP's title track. The song takes the quiet/loud template to its logical conclusion, interspersing subtle, almost ambient sections led by D'Amour's bass harmonics with chaotic, riff-heavy parts. Keenan took on the religious right, with his plea to Jesus Christ to save his life or blind him with his light and lies being as catchy as Tool got at this early stage in their career – although more than a few people failed to hear the last few words. As Adam recalled, "'Opiate' [is about] the corruption of Christian religion being forced down our fucking throats. A lot of people take that as like a pro-Christian song, and these Christians come up to us going, 'Dude, you know, that song saved my life, and thank you Jesus' and I go 'OK, cool'."

There's a hidden track on the *Opiate* EP called 'The Gaping Lotus Experience' (which itself sounds like one of the band's many invented titles, thrown out in interviews to dupe people like you and I). It starts at 6'06" into track six (in other words, 666) and is a rather lovely, Doors-like reverbed drone in complete contrast to the rest of the record. Cleverly, the band hid it on the vinyl version of the EP within the song 'Cold And Ugly' – etching a second groove next to that song's own spiral scratch, so that one of the two songs played randomly, depending on where the user dropped the needle. Throughout the song, guitar solos drone, reversed for an eerie effect.

Whatever the listener's opinion of the music, the artwork was equally riveting. This is where any analysis of Tool enters another plane: one populated by conspiracy theories and spooked fans posting their revelations on websites, studiously ignored by the band – who rarely, if ever, offer an official clarification. The front cover image, a man wearing an alien mask and clergyman's dog-collar in a praying posture, hints towards the title of the EP – which refers, in the words of Karl Marx, to religion being the opiate (or addiction) of the masses. Maynard confirmed the reference in a discussion some years later, saying: "Yes, that's right. My views against Christianity or religion in general are directed towards the 'middle men' – those who are in power and use religion as a market force by which to manipulate human beings for their own personal gain. I was raised a Southern Baptist. I witnessed first-hand the hypocrisy of this particular form of Christianity. But it was a gradual thing. As I got older, I began to see people claiming one set of beliefs and acting in ways which directly opposed those views."

If you want to take the speculation further, don't forget the presumptions peddled by conspiracy theorist and former TV sports presenter David Icke and others that we are all ruled by a military-industrial complex controlled by the Illuminati, who are rumoured to be an obscure religious sect deeply involved with world finance – either that or a lizard race from the planet Vulcan, an Earth-like world permanently invisible to us because it orbits the Sun at a perfect 180 degrees from us ('behind' the Sun, in other words). The alien priest on the cover seems to reflect the Illuminati idea.

Why stop there? The interior artwork, a sepia-toned three-dimensional collage of objects in a wooden box or coffin that takes up the entire three-panel booklet, is crammed with references. Photographs of the four members as teenagers stand at each corner. Teeth, skull fragments, a dead scorpion and a glass eyeball add a macabre touch. Small models of cherubim, one with a demon head transplanted onto it, and a crucifix clutched by a demonic hand, provide an anti-religious flavour. Most infamously, a photograph of a man in a baseball cap simulating intercourse with a decayed corpse stands at the centre, which worried more than a few Tool fans – even when the theory was later accepted as fact that the 'corpse' was a prop from Adam Jones' special-effects day job and the man was his colleague Kevin (the letters E and V of 'Kev' are visible on the photo's border). Keys, coins, broken wood and rusty screws make the whole thing somehow more deathly, like a coffin filled with the daily ephemera of the deceased person. And this was only Tool's first EP.

Rumours of Tool's weird approach to just about everything they did began to circulate. Here was a heavy metal band who rebelled utterly against heavy metal convention. Were they Satanists, malcontents, drug freaks? The last category at least began to seem plausible when the band referred to their drug use in interviews. These references ranged from simple statements, as when Carey explained: "Our main goal when we're together is to write music in a forum where we can involve our subconscious as well as our conscious. To make that happen we use every tool available to us, be it sigils, mind-altering chemicals, fragrances, or whatever modern technology can supply", to more direct recommendations, like Jones' question to one interviewer: "Have you ever done ketamine?... Come check it out, man. Fucking changed my life. Changed my whole thinking," and Keenan's atypically revealing admission that, "One of the songs on *Opiate* was written when my friend and I sat up all night listening to our entire Joni Mitchell catalogue on acid. When we started listening, we were facing the inside wall. When we looked outside, it had snowed a full seven or eight inches."

The depth of the band's collective thinking when it came to drugs should not be underestimated, however: their approach to stimulants was about as far from the cocaine-and-champagne foolishness of the hair-metal bands as could be. Carey later warned, "I'm not for one minute suggesting that people should go out and do drugs. It's not so much what you take as the circumstances you do it in and what it is that you bring back with you. I mean, if you just go off on your own and freak out, you maybe don't have anything to bring back."

As anyone who has taken a hallucinogenic drug knows, once inside the experience it's possible for the user to pass through doors that, once opened, cannot be closed. Or, as Maynard expressed it, "I think there's a huge range of things that could be considered near-death experiences. Some shamans will go out in the middle of an ice tundra in a small igloo, with a cup of water, and get to the point where they're near starvation and they have that revelation of sorts. Other people do a whole baggie full of mushrooms, which is a similar near-death experience. It's a matter of shifting your focus, seeing things from a different light, and re-addressing your conscious frequencies, so to speak... There's definitely an orientation behind the eyes of people who have faced death."

All this drug talk was dismissed as hippie nonsense by those music fans who didn't take Tool seriously, and who can blame them? In the early Nineties, only dance acts talked about drugs, and then it was largely Ecstasy: mainstream rock bands didn't admit to any kind of drug use unless they were showing off or using a stint in rehab as a publicity move. Acid, cannabis and the other psychoactive drugs were old hat – relics from the Seventies – a point that differentiated them from the *de rigueur* cocaine and heroin beloved of the hard rockers. Carey showed his understanding of this point when he explained: "I think it's unfortunate that [hallucinogenic] drugs are lumped along with the really destructive ones that are tearing the inner cities apart. These drugs have a shamanic use. Also, nobody gets rich off of them. You don't get people who become millionaires as psilocybin runners, you don't get mescaline dealers shooting people... We're a total drug band. We're as psychedelic as a band can get, but we're articulate about it, I suppose. That's the difference between us and some other groups."

The members of Tool have often talked about the value of perspective, and how changing perspectives can enrich a person's life – whether through drugs, music or another channel. Tool's complex, ever-changing music and obscure lyrics with multiple meanings obviously require an open mind from those who wish to understand them, and drugs might be seen as a way into that open mind – but again, the band have always been circumspect about the best method. "I think psychedelics play a major part in what we do," said Keenan. "But having said that, I feel that if somebody's going to experiment with those things they really need to educate themselves about them. People just taking the chemicals and diving in, without having any kind of preparation about what they're about to experience, tend to have no frame of reference, so they're missing everything flying by and all these new perspectives. It's just a waste. They reach a little bit of spiritual enlightenment, but they end up going, 'Well, now I need that drug to get back there again'. The trick is to use the drugs once to get there, and maybe spend the next ten years trying to get back there without the drug."

Once the channels of communication were open between band and listener, the group reasoned, there would be a more complete understanding all round. This meant, from the very beginning, that Tool's lyrics were not printed in the booklets of their CDs, a move that has consistently frustrated many of their most devoted followers. However, the band were aware of the old Pink Floyd trick that was perpetuated more overtly by R.E.M. – that if you don't print your lyrics in your album, the listeners will try their damnedest to figure out what you're saying, thus paying attention to both the music and the words (when they finally work them out). As Adam put it, "We don't print our lyrics because we want people to really sit closer to the speaker and try and hear what Maynard's saying versus what's going on in the music... we treat everything with as much importance as the lyrics."

All this outlandish stuff attracted rock fans' attention to Tool, who played their first major dates in the summer of 1992 to support the *Opiate* EP. As their LA fanbase grew, a new band called Rage Against The Machine began to make their presence felt on the Californian rock scene, led by Jones' high-school friend Tom Morello. The two bands shared certain musical ideas in the early days, with Jones' guitar tone similar to Morello's on Tool's more aggressive songs: when Rage invited Keenan to sing some backup vocals on their incendiary self-titled album, released in November 1992, it seemed like an obvious step.

The song, 'Know Your Enemy', featured a softly played midsection between the heavy riffage of its beginning and end, with Keenan's confrontational lyrics building to an extended roar. It's interesting to note firstly that this song, one highlight of this huge-selling album, was Keenan's best-known recording for the next couple of years until Tool really took off, and secondly that the lines are definitely 'Maynard-like' despite their much more openly abrasive context. Rage Against The Machine were never known for their lyrical subtlety: their singer, Zack de la Rocha, often made the target of his wrath explicit, but the short stanza of 'Maynard' is more opaque, naming no one in particular and merely venting a general dissatisfaction with the system against which Rage pitted themselves. This is the essence of the difference between the two bands, who shared so much in 1991 and '92 and moved in much the same circles, attracting the same demographic of listeners. Adam made this clear when he said, "We're not a band like Rage, who I respect a lot, but they're very political... they're trying to change people's thinking and all that kinda stuff, and all we're doing is going, 'Hey, this is what we're about'... I can't do anything. All I can do is just try to open my own mind. And that's what we're expressing through our songs."

Taking an open mind to the people proved to be a tough task. Between February and August 1992 Tool played a few-dozen club shows, mostly on the liberal West and East Coast rock circuits, but also ventured into the great American interior for shows in Nebraska, Kansas and beyond. A hint towards the band's future aesthetic was evident in their stripped-down performances, featuring basic light shows and little of the bombast that typified the metal scene of the day. The band also played a few shows supporting Road Crew, the short-lived band of ex-Guns N'Roses drummer Steven Adler, but this hardly did them any favours: as Carey laughed, "On our first tour we were put with some bad bands... We did this show with the ex-Guns N' Roses drummer's band... We ended up with a bunch of people with big hair watching us with their mouths open. Some of our shows we had five people. Every band needs to go through that. Hey, we needed the rehearsal time. We weren't that good back then. We played the songs well, but we were pretty green...."

More useful exposure came in the autumn when Tool toured with hardcore punk icon Henry Rollins, who had become beloved as a solo artist on the alternative-rock scene after the split of his previous band, seminal punks Black Flag, in 1986. Hard-working and streetwise, Rollins and his band and crew knew how to get the job done on tour, down to the finest details. "We learned a lot from being around those guys," said Danny. "They're such seasoned players. We saw how to deal with crew people, how to get where you're going and do what you have to do, how to fit things into your schedule. The worst part was the little punk rockers who'd complain that we didn't play fast enough, but that didn't happen very often. Maynard would just tell them to listen slower."

1992 ended on a high for Tool, but it was a strange time for modern music in general. Grunge was now the buzzword in music circles, now that Nirvana had spearheaded a movement out of Seattle onto the world stage. Neither metal nor conventional rock, the grunge bands were regarded with suspicion by the mainstream – although by this point, they had almost *become* the mainstream. Needless to say, their emergence affected Tool, whose uneasy brand of rock had no name back then (the idea of progressive metal was niche at best in 1992). "We never said we were a grunge band," sighed Paul D'Amour. "We're just a bunch of guys who listen to Judas Priest and Yes and Tom Waits and Minor Threat. We got together, and we just play what we know."

Eighteen months after the release of Nirvana's *Nevermind*, the phrase 'alternative rock' was beginning to adopt parallel importance to 'grunge'. But that too began to lose its flavour after a while: record companies fought to sign the next Nirvana and a sense of disillusionment settled in. "[Seattle] isn't even alternative any more," complained Carey. "Look at bands like Pearl Jam. That's not alternative. Their songs are just as poppy as anyone else's. They just got lumped in with that crowd. Any hardcore punk band is a lot more alternative to me."

It was clearly time for something new – and Tool were about to deliver it.

Chapter 4

1993

"I really like the idea of an undertow," said Maynard James Keenan. "That feeling that you get when you're standing out in the surf, you just feel like you're being pulled under and out, whether you like it or not. I would hope that the music takes you to that place, it kind of pulls you under and throws you around and you go with it."

Even 15 years later, *Undertow* is a frightening album, full of songs that paint a bleak picture of the physical world and an even bleaker one of the inner world of the mind. Delivered by a young band who had had plenty of time to hone their anger into a concrete form, the album caused much controversy in a country that had not yet become accustomed to the concept of intelligent heavy metal.

Undertow was recorded over three months in late 1992 at Grand Master Studios in Hollywood, with the veteran producer Sylvia Massy (who had worked with Green Jelly) taking a co-production credit. Released on April 6, 1993 in two different covers – one depicting a sinister ribcage sculpture and the other a bar code with a sarcastic message from the band – *Undertow* was, like the *Opiate* EP of the previous year, impossible to digest in a few listens. The fact that it has gone on to sell over two million copies is testimony to the changes that have taken place in the metal arena in the years since then, with listeners increasingly ready to invest time and mental effort into appreciating music with depth. It was also one of the first albums to convey a message made up of equal parts humour and horror, a quintessentially Tool-like approach shared by a small number of bands, notably Radiohead, Tool's contemporaries in many ways.

The album begins with 'Intolerance', a straight-ahead metal tune similar to others on *Opiate* in tone and sentiment. The tonal similarity between Adam Jones' rhythm part and that of Rage Against The Machine's Tom Morello remains: Paul D'Amour's trebly bass-line also bears comparison with the work of Rage's bassist Tim Commerford. Lyrically, of course, Maynard James Keenan keeps the message obscure, although he again invokes religious targets. The theme of corrupt religion is one that Tool spent some years addressing, in all likelihood due to the suffocating Southern Baptist childhood endured by Keenan.

The next song is one of the most powerful that Tool has ever written, and not one that is easy to write about, even today. When the video for 'Prison Sex' was first aired on MTV that year, the reaction was confused: even if people didn't know what it was about, they found the visuals disturbing. MTV stopped playing it after a while, predictably.

'Prison Sex' is about child abuse, and how it endures from generation to generation. Maynard has never explained specifically who the song is about, but he has discussed the fact that he was abused as a child on many occasions. He sings the lyrics from two points of view – the abused victim and his/her abuser, who he referred to as 'the Antagonist' in some interviews. Its in-your-face lyrics make it clear what he's referring to, and he switches between the two narrative voices with the words "Do unto others what has been done to you" and "Do unto you now what has been done to me".

The song begins with an ambient intro, recorded when Jones depressed his guitar's whammy bar until the low E string flapped against the pickups and strummed it, making a thick, swampy sound laden with reverb. The bulk of the song is dark but not particularly threatening until three minutes in, when the crisp riff that dominated until that point is replaced by a slower, bass-driven section of great power. This is the background to Keenan's pained, emotional lyrics, which were widely misunderstood until he explained what he was singing about. For example, the *Omaha World Herald* wrote in April 1999 that the "lyrics chronicle an impeding rape in prison from the viewpoint of a former rape victim". Addressing this common misconception, Maynard said: "Instantly they think of San Quentin... being buggered by your cell-mate. It's not about that at all... and it's not saying that sodomy or sexual abuse is in anyway OK. It's not. It's just a story of someone who is having it happen to them now because they're fucked up, because they don't know how to deal with past abuse."

The song specifically deals with the cycle of dysfunction, which propagates itself when an abused child grows up and abuses another child in turn – hence the dual perspective of the singer. "A lot of time when a child is sexually abused they put it out of their mind," said Keenan. "Then they grow up and they don't understand this unrest that they have in them. They turn to different ways to try to channel it. They become alcoholics or become co-dependent or whatever. So what our video deals with is someone who has that happen to them. To channel it, they sexually molest another child... In the song it talks about 'I become full circle'. And that's what that means: 'This happened, I grew up and now I'm doing it to someone else'. That's why it's written from the Antagonist's point of view... like, 'This is what happened to me'."

Clearly, 'Prison Sex' was never likely to find a home in any niche of mainstream culture. Its subject was and remains hard for most people to consider, let alone discuss. There were some ironic repercussions, such as the song's use (and swift removal from) a 30-second radio ad recruiting prison officers in Davenport, Iowa, as well as more serious issues that arose when media channels refused to play it. The Canadian music programme *MuchMusic*, which occasionally refused to show video clips that it deemed offensive, wouldn't play 'Prison Sex', although they did feature it on *Too Much For Much*, a show that discussed the banning of such content with guests. Keenan appeared on the programme and was invited to defend the video, but in the brief 30 seconds or so allocated to him was not able to do much more than admit that he had been a victim of abuse. Afterwards he fumed, "What I heard was, this woman who was head of programming watched 'Prison Sex' and she didn't know whether or not we were pro or anti sexual abuse. That was the most asshole thing I've ever heard... That was what the song was all about, recognising the cycle of abuse. To deny people access to someone who has worked through that process is bullshit... I didn't really have a chance to explain any of these things."

The video clip's artful, non-graphic evocation of child abuse – done largely in metaphor – was a world away from the standard 'banned' video of the day, which (then as now) usually caused offence through excess nudity or violence. 'Prison Sex' was just frightening. It's ludicrous that anyone banned it, although it wouldn't have been unreasonable to pre-cede it with a parental-guidance warning or broadcast it at night when children were unlikely to be watching. "What got to me about the whole situation," said Keenan, "was [that] you have these other videos where Steven Tyler's daughter is stripping in front of old men, or where Janet Jackson is practically having oral sex. I kind of find that disturbing, yet it's something that's just thrown in people's laps and they don't think twice about it. So I guess anything that deals with that sort of subject matter [child abuse] is going to end up hitting roadblocks."

So what was in this supposedly offensive video, exactly? Look it up on YouTube. It's a Claymation video, which usually has connotations of friendly children's TV or comedy – which makes it all the stranger. It opens with blurred shots of the walls in a room alternately occupied by two characters: a legless baby who drags himself along the floor by his hands, and a jet-black female creature, the Antagonist. The former is made of what looks like cracked porcelain and wire and has only one eye, which rolls up and down; the latter is the stuff of nightmares, a clawed, serpentine female not unlike the monster created by HR Giger for the *Alien* film series. She darts in and out of shot, occasionally pick-ing the baby up and laying him on a table, where she strokes him and paints his torso with a brush.

There is no violence in the video, but the suddenness of the Antagonist's appearances and disappearances, her occasional anguish as she shakes and vibrates, the close-ups on her elegant, spiderlike hands and the stark pools of light that illuminate the room all combine for an unsettling experience. A robot figure comes and goes, made of bits of junk, with a face made from a spinning photograph of a small boy. At one point, the legless baby pulls open a drawer from the wall, out of which emerges a small, manlike figure made of lumps of rotten meat or excrement: the Antagonist stamps on it, crushing it to the floor. At the end of the clip, after the Antagonist has removed the baby's face to reveal the mechanical workings of the brain within, the victim tries to reach out to her (his mother?), only for her to push his hand away.

It's powerful stuff, for those who care to invest time in it. Tool were apparently trying to portray the mutual anguish of the abused and the abuser, as well as the psychological demons that accompany the process, and in creating this small, horrific world where everything is implied and nothing is explicit, they pulled off a serious artistic coup. Perhaps they went too far: the 'Prison Sex' video is painful to watch.

None of this would have been possible, it's fair to say, if Tool had shot a standard live-action video of them performing. In fact, the band was rabidly against the idea of appearing in their own clips, as Keenan explained: "People focus on... what the people look like, so they're going, 'OK, let's develop this person's personality'. What the fuck does my personality have to do with what this song is saying? I don't want to do that. I don't want people to latch on to my movements or the way I sound or the way Danny hits his drums. That's a distraction from the piece at hand... When you look at the Mona Lisa, I don't have any idea what the artist looks like or what he's about. I have no idea what that guy is up to, what his personality is. I don't care, looking at that piece. Is she smiling? Is she frowning? What is she doing? All these things are entering into it, and that's the same way you should look at... a video [like] 'Prison Sex'. You should be looking at it in terms of the music and the medium that's being presented to you. Don't worry about the rock guys that are doing that shit. It's not really important."

The 'Prison Sex' video shoot featured art direction by Adam Jones, whose experience in movie special effects was an obvious asset. The group wanted to keep their creative efforts in-house without recruiting artistic talent from outside, said Danny: "We can't see the point of farming out various parts of the band to other people, so we do it all ourselves. If we did pass things on to other people, there is a chance that the impression we want people to get of the band may become distorted. I guess we're lucky because we have the ability to execute everything we need to: if we don't feel that it is important, then the record company can step in and take over that one element."

Jones' artistic vision was as evident on *Undertow*'s next song, 'Sober', as it had been on 'Prison Sex'. Also released as a single, the song features another unorthodox, disturbing video. Musically, it's more disjointed than the previous track, all loping rhythms and scratched guitar solos. Paul D'Amour's overdriven, staccato bass part anchors the song, which reduces at times down to Maynard's impassioned vocal and the rhythm section. The chorus of, "Jesus, won't you fucking whistle / Something but the past and done?" infuriated a few religious listeners, a line that Maynard explained as a wish to move on from the past. Meanwhile, when he sang, "Why can't we not be sober?... Why can't we drink forever?... I am just a worthless liar", he appealed to many listeners struggling with addiction, some of whom approached the band to explain this over the years. "It's about doing drugs, and why can't we do drugs if something positive happens?" said Adam. "And we get a lot of people who can't handle drugs that think it's about not doing drugs, and being sober, and they come up going, 'Man, I really relate to that song' and I go, 'Great, if that's what you get out of it'. But I don't wanna go, 'Oh, we're such an edgy band and everyone must get us' and all that kinda thing. Like I said, it's just personal, and if you get it, cool, if you don't and you like it, cool. You know, as long as it's all positive."

The song rises and falls into a short instrumental section of great subtlety before expanding again and ending abruptly, leaving the first-time listener usually puzzled: the video doesn't illuminate the song much either, although it is a fantastic piece of art. Like 'Prison Sex' it's a Claymation clip, and shares much of its textures with that previous video: the tones are dark, with greys and browns prominent. Set in a claustrophobic room and surrounding corridors, the film follows the figure of a bent old man with a strange, beetle-like head: he is shown either sleeping, standing still or poking around under the floorboards and in cupboards. He opens a box by cutting through the ropes that hold it shut, opens a door in the wall to reveal a robotic creature, made of rust and nailed to the wall behind; sits slumped on a chair and levitates into the air; and, as the song reaches a peak, falls backwards onto the floor, where his head melts gruesomely. Another figure made of rusty metal and wire manipulates a strange, intricately detailed machine that resembles a cross between a cannon and a telescope – and most memorably, the main character approaches a large horizontal pipe, pulls off a chunk of it and sees within it large chunks of meat, unpleasantly faecal in appearance and relentlessly pushed along inside. The video includes brief shots of a person – a real one – shaking and crouching, the only non-Claymation figure apart from some brief, blurred sweeps of the band playing their instruments near the beginning.

Once again, the video made an impact on critics and fans. The band were proud of the truly alternative direction which they'd taken with their clip, as D'Amour said: "We just kind of went into it with the attitude of, 'Who wants to see another fucking video by a bunch of guys in a warehouse playing guitars with graffiti on the walls?' It's a bunch of crap with just some wild editing. We said, 'Let's make a film with a great soundtrack'. If you want to see the band perform, go to the fucking show."

Keenan was more circumspect, explaining that videos *per se* were almost pointless these days: "If I had any advice to younger bands that are all star-struck with the whole industry, I would say, 'Don't make a video', because there's no outlet for them. Unless you're gonna make some crazy, awesome video that you don't care if it ever gets played on MTV... There's no longer any real actual outlet for your video to promote your record – unless you're just gonna do it on your web page... at this point, there's no way to really make your money back on those videos and they don't necessarily promote your record nowadays. It's not like a make-or-break situation, and the way things are going, budgets for videos are huge now. Nobody's being real creative with their budgets. It really comes down to ideas. If you have cool ideas, you can make it work with 100 bucks. But nowadays everyone's going for the big budgets and I think the creativity is lacking, because you give yourself so many choices that you kinda get paralysed in a way." Asked about the equally incomprehensible song and video, perhaps Jones put it best when he said: "So many people [said], 'Dude, I related to 'Sober' so much. I've been sober seven years and I'm a liar. That's me, dude, I'm a liar'. You know, that line in the song, 'I'm a liar'? And that little guy brings that box. But that's not what the song's about. The song is actually about doing drugs – just leave me the fuck alone and let me do my drugs."

Undertow continued after these two jaw-dropping songs with 'Bottom', on which Henry Rollins supplied a guest vocal. "He had a gambling debt for a while with us," said Keenan, lying with a straight face. "He's kind of a bad poker player. He lost a lot of money... like $3,000. Turns out he was losing the T-shirt money. He was borrowing from the merchandiser to play poker with us and he's really bad at bluffing. So we pretty much nailed him, and that's actually how we got him to play on the album."

The song rests on an unlikely rock riff that sounds more jaunty than anything Tool had recorded so far – almost Bon Jovi-esque, in fact – but never fear: the song soon descends into far darker territory, with lines that promise "I'm naked and fearless, and my fear is naked". The song closes in a complex end montage that includes an uncharacteristic shred solo from Jones: its final message seems to be Keenan's repeated mantra of "Shit adds up at the bottom" – the thoughts of a man at his lowest ebb.

'Crawl Away' is preceded by a snatch of what sounds like South American pan-pipe music, before it launches into an uptempo riff pattern filled with layers of guitar, a different approach to the simpler 'Sober' sound. There's an ironic appearance of the line, 'Got you in a stranglehold, baby / Get up, get up, get up now" (the chorus from the Ted Nugent song 'Stranglehold'), and Keenan hints at sinister motives as the song develops. This is Tool, however, and as with so many of their songs, what Maynard appears to be saying may be worlds away from what he really means: if their goal – as has been so often stated – is to encourage their listeners to think for themselves, then encouraging us to question their songs' meanings is a good start.

Whether the swamp in question in 'Swamp Song' is real or metaphysical is impossible to gauge. Keenan's vocal melody follows the guitar riff in the chorus, making this song one of the most difficult to shake if it's stuck in your head, as so many Tool songs eventually become. The songs on *Undertow* often follow a particular loud-quiet-loud pattern, in which a riffed-up beginning and end are separated by a mellow, even ambient midsection, and 'Swamp Song' is no different, allowing Jones to layer a guitar solo with a delayed line echoing after it. 'Undertow' itself is more complex, rising and falling with different dynamics, reversed vocal echoes and a razor-sharp guitar line from Jones. Lyrically, Maynard is a little more obtuse than in the big thematic hitters of 'Prison Sex' and 'Sober', referring obliquely to a voice beneath the water that calls him and sweeps him away. Is it God he's talking about, or organised religion, or a drug? All three have been posited, but the most likely answer seems to be that – like in so many Tool songs in the first few years of their career – he's reacting against perceived norms of thinking, the individual protesting against a wall of resistance.

The Tool songwriting method at this point in their career – of titling a song, then adding lyrics that relate only spuriously to that title, then explaining that the song meant something else entirely, as with 'Prison Sex' and 'Bottom' – peaks with '4°', which some assumed was meant to refer to degrees of an angle. In fact, Maynard is alleged to have explained that the song refers to the anal cavity being four degrees warmer than the vagina. Lyrics about penetration back up his statement in typically graphic detail. 'Four degrees' is also said to be West Point slang for a rookie student, however, which is obviously a plausible explanation, as is Maynard's supposed assertion that the song actually represents a state of openness rather than any sexual expression.

'Flood' is the heaviest song in purely sonic terms on *Undertow*, beginning with an extended section of droned, down-tuned riffs and stamping drums akin to modern doom metal. Unhurried and menacing, the song clambers along, with Keenan wailing "Here comes the water!" Later, he invokes the rising waters as a tide that will wash away his entire consciousness. When the song really begins after almost five minutes, it accelerates nimbly, droning along with cold commitment with Maynard's wailed paean to oblivion. This resolves into a 40-second silence – and leads into one of the first hidden tracks ever included on a heavy metal CD.

Although this last track, 'Disgustipated', is listed as track ten on the *Undertow* sleeve, when the original US CD pressing was inserted into a player it appeared as track 69, after quickly scrolling through 59 empty tracks. Yes, more Tool games... the song itself is largely ambient noise and a rhythmic beat made up of found sounds. A chanted whisper of, "This is necessary" and "Life feeds on life, feeds on life, feeds on life…" leads into a cacophony of sounds and drumbeats. Maynard then launches into a preacher-style sermon, adopting a Southern accent and telling an apocalyptic tale of intelligent vegetables awaiting a harvest in terror. The bleating of sheep can be heard: *BAM* magazine explained that this was inspired by a brush with Scientology, as follows: "In May 1993, Tool performed at Scientology's Celebrity's Centre, apparently not knowing that this was the home of the cult. Once they found out, they were not taking it nicely. Between songs, Keenan, staring first at the lush grounds paid for by devoted L. Ron [Hubbard] followers and then into the eyes of his own audience, bayed into the mic like a sheep looking for his shepherd's gate. 'Baaaaa! Baaaaa!' the singer bleated."

Four and a half minutes of crickets making their sonorous night-time noises follow. The sound is blissfully peaceful, and you barely notice the quiet sound of a man recounting a story, starting with the words, "It was daylight when you woke up…" The last part of 'Disgustipated' is an answerphone message from a man credited in the liner notes as 'Bill the landlord', and the song fades after almost 14 minutes, although some versions of the CD have a shorter, edited version.

Once again, Tool's album artwork was a trip in itself. The cover of the uncensored version of *Undertow*, with its ribcage image, is dark but not particularly disturbing. However, the rear of the CD bears an image of a pig, supported by a raft of upright forks, with the album title shaved into the hair of its visible side; an obese, naked woman is pictured lying in a foetal position; the same woman is pictured lying on her back with a slim man lying on top of her, face up, with his penis visible but semi-obscured; D'Amour is pictured with acupuncture needles protruding from his face; and Keenan appears to be wearing some sort of S&M torture device on his face and neck. There's also an X-ray image of a human abdomen, into which a vibrator has been anally inserted. Defending the artwork, Jones said: "I like a picture that makes you uncomfortable on one hand and it's beautiful on the other. Something kind of gross, but you look anyway. Something you'd never want to see, but it's kind of beautiful." D'Amour added: "The images work with the rest of the album – soft and womb-like… an example of the beauty of atrocity. At first you'd say, 'Ooh, she's fat', but if you keep looking, there's something about it."

With wearying predictability, K-Mart and Wal-Mart refused to stock the album because of its strong images, leading the band to manufacture the bar code sleeve: as Carey explained, "[There]'s a pretty big market that might not get a chance to hear our music, Middle America basically… We made the censored cover for those kids who don't have skate shops or cool record stores in their town, and all they have is the lame mall record store or Wal-Mart that doesn't always carry everything. Besides, we'll miss out on all that money." He laughed as he uttered the last line: Tool were fully aware that a successful album doesn't always translate into material wealth. "We're not naïve about how the business works – it's not like we walked into a casino and pulled a lever and hit the jackpot, and all the money just pours out into your hands," said Keenan. "Just because we've got a successful record doesn't mean we're gonna get paid. It's wonderful to see the success – we go out and party, and it's a real milestone for us – but it doesn't mean the work is over."

Indeed: the work was just beginning for 1993, with a long trek on that year's two-month-long Lollapalooza tour booked for Tool. The tour that would break them in America also featured a raft of alternative artists, with Primus (then at the peak of their popularity) headlining the main stage, followed by Alice In Chains, Dinosaur Jr,. Babes In Toyland, Rage Against The Machine and others. Tool initially headlined the second stage over Sebadoh, Mercury Rev, Royal Trux and a long list of lesser bands, but were moved to a spot above Rage on the main stage after four weeks on the road. Of the enthusiastic reaction from the fans, Carey mused: "We've done well for ourselves because of our fanbase. It's been very underground, and the lack of advertising and marketing with the band [has made it] more of a thought process… people getting in touch with the music and taking it a lot further than just being the hot pick of the week, or taking it further than just the catchy song lyric."

Although Tool had long since secured management with Ted Gardner, the festival co-founder, his decision to move them up a level didn't make the band entirely happy. As D'Amour said, the endless press was starting to get them down: "It's the dumb questions… The stoned college kid from some fanzine asking, 'Like, are you an alternative band?' I don't like venues like Lollapalooza because it's just too big… The vibe was good, but there were too many fans and creative people. In a smaller venue it becomes a personal experience where I can see the kid in the back row, and touch the people and sweat on each other."

Getting through the tour was made easier for Tool thanks to the experience the previous year of touring with Henry Rollins, recalled Carey: "Henry Rollins was great for us. He was like this seasoned pro. He showed us the ropes and took us under his wing. It helped us make it through Lollapalooza. The frustrating part about that tour was being put in that environment. It's more satisfying for me to play a club with 1,000 people than a big thing like that. That is why we enjoyed the second stage more. It was more sincere."

Another equally important mentor for Tool was the comedian Bill Hicks, who is credited in *Undertow*'s liner notes. "He came down to Lollapalooza in Los Angeles and introduced the band," recalled Keenan. "We saw him a couple of times after that, talked to him a couple of times more… His ideas were what really resonated with us. I think that's what he really liked about us as well – that we were resonating similar concepts. Unity is the philosophical centre. Evolution. Change. Internally and externally. Individually and globally. That's pretty much the gist of his comedy no matter what he was talking about – music, porno, smoking. Whatever it was, it came back to the idea of unity and evolution. Evolving ideas."

All this high-profile activity elevated Tool to the cutting edge of the American rock scene, which was still in flux and looking for a voice. *Undertow* had gone gold by the end of 1993 and went platinum two years later, despite the lack of support from Wal-Mart. By the end of the year the band had racked up over 130 live shows, a considerable target for any outfit, including major festivals in Europe, club shows all over the UK (including a date at London's Astoria) and the continent, an American trek in the summer, the huge Lollapalooza sheds and anywhere else that would have them. Enough to drive a man to tears – and funnily enough, tears were high on Tool's agenda as 1994 dawned…

Chapter 5

1994–1995

"Lachrymology is like a life philosophy of dealing with yourself, and dealing with the pain or whatever bullshit you've got inside you, but you have to do it on your own. That's our philosophy. All these twelve-step programmes and churches and religions, Scientology, whatever, are not the way to deal with it. You have to go back within yourself and do it yourself."

Thus spake Adam Jones in 1994, very plausibly, causing Tool's ever-expanding fanbase to prick up its collective ears and visit their local library to research the philosophy of crying (yes – in the pre-internet age, people actually did that). As more and more people bought into the idea and Jones was asked for more information, he told *BAM* that the idea of self-improvement through crying had been invented by Ronald P. Vincent, a crop-spray contractor, who moved from Kansas to Hollywood after his wife had been dismembered in a snow-plough accident. Racked with mental agony, Vincent wrote a book, *A Joyful Guide to Lachrymology*, which shared some themes with Sigmund Freud's *The Pleasure And Pain Principle*. "The philosophy of that book is basically using your pain to a profit, rather than letting it drag you down," added Danny Carey. "A lot of people who can't master that art end up jumping off buildings."

Utter rubbish, of course. There was no such person as Ronald P. Vincent, no philosophy of crying and no book on the subject. The whole thing was a glorious joke that lasted for several years, with the members of Tool carrying it off with straight faces, and in doing so establishing a basic relationship with their fans that involved untruths and jokes as much as it did serious messages. After all the grimness of the *Opiate* EP and the *Undertow* album, it seemed that Tool wanted to lighten up a little: as Danny explained, "We've been misquoted and perceived the wrong way for a long time. They [the press] make Tool seem like we're all about the horrors of life. While there certainly is a disturbing side to what we do, it's just one aspect of it, not the entire story. We're one of the few bands who haven't had to play any lame fashion games. We've always been able to put art first."

Still, at the same time the band was not averse to a bit of philosophical musing – seriously, this time – when the mood took them. Maynard James Keenan, who was apparently beginning to find the endless round of press slightly fatiguing, offered up this nugget: "I heard this theory the other day. I'm not necessarily saying this is what I believe, but I think it's a very interesting point of view… God had his right-hand man, OK, which was Lucifer, and he decided that this guy was getting out of hand so he had to be taken out of heaven. So the theory goes that, perhaps, what we all are is fragmented souls of Lucifer living on Earth, and each piece is self-aware. The goal for us then is to understand that we are all a piece of this larger idea and we're all working to get back together, and this particular planet we're on keeps encouraging us to stay separated… I think that is kind of a cool idea."

Keenan was starting to dislike doing press. Perhaps the inherently selfish record industry was starting to get to him, with everyone around him looking for a piece of him. It seemed that way when he said: "I think that we're fragmented… I think that alienation is inherent. People think that when they are together with their group of people, they're together. They're not really, they're an individual in that group. So no matter how many people are around you, you are definitely alone." Life in Los Angeles, always slightly inimical to Maynard's basic values, was also starting to wear him down, he said: "Just living in a big city, there's so many strange things going on… The more you uncover, the more you find out, the more helpless and trapped you feel... Fuck! It's just everything. The dying oceans, the ozone, people hating each other for some fucking reason, I don't know why. I mean, I hate humans in general, but I don't single out any individually... I like to spread my hate equally."

Modern culture, it seemed, was disgusting Keenan. He mentioned the film industry, saying: "Look at so many of today's films and the sexist nature that goes on in them. *Basic Instinct*, why the fuck does that have to be made? I mean, are we evolving or not? We don't need to see that shit any more, the only reason we do is because it sells and people have a very temporary view of their existence, and they're going to cash in and make their lives more comfortable as quickly as they can."

He also targeted hip-hop, which in 1994 had made the leap from gangsta rap to G-Funk, marking the beginning of the heyday of the wealthy rapper festooned with bling: "Even the guys in the hip-hop scene that portray themselves as being the homies down in the hood, packing their guns, and having to look over their shoulders. That's garbage, most of them live up past Bel Air and Beverly Hills in these beautiful homes, and their friends in their BMWs and Mercedes come over on the weekends in their polo sweaters and they sit around and have a barbecue. Not packing anything but a fat wallet, while there's a million kids out there buying the fashions, packing the guns and shooting each other over these fucking idiots. They're just fucking lying, and there's no reason for that shit any more. I just guess these people don't believe in an afterlife or a karmic balance."

Indeed not. Maybe Keenan was burned out from a year of touring; perhaps he was depressed by the nature of the industry he found himself in; possibly he just couldn't answer any more stupid questions. Or maybe he was unnerved by the fragile state of the music scene, which once again found itself on the cusp of a new age. In April 1994, Nirvana's frontman and mainstay, Kurt Cobain, had killed himself – destroying grunge at the same time, many felt. Alternative music had suddenly lost its most important figurehead, and both fans and industry were looking for something new.

Heavy metal in particular was about to be rebranded as nu-metal, thanks to the debut album released in October that year by Korn, a five-piece from Bakersfield in California. By mid-1995 Korn's brand of hip-hop-influenced beats and low-register riffs played on seven-string guitars had become hugely popular, along with their tendency towards extreme emotional openness in songs such as 'Daddy', which detailed singer Jonathan Davis' experience of child abuse. The parallels with Tool and 'Prison Sex' are evident, even if Korn's lowest-common-denominator riffs and mall-rat audience made Tool look like university professors in comparison. The band members understood this perception, with Carey saying: "Every other band in America either seems such complete idiots or they're just underestimating people. You put something with a little bit of intelligence out there and a lot of people are going to buy it. I guess that's the kind of crowd we pull in. We pull a lot of metalhead idiots too, we've got a certain percentage of those, and that helped to launch us. But the videos were the biggest thing, because MTV is so powerful."

For the first time, Tool's music began to seem like something entirely *other* – an artistic expression that didn't conform to anything happening in the mainstream. The word 'progressive' was first applied to their music at about this time, as the band's vision expanded: in fact, it was their constant name-checking of the prog-rock bands of their youth that prompted it.

"When I was a kid, some of my favourite records were by Pink Floyd, King Crimson and Yes," said Jones, "and there were never any pictures of the band [on the LPs]. The music was all that mattered… I've never wanted to be a conventional guitarist in any way. When I started playing guitar, my heroes were all about riffs, not leads. Then I got into more experimental players, such as David Sylvian, Robert Fripp and Steve Howe. But I also liked Devo and Brian Eno. At the time, it seemed like everyone else was playing lead guitar, and I just got sick of it. I never went down that path myself." Carey added: "When I was a kid, I never thought once about whether a song was too long. Led Zeppelin, Yes, Pink Floyd, King Crimson did these huge, epic things, and when they were done, I always wanted to hear more. Tool has never compromised the length of a song just because we're concerned about what people want to hear. We just go with how we feel. That's why we won't do edits for radio – they corrupt the song. We're only concerned about getting from one place in the song to the next, and then to the end. At that point we ask, 'Well, did it resolve itself or not?'"

Talking of old rock bands, Tool were invited at this time to record a song for a KISS tribute album called *KISS My Ass: Classic KISS Regrooved*. Maynard sang vocals in a veritable alt.rock supergroup called Shandi's Addiction (named after the KISS song 'Shandi' and nodding to fellow rockers Jane's Addiction) which also featured Tom Morello and Brad Wilk of Rage Against The Machine and Billy Gould of Faith No More. The song they covered, 'Calling Dr. Love', was about as uncool as classic rock could get in the era of nu-metal: you can almost imagine the musicians laughing sarcastically as they laid down the track...

Much of 1994 was taken up for Tool by touring in the UK (where they played at the Glastonbury Festival), Europe and the US, as well as venturing into Canada and Mexico and performing a show in Hawaii. The average Tool show had developed from the stripped-down performances of their early days to a spectacular array of lights, backdrops and projected film, with Keenan often dressed extravagantly. The long Mohican haircut he wore gave him an intimidating appearance despite his small stature, and his complete emotional immersion in the performance often gave him the look of a man possessed. Tool debuted a version of Led Zeppelin's 'No Quarter' this year, a stretched-out performance of the 1973 John Paul Jones showcase from *Houses Of The Holy* that took on many different textures, from full-on riffage to the most delicate harmonics. To keep things fresh, Tool switched the songs in their live set around, even playing the largely ambient 'Disgustipated' and introducing new songs called 'Stinkfist' and 'Pushit'. A London show featured a guest spot by the bass player of a local band, Peach, on 'Sober': his name was Justin Chancellor.

Audiences rarely knew what they were going to get with Tool, who took pleasure in playing with their crowds' patience. They would start a show with a lengthy bass drone before the band came on stage, dragging it out for minutes on end while the concertgoers grew impatient and called for them to hurry up. "We try to push [their] sense of time," said Jones. "When the show begins, the rumble goes on and [a] video comes up. We leave it up for a while, and I can hear people in the crowd yelling, 'OK, OK, come on!' Some people are thinking there's a problem because we're not coming out yet. It's pushing the element; there's the long fix and the quick fix. Which one's better? Neither, but they're both powerful."

Another amusing trick was one that Bill Hicks had introduced to Tool's Lollapalooza shows the previous year, when he asked the audience – sometimes over 50,000 in number – to stop what they were doing and look around for a contact lens he had lost. Maynard continued the gag, executing it during several shows this year.

Most unexpected of all was Tool's onstage setup. More often than not, Keenan avoided the front of the stage, skulking at the back, close to the backdrop or video screen, when there was one, while Jones and D'Amour were spotlit at the sides of the stage. Even when Maynard chose to place himself at the front of the stage, he often stood with his back to the crowd – an entirely unorthodox practice, but one rooted in practicality, he explained. "That setup came about simply for reasons of sound," he said. "When I'm up the back like that, I don't have to battle with Adam's guitar and [the] bass so much to hear myself. With a lot of the new songs, I need to really hit notes that are pretty difficult, so I need a clear, uncluttered sound on stage. This setup has worked really well so far for that reason – it just gives a much better onstage sound."

Once you understand the reasons for his onstage position, and consider the band's constant emphasis of the music over the musicians, then it begins to make sense. "There are no rules to this," Keenan added, "and when you start making rules it gets convoluted. Everyone wants to supply rules to it, and that takes away the magic of doing something musically that can remind someone of a sensory experience, a smell, a thinking process, whatever. It's about exploring, any way to touch the senses."

"I want Tool to be a powerful escapism," said Jones, backing up Keenan's point. "I want Tool to be like a drug. Take Tool and kick back into your own little world, or get aggressive, or get all sweet and nice and go ice-skating – whatever floats your boat. The bottom line is that we're pretty selfish; this is our thing, and it's what we want out of music. The fans are pretty secondary to that. It's nice that they're there and they can appreciate us opening with a 14-minute song. I'm in this to be happy."

In 1995 Tool were the hot new band on the block, with two years of high-profile touring and releases behind them and an arguable tag as the brainy kids of the alt-rock gang. This meant that opportunities outside the musical arena opened up for the band – notably for Keenan, who made several TV appearances as an actor around this time. With his stand-up comedy experience, several hundred gigs and the same number of radio and TV interviews under his belt, inhabiting a role was hardly a huge challenge for him. He made frequent appearances in the HBO series *Mr Show*, most memorably for Tool fans as the leader of the non-existent band Puscifer, a role he executed while wearing an incongruous wig.

Keenan's life changed significantly in the summer when his partner, who values her anonymity, gave birth to his son, named Devo H. Keenan. He hasn't explained yet if the boy's first name is a tribute to the famed art-rock band of the same name, but he did once explain that the H is just the latter H and not a name – which could, of course, just be another red herring. Maynard immediately took great care to protect his son's identity, to the extent that he began to vary his own onstage appearance in order that he would be less easy to recognise. From this point on, his stagewear became more extravangant, which he explained by saying: "That started when I had a son. That's the main reason for the make-up, the wigs, the bras, whatever you've seen [me wear on stage] with Tool. I just like the incognito aspect, because now I can wander around, even where I live, and not really be hassled too much. I just think it's really unfair for my child to have to be victimised by my career – you know, here you are signing autographs in the 7-11. It seems ridiculous to me. And I try not to be in my videos."

In September, Tool regrouped to record their next album, the much-anticipated follow-up to *Undertow*. However, Paul D'Amour had gradually become disaffected with Tool's musical direction, leading to inevitable friction between him and the other three musicians, and it didn't take long for the two sides to agree that it was time to part ways – even though the recording of the new album had actually begun.

Adam explained: "The trouble started when we were getting the material ready for [the new album], there was a massive difference in direction. Paul was pulling in one way, we were pulling in another. He's doing another project and when you hear it you'll know why he left Tool."

Immediately, interviewers wanted to know if D'Amour (who has remained largely silent on the subject in the subsequent years) had jumped or been pushed. "He really did want to do his own thing," Jones insisted. "It's good, it's just different from Tool." Keenan added: "If you were to take David Bowie, Syd Barrett, Flaming Lips, Steely Dan and The Beatles and mix it up you'd have what Paul is doing right now. Which is not what we're doing."

Paul played gigs with the band until the end of the year before going his own way. His replacement was announced as Justin Chancellor, the British bassist who had played with Tool in London the previous year when his band, Peach, supported the American act.

Though personnel changes in bands tend to be dramatic affairs, the D'Amour/Chancellor switchover was executed with consummate ease. D'Amour didn't bad-mouth his ex-bandmates or his replacement, then or since; Chancellor took up his place in Tool with nothing but good humour and a solid work ethic; and relationships between Paul and his erstwhile partners Carey, Jones and Keenan remained positive. The other members of Tool made a point of praising the music he went on to make, and Carey has even guested on D'Amour's new band's albums. It was all serendipitously smooth.

How Tool came to choose a Brit to join them is quite a tale. They're an American band to the core, having endured the privations (or privileges, depending on your point of view) of small-town USA in their youth, and reflecting those same tests in the shape of their music. What's even more astonishing is that Chancellor, an affable chap with no art-rock pretensions whatsoever (he told the author in 2001: "You can't get a decent pint of Stella out here", a reference that British readers will appreciate), went on to become a spokesman for Tool, doing more interviews than any of the others as the years passed.

"My brother was travelling in America and met this guy, Matt Marshall, who would later turn out to be the Zoo A&R rep who signed them," recalled Chancellor. "Matt and my brother lost contact for a while, but when they met up again, they were both working for labels and would exchange demos, one of which was Tool's. It just kicked my ass!... I met Tool through some mutual friends when my band came to LA," he says. "My brother had managed to book us some gigs through friends of his, so we smuggled our guitars into the country and pre-tended we were just on holiday."

After the guest spot, which he played in 1994, Justin was called by Adam, who told him that the band were looking for a new bass player and invited him to audition. "He asked if I wanted to try out," explained Justin. "I was really freaked out and shat myself. I know it sounds really corny, but Tool was literally the epitome of everything I liked about music, it was very unique to me. At first I actually turned it down… Peach had split up six months before, and I was in the middle of getting a new band together with a friend of mine. I didn't want to let my mates down, my head started spinning and I thought to myself, 'No, I've got to think about this'. I soon realised that if I was honest with myself, I'd fucking kill myself if I didn't give it a go, so I called Adam back and told him I was into it."

During his week-long audition, Justin was expected to come up with new songwriting ideas for the band as well as play songs from their cat-alogue – and he faced some stiff competition, including Filter's Frank Cavanaugh, Kyuss' Scott Reeder, and Pigmy Love Circus' Marko Fox. "I thought there was no way that I was going to get the spot," he said later, "but at the same time, I was totally happy to have made the decision to go for it." The pressure on him was reinforced by the decision of his bandmates to kick him out when they heard that he was trying out for Tool: fortunately, he impressed Jones et al with his phenomenal bass skills and was offered the job, and has remained with them ever since. The setup in Tool suited him perfectly, he said: "I've always been in bands that have been pretty democratic, but there's always some sort of control figure. This experience is very much four ways. I think everyone in the band is unique in character and offers something different. I hope it continues to work that way, because you can really feel the diversity in the music. It burns in such a cohesive way that it gives the music real strength."

Despite his skills with American psychobabble, Chancellor brought a particular down-to-earth quality to Tool, especially when talking about the music scene back home – which was, admittedly, in a fractured state in 1996, with the brash tones of Oasis and the rest of the Britpop bands starting to seem more than a little puerile. "The UK is really fucked," he said. "It's just this massive pop market. If you're not writing really stupid songs and making a lot of money – which we could do easily – then the industry is not willing to support you. We have some fucking integrity. It's a real shame for our fans in the UK that we're not getting the support we need. I'm not saying America is the perfect place for us, but in the UK it's all about making money and shifting units: maybe if I owned a record company I'd think differently, but that's the way I view it. That's why we're not releasing a single over there… we're not a pop band and we're never gonna be a pop band, so I guess we're not gonna be able to compete."

Evidently on a roll, he went on: "Even the underground scene in the UK sucks – I mean Mint 400 were a fucking amazing band, but they got stomped on because they weren't immediately accessible, a bit like us, and the music industry couldn't handle that in the UK. Everybody in Britain is up for making a fast buck [but] some things don't make money right away, they need investment and nurturing, the industry over there can't grasp that idea. I just feel sorry for the bands that don't play pop."

Justin suited the other musicians' personalities, too: as Jones said in rather flowery terms, "I love Paul and all that, and I wish him well, but I'm so happy that happened… Justin Chancellor is the most amazing person I've ever met. His favourite band was Tool, he was my best friend in England, he writes like Tool, he thinks like Tool, he likes all the same kinds of music I do, he just fit the glove – perfect." He added, "And he looks like the devil…"

As for Paul D'Amour, he went on to perform in several projects before sliding into semi-obscurity a few years ago. With hindsight, it's hard to understand how petty musical differences would cause anyone to leave a soon-to-be-huge band such as Tool, but it's true that the music he went on to make was vastly different from that of his old band. The Replicants was one of his projects, formed with Tool's erstwhile video director Ken Andrews of the band Failure and Chris Pitman, sometime Guns N'Roses keyboard player: they released a self-titled covers album in 1995 that featured a guest vocal from Maynard on the track 'Silly Love Songs'. D'Amour also formed a psychedelic rock band, Lusk, and worked under the name Feersum Endjinn, the title of an Iain M. Banks sci-fi novel. While all of these projects have attracted a cult audience, his profile remains low.

Chancellor admired Paul's work in Tool, saying: "I wanted to get Paul's sound and style – I loved it." While writing and playing in a similar style to D'Amour, he also brought in his own influences – a range of sounds from Rush to Fugazi, bands he had admired as a child. Born in 1971 in Kent, he was already listening to rock music by the Eighties, as he recalled: "I actually got my first guitar when I was eight. I was living in Germany at the time, and my first lesson was 20 people in the room, with a teacher up at the front showing us these chord shapes. And then all you'd hear is this horrendous racket as 20 people tried to copy him…."

On joining Tool, Chancellor was required to contribute as much as the other three members. "It was quite daunting because they'd already had a successful record and I'd never been part of one," he said, "but I was a full member from the start. I had to pull my weight. We're not really schooled in music theory, and we can't read music, but we understand the language and it's useful for making sure that we're all in the same ball park." Jones in particular influenced his bass style, as he added: "Before playing with him, I was… just pumping away as a bass player. He's inspired me to not be scared to be a little more sensitive. People often have a very narrow view of what the bass guitar can do, but there's an unlimited world for the instrument you're playing. And that applies to all instruments."

With their new member in place, Tool went back to work on their new album. Asked how it was progressing, Jones explained in typically evocative terms: "Well, it's hard for me to say. It's like living in a room and the cat always pisses on the rug. Your friend comes in and goes, 'Man, it smells like piss in here'. And you go, 'Really?' because you live in the room and you're used to it. We're around the music so much, so it's kind of hard to comment on it."

Would the smell of the new album be a sweet one?

Chapter 6

1996

Ten months of touring passed before *Ænima*, Tool's frankly startling second album, was released. In that time, the new line-up honed their act, assimilating Justin Chancellor and expanding their live show in many ways. The band was now using a large projection screen as a backdrop for surreal, frequently psychedelic film work, and both Maynard James Keenan and Chancellor often appeared with their torsos painted blue or in spots.

The tour swept through California, where Justin played his first show in Pomona; into the American interior; across to the East Coast; into Canada; into the deep south; and back to LA, with the band executing endless press duties at the same time. In between squeezing in the occasional comedy vignette, such as a cameo in the *Mr Show* episode *The Velveteen Touch Of A Dandy Fop*, Maynard was developing a reputation as a difficult interviewee. The rest of the band, the affable Chancellor aside, didn't make it too easy for the press either: as a reporter for *Kerrang!* wearily reported after yet another tense photo shoot, "Tool aren't big fans of *Kerrang!*... they reckoned we had stitched them up in [print], misquoting them and trying to make them look stupid. During [the] photo session, it would appear that our worst fears are being realised. Tool make it clear that they don't like certain types of lens. They won't pose in certain ways. They look about as interested as the Pope in a whorehouse. We haven't flown a couple of thousand miles to make Tool look like cunts, but frankly, they're not doing themselves any favours..."

At this crucial stage in their careers, Tool had realised that the most efficient avenue of communication between band and fans lay in their music rather than via the press. When *Ænima* appeared on October 1, it both revealed and obscured huge amounts of information about the world-view of the reticent foursome, from its artwork – a scintillating barrage of symbolic detail co-created by Adam Jones and artist Cam de Leon, who had also assisted with *Undertow* – to its lyrics and music. The band was at least willing and able to explain the album's title, although to this day no one really knows how to pronounce it. "Anima is a term for the female side of your psyche," said Chancellor. "It represents the stuff guys try to avoid but [which is] always there – the shit you've got to confront and deal with. The 'enema' part of it is a slightly different theme that's more self-explanatory. A lot of the album's songs are about evolution and trying to pry open your third eye."

'Stinkfist', the album's opener, is a hugely riff-heavy tune that begins with some ambient noise before Keenan assures his protagonist that whatever he's about to do won't hurt very much. For reasons best known to himself, he mutters "Chupa minha pica pichu; chupa minha pica pinto" at two minutes and 45 seconds into the song, a bit of Portuguese slang that translates as 'Suck my sweet dick; suck my sweet prick'.

Various people, including the controllers of MTV, objected to the connotations of sexual extremity associated with the title, but once again Keenan had done a good job of shocking people with a title of many different meanings. The title was a metaphor for evolution, he explained. "It's like that scene in [the 1994 sci-fi film] *Stargate*, where James Spader is sticking his hand through the stargate and he's kind of moving into the next world. First you're finger-deep, knuckle-deep, elbow-deep; [then you] move into this whole new perspective. This whole other reality of the sensual and physical. That's the thread that pretty much sews the whole album together, this idea of evolution and change and alternative perspective."

On examining the lyrics, and Tool's previous conceptual work, 'Stinkfist' doesn't seem to have an unreasonable message. However, MTV changed its title to 'Track No. 1', a reflection of its position on the album and as the first single released from it. Adam Jones joked sarcastically, "You know, I'm sure if Madonna put out 'Stinkfist,' they would have called it 'Stinkfist'. If she put out 'Bloody Cum Fart,' they would have called it 'Bloody Cum Fart'. I think MTV was even asked about that – what the difference is – and they went 'Well, that's Madonna'. It comes down to making money. And that's fine. It's their rules, it's their game. If they want to play our video, great... You know what? There's nothing you can do. All you can do is just try and keep your dignity. You try and explain things, you try and speak in metaphors and poetic ways and prose, and all some people do is try and think of ways to prevent other people from getting into it. There's no control over that. That's the monster, you know. We'll let the monster rage, and we'll stay where we're at and do what we're doing."

The video for 'Stinkfist' was denser and more abstract than the clips that had preceded it. Mostly live action but also featuring plenty of the expected sinister Claymation, the clip followed a group of hairless humanoids around a dark complex with corridors and strange machines, similar to the one in the 'Sober' video. One man is pictured swallowing rusty nails, which re-emerge from his stomach; another's arm breaks off and has its skin peeled back to reveal the red flesh beneath; a half-person with no legs is plugged into an electric wall socket; three more humans are revealed, suspended in water tanks; a female figure gently caresses a male, slipping a finger deeply underneath one of his eyelids; a large, bloody maggot or snake is pictured slithering across the floor. It's a fascinating, slightly repellent gathering of images that complement the song's sinister, droned riff perfectly.

Of the mild violence in the video, Keenan shrugged: "To me, when you see some movie about somebody doing some horrific deeds, in a way, by watching the movie you have related to and expressed that emotion and that desire, and therefore you don't need to go do it. It's kinda like letting the steam out in a way. But the more you repress it and deny it, it's gonna come up somewhere, and it's not gonna be pretty when it happens and it'll be real when it happens, rather than just a book, a story, a film or a song... those kinds of social frustrations that come about, with people lashing out, is because of unaddressed aggression, repressed emotions and that kind of stuff."

'Eulogy' is *Ænima's* next song, an eight-minute epic that has never been fully explained. Keenan sings about a recently dead person who, it seems, failed to fulfil their promises. Anchored by Chancellor's razor-sharp bass, the song includes several different guitar effects from Jones, including a heavy chorus sound and pick slides. "He had a lot to say," sneers Keenan as the song ends, "He had a lot of nothing to say..."

'H' begins with a distorted bass riff and builds with restrained menace to an atmospheric plateau, over which Keenan sings with subtle emotion about a snake that tempts him to unnamed deeds. He once told an audience before singing this largely unexplained song, "Any of you ever seen those old Warner Bros cartoons? Sometimes there's that one where the guy is trying to make a decision, and he's got an angel on one shoulder and the devil on the other. Seems pretty obvious, right? The angel is trying to give him good advice while the devil is trying to get him to do what's bad for him. It's not always that simple, though. A lot of times they're not really angels or devils, but friends giving you advice, looking out for your best interest but not really understanding what's going to be best for you. So it kind of comes down to you. You have to make the decision yourself."

After 'Useful Idiot' – a few seconds of the crackling of a vinyl LP titled, it is rumoured, after an old Soviet label for the perfect, unquestioning citizen – we come to *Ænima's* most complex song, 'Forty-Six & 2'. It's not immediately clear what Keenon is singing about when he refers to 'pickin' scabs', but towards the end of the song he seems to be looking forward with a touch of optimism to what may lie ahead. The song alternates from melodic mellowness to solid riffage, underpinned by a staccato bassline.

After much debate among fans, Keenan clarified the song's meaning. It's about the 44 chromosomes in the human body and how evolution will lead us to develop another pair. "It's in our geometry. It's there. We are moving," he said. "It's what all those people before us who were smarter have been telling us over and over. Every possible piece of architecture they left for us. Every drawing they left us. They were more in tune, and they understood where we were and where we're headed. They've left all those cute little clues everywhere for us, so hopefully we'll wake up one day and go, 'Oh fuck, that's what that meant!'"

The song reinforces the overall theme of change on the album, although this isn't particularly clear on the next track, 'Message To Harry Manback', based on a funny – if threatening – answerphone message left on Maynard's flatmate's machine. An unidentified Italian leaves a long, rambling threat of retribution accompanied by a sweet piano melody that makes it sound almost like a love poem – until you hear the words. "Pezzo di merda, figlio di una puttana" he mumbles ("Piece of shit, son of a bitch"), before pointing out that one in three Americans die of cancer and that his enemy will be one of them. Admitting that he doesn't have the courage to fight Keenan's friend, the man promises nonetheless to do exactly that if he ever meets him outside America.

Bizarrely, the message appears to be genuine – insofar as we know anything about what is real and what is not in Tool's work. Danny Carey once explained that the Italian in question was a scammer who had claimed to be a friend of Keenan's room-mate, and had stayed at their apartment while eating their food and using their phone. On finding out the truth, the residents ejected him, hence his vengeful words. The piano was played by *Ænima*'s producer David Bottrill, who said, "The threatening Italian person was leaving a real answerphone message… Basically it was from a guy who had recently been kicked out of the house for being the guest from hell." Carey added: "A so-called friend of a friend of a friend of Harry's… Before we finally managed to figure out that nobody really knew him, he had already emptied the fridge and run up a huge phone bill. He got kicked out of the house."

The next song is a Tool classic through and through – 'Hooker With A Penis'. "Title aside," said Keenan, "[this] is a very simple, very obvious song about a situation [where] somebody is arguing about the element of selling out. But the underlying principle of the song is we're all naked in this together. It's a song about nudity. You can say the song itself has a surface thing that you are getting into, but then it has kind of a 'bonus'… The record is written so that there are layers for [the listener] to get into. He'll hear 'Hooker With A Penis' and initially think it's a 'fuck somebody' song, [but] it's about unity, realising that everything is connected.

It's about breaking down the process of pointing the finger. He'll get it in about five years."

Despite its title, the song is one of the most digestible on the album, based on Keenan's dialogue with a young fan who once told him that he thought Tool had sold out. The reference to 'OGT' is presumably supposed to mean 'Original Gangsta Tool', as in one of the very first Tool fans. In the song, Keenan doesn't take this criticism lightly, calling the kid a 'dumb fuck' and 'dipshit', apparently for buying the record in the first place.

Naturally, many people took the song title at face value and assumed that Tool were singing about a transsexual. This irritated Jones, who sighed: "Most people take everything literally," he says. "They don't want to think. If you throw something at them, they just look at the surface level. If they don't understand it, they immediately think it's evil... On the surface, ['Hooker...'] sounds like the heaviest song, but really, to me, it's the light relief of the album. It says 'Shut up and buy our record' to all those little kids who even suggest that we've sold out. Just the idea of selling out – what does that really mean, since everyone is bowing to the man? The song is a little break in the record, but in the heaviest possible form. If you're going to get any relief from Tool, you're going to get it right in your face." Based on a dark, almost stoner-rock riff, the song sounds like Kyuss or early Queens Of The Stone Age and is musically as well as lyrically among the most accessible on the album.

After 'Intermission' – 56 seconds of amusing, fairground organ-style music – we hear 'Jimmy', with a central riff that is a guitar version of the same organ melody. It's a quieter, more introspective song that is thought to centre on Keenan's memories of his childhood and a specific pivotal event.

'Die Eier Von Satan' is the sound of Tool interfering with their listeners' preconceptions once again. A sinister voice speaks in German, while an industrial sound clatters and wheezes in the background. The voice slowly builds in volume and malice until it is shouting, accompanied by mass audience applause. The overall effect is like a Hollywood version of a World War II Nazi rally, and probably disturbed quite a few people – until its true meaning was revealed. As with 'Message To Harry Manback', Tool had taken words in a foreign language and surrounded them with a musical backing that was at complete odds to their meaning. The title translates as both 'The Eggs Of Satan' and 'Satan's Balls', 'eggs' being German slang for testicles. The aggressive German rhetoric, meanwhile – supplied by Marko Fox of Pigmy Love Circus – is nothing more than a recipe for hash cookies.

The supremely sinister drone of 'Pushit' ("Pushit on me, shoving me, pushit on me... shit on me, shit on me") is a highlight of this album: Jones' layers of low, doomy guitar tone and the opportunity for Maynard to showcase his vocal range make it one of the most gripping Tool songs yet. The song is as memorable for the band's advancement into prog-rock territory as it is for the virtuoso vocals, however: at almost ten minutes in length, 'Pushit' allows Tool to stretch out and enjoy the space, especially in its long midsection, made up of atmospheric echoes and dramatic textures. It's a huge leap forward for the band – who had been writing rough-and-tumble metal songs just three years before – and marks the point at which Tool truly found their own sound, assisted in no small measure by producer Bottrill, whom we'll come to in a moment.

After the two-minute ambient drone of 'Cesaro Summability' (named after a summation technique invented by Cesaro, an Italian mathematician), we're into 'Ænema' – almost the title track, one vowel excepted. It's the most uncompromising song here, both musically and lyrically. Anchored by a prominent, aggressive rhythm arrangement, the song veers from mood to mood, with Jones on incandescent form and Keenan multilayering vocals and comments by the band's friend, comedian Bill Hicks, on the possible aftermath of Los Angeles falling into the Pacific Ocean.

As Keenan explained, "People realise that if LA were to go underwater, within 48 hours the economic systems across the world would collapse because they're all so integrated and reliant on each other. Just think of the chaos that was going on in the southwestern United States when all the [electricity] went out for, like, an hour. No power for an hour. People were running into each other in the street. Insanity. And that's just some power. Imagine if the banking system went down because of it... The underlying thing isn't so much, 'Learn to swim because LA's going into the ocean'. It's more like, 'Get back in touch with the collective unconscious and learn to swim with everyone in there. Know how connected everything is. Literally, figuratively, spiritually."

Critics and fans didn't like this, understandably, particularly in California. Keenan was unapologetic, however, merely saying: "If you're an advocate, or put any kind of faith into. Earth changes and pending changes, you have to figure that those are going to be, at first, relatively chaotic and violent. It's gonna be chaotic because there are new ideas, and there is of course resistance to new ideas. The idea of holding yourself together and walking through that chaos takes a lot of focus and faith and clarity. When you realise the whole unity of it all, it just gives you a better perspective."

"The Earth has its own frequency," added Chancellor. "I'm not a scientist, but change, on massive scales, has occurred on Earth for millions of years. Some people think we're approaching another time of change... Anyone who thinks we advocate the destruction or sinking of California is taking the lyrics very literally. We're saying that, of all places, this place could do with a good enema; it could do with being totally flushed out. It's suffering from the weight of so many fucked-up things. People have lost touch with their own existence, they're unaware of the big picture because of industries that thrive here. We're saying, prepare yourself for change. Flush it all away and learn how to swim."

Much of the song was to do with the idiotic materialism of Los Angeles, Keenan revealed: "It really comes down to discovering what matters. Do you really need your Porsche? Do you need all these things to really evolve who you are? Perhaps the next step of evolution would be the next piece in us that the children that we're bearing today already have. They're going to grow up understanding that unity inherently. I would doubt that our generation has that, but who's to say that the next generation doesn't have that quality in them? It's already being put into them, and they understand it. When you were a kid, were you recycling? Now, we're just completely Earth-aware, and we're understanding our responsibility to this globe. Perhaps our children are going to understand [that] yes, in fact they don't need their Porsche. They can understand alternative medicine and alternative energy sources that don't necessarily cure cancer with cancer."

The importance of this concept – that humankind should rediscover its unity and evolution through a mental or physical cataclysm – is reflected in the artwork for the American pressing of the album, which was nominated for a Grammy Award for Best Recording Package (although it didn't win). The CD cover came with a lenticular viewer, presenting the user with the illusion that the images beneath it moved in three dimensions. The cover itself was a white rectangle on a black background with white flares erupting from it, referred to by the band and the artist, Cam de Leon, as the 'Smokebox'. Eyes surrounded it, and smoke appeared to emanate from the rectangle. There was also de Leon's picture *Ocular Orifice*, a close-up of an eye with two irises (which 'moved' under the lenticular viewer); a picture of a naked person contorted in such a way that his or her face appeared to be performing oral sex on his or her self, with the band seated on a sofa and Keenan throwing a rose at the figure; and a painting of the late Hicks (who had died of cancer in 1994, aged only 32), captioned 'Another Dead Hero'. Relevantly to the song 'Ænema', a picture of California before and after an earthquake is situated in the jewel-case tray. The packaging also contained the inscription: "Beliefs are dangerous. Beliefs allow the mind to stop functioning. A non-functioning mind is clinically dead. Believe in nothing'..." Keenan explained: "Danny picked that out. That gives you a wider perspective on the band's ideas because [since the other members] don't write the lyrics, their ideas aren't necessarily being expressed in words."

Four minutes of '(-) Ions' (that is, 'negative ions') – a sheet of metal manipulated by Carey and Chancellor to make a thunderous rumble, treated in the studio and underpinned by a drum pattern – precede the epic 'Third Eye', the 13-minute song that ends the record. It has multiple sections, which start and finish without warning, notably a long, almost silent part in which Keenan whispers over Carey's quiet bass drum, apparently addressing the subject of the mysterious pineal gland situated at the top of the human head. Of all the songs on *Ænima*, this one contains the deepest philosophical explorations, with the band spending a lot of time explaining it but finally leaving most of the theories to the fans.

"'Third Eye' is the ultimate song to me," opined Chancellor, already well aware of the rumour-mill that surrounded Tool and their lyrics. "It takes you on a trip without the necessity of taking any drugs at all. It addresses the fact that there is so much misinformation about drugs. They can open a lot of doors if treated the right way. For us, everyone does their own thing, everyone's up for new experiences, but only in order to draw something out of that. Luckily, we have a job that allows us to address the things that have come out of those experiences."

The song begins with Bill Hicks' famous discourse about drugs, in which he states that if anyone doesn't think that substances have been beneficial to society, they should go home and burn all their CDs, because the musicians who made them were "really fucked up on drugs". Of Hicks – whose profile was less high in 1996 than it is today – Keenan said: "[Our fans] will search him out. That's why we put the picture on the album, so they can get a wider idea. It helps people understand where we're coming from as well, if they can get perspective like that. They'll get Bill's tapes and listen to what he's talking about, listen to our album, and then hopefully have enough intellect to make the leap and say, 'I see where the connection is'."

He went on, getting into a spiritual theme: "If you look at Bill's work and really understand where he's coming from, you start to realise he's not really gone, he's just going through a change. Which is what he said throughout his entire work... He's just gone through a change, whatever aspect of him that was, whatever part of his soul was in that physical form at that time has just changed form... When he's talking about the young man on acid realising that all matter is merely energy condensed with soil vibration, he says there's no such thing as death... Perhaps his soul decided it was time to check out. I think in the particular medium [i.e. comedy] he was working in, it was almost more powerful. It will be more powerful and more effective if he's not here. It may be one of those things that ends up transcending itself."

Note that Keenan had come a long way, intellectually: no longer was he 'only' a heavy metal singer. He was now something of a philosopher – and to his fans, on whom *Ænima* made a vast and ongoing impact, he was rapidly becoming a prophet. This was helped along nicely by ruminations such as, "'Third Eye' is a metaphor for that alternative perspective I've been talking about. It's a metaphor for that state you would get into if you were really exploring the idea of meditation and alternative realities [via] breathing and meditation, but also, there is a third eye in your head, physically. It's a gland, where if you were to put your finger in the very top of your head, in the dead center of your forehead and back right there, there's a gland, and it basically is an eye. It's the pineal gland. It has a lens, it faces straight up, and it has all the rods and cones necessary to focus light, but it's not something we've used for a long, long time."

Keenan was obviously aware of the mockery that might accompany such musings, adding: "If you're one of those New Age freaks who believes that whales and dolphins are more evolved than we are, then you start recognising the physical characteristics of what that means. They do breathe light through that top part of their head, where that third eye is present in our skull... In our recorded history it took us about 4,000 years to gather a certain amount of information, and then all of a sudden within 1,000 years we doubled that, and within 500 years we doubled that, et cetera. We're leapfrogging with some of the discoveries that we're coming up with. Just think of the everyday things you're into, and just try to place them 20 years ago. Think of the chaos. If somebody were to say right now, 'The mothership has just landed on the White House lawn', people wouldn't freak out nearly as much as they did when there were radio broadcasts for *The War Of The Worlds* and people were jumping off buildings."

Despite his ruminations, Keenan laughed off the idea that he was a spokesman of any kind, saying: "I don't have any original ideas. I'm just expressing what I've read and how I feel about things. I'm taking age-old ideas and expressing them in a medium I'm familiar with, which is rock... I have my beliefs, but I can't even discuss that with the average person, because they just think I'm nuts, which is fine, cos I am. I'm really left with a choice. Do I want to go out on a limb and alienate people, or do I wanna filter out some of those ideas that I'm into that will at least keep people interested enough to explore for themselves?"

Maynard did acknowledge the influence of his upbringing on all this enlightened theory, adding: "I grew up Southern Baptist, and where I grew up, there were no Christian churches around that were teaching anything about crystals or chakras or community, any kind of wacky New Age stuff. But now there are so many churches that incorporate that kind of stuff, and understand more psychology, and incorporate it into what they consider their dogma."

The new incarnation of Tool – from metalheads with body-parts metaphors to progressive-rock social commentators – went down well with the fanbase, who took *Ænima* to number two on the US albums charts. It sold about 10,000 copies fewer than Nirvana's *From The Muddy Banks Of The Wishkah*, due at least in part to the fact that the retail giant Wal-Mart refused to stock it because of the connotations of 'Stinkfist'. Asked how he thought the album would sell, Keenan said: "I've just got a feeling that a lot of the fans who got into us and heard a lot of Pantera in the sound are definitely not going to like the new record. The first thing we put out was *Opiate*. That was a pretty aggressive record, but it needed to be angry because that's where our heads were at – it was our primal scream, so to speak. But I think that's mellowed out, and there's a lot of different stuff on our minds right now that doesn't have much to do with anger and frustration. Personally, my thoughts are more intro-spective. Well, we've travelled overseas, and you see so much more when you open yourself up to different countries, different people and music being played by different musicians. When you see how other people live, and their struggles and aspirations, you go through a change. You tend to come to terms with a lot of the shit going on in your own small world. It's like, 'Wow, I was moaning about all the junk in my life, and it was such a waste of energy'."

The band knew that *Ænima* was far from the usual rock album template of 1996, but shrugged off any concerns of it being too challenging for the public. Chancellor said, reasonably enough: "We just tried to keep our heads down and continue the evolution of ideas, and not notice what was popular and what was current. If we hadn't done that, things would have gone horribly wrong. But it's not in any of our natures to worry about being a hugely popular band, and I think the people who have been into the music in the past expect us not to stand still… Personally, and it goes for the rest of the band as well, I'm always trying to hear things that I've never heard before, when it comes to approaching songwriting. Who wants to be clichéd? We're also very open about just letting an idea breathe and just going wherever it's going to go, rather than just stopping it at a certain point and then using that…

If you let things go, you can stick ideas on top of each other that don't make a lot of sense unless you let it go far enough, and then it has this cycle to it that can be original."

Very eloquent. However, the usually relaxed Justin could be abrasive when he chose to be. Of his English background, he seethed: "The music scene is run by the two papers [the *NME* and *Melody Maker*], with no scope of radio play. Everyone's looking over their shoulder. They will only commit to something if someone else does. That's how you get a movement going, like shoegazing or Britpop. If you don't conform to that, you are irrelevant. People in England say that Tool is not relevant... By virtue of that comment, we're completely relevant."

He was right. Not only was *Ænima* entirely a product of the shifting metal scene of the day, it drew the rock-consuming fanbase towards itself like some arcane spider to a fly. Anyone willing to listen to challenging music that offered more than the usual chart nonsense could find something in the album that thrilled or stimulated them. Some of this came from the mystique of its images and lyrics; some from the refusal of the band to explain their work in too much detail – and some from the exploratory sounds that came from the record.

Credit for this last aspect of *Ænima* must go to producer David Bottrill, better known for his work with Peter Gabriel and King Crimson than in the world of heavy metal. The reasons for his recruitment to the Tool cause became clear after the album's release. As Chancellor explained, "We met a lot of people who were the hot producers of the moment, and they all seemed to be able to do a good job – but they had a lot of attitude. We wanted someone who could push the sounds a bit, and we all enjoy King Crimson; that's how we came up with the idea of using David. This new material is a bit broader and more sonically challenging, so we didn't want to use someone who would just nail down a heavy rock sound. He was really the right person."

Bottrill himself recalled, "Funnily enough, they called and asked if I would work on [their new album], and they sent me their *Opiate* [EP] and *Undertow*... I listened to them and thought, 'I've never done anything like this before... why would this kind of American metal band be sending me things, when all I've done was English art-rock music?' At first I thought they had me confused with someone else, so I spoke to them and asked if they were sure they had the right guy. As it turned out, Danny, the drummer, was a huge King Crimson fan, and Adam the guitar player's favourite album had been *The First Day* [by Robert Fripp of King Crimson and David Sylvian of Japan, 1993]. The singer Maynard was a huge Real World music fan. A lot of the stuff I worked on happened to be their favourites, even though they were musically doing different things."

He added, "They thought I wasn't an 'American rock producer', but they figured they already knew what area they wanted and that I would bring something else to their music. So I met them in Los Angeles, sat in on one of their rehearsals, and right away we hit it off. It was an exciting rehearsal, despite the fact that I sat beside Danny's ride cymbal, which made me deaf by the end of the day. They knew what I could do, they knew what they and their fans wanted, so I went along with their confidence."

Confidence is the key word here. By now Tool had evolved into a musical phenomenon of enormous creative and performing power, with each member contributing something unique. Carey provided a solid backbone and an inquisitive spiritualism; Chancellor was the pragmatist, but with plenty of youthful optimism; Jones was a sonic expert, happy to experiment in all directions; and Keenan was and remains the enigma, a man whose ideas veer from the absurd to the fearsome in a moment. Bottrill's triumph was that he harnessed all these talents and created a whole that was as great as the sum of its parts – no mean feat.

Keenan in particular realised that Tool was no longer just a metal band. The rage that had driven their early work had refocused on *Ænima* into a more positive energy that pushed up and outwards with equal power, but also with a subtlety that many people entirely missed. As Maynard put it, "You can only scream your head off for so long before you get kind of tired of screaming... Anger is definitely a very cleansing emotion, but there comes a time when it stops being all that useful." He still experienced a violent need for expression, however, explaining: "Go down and try to get through the intersection at Santa Monica and Western [in LA] without having to wait a half-hour. Try to talk to anybody in this town about anything that has to do with anything, and see what kind of opposition you get with your friendly nature. Try to sit down with somebody who has been repressed all their life, who has had to deal with racial prejudices and has had so many hurdles placed in front of them all [their] life... it's enough to drive you nuts. There's plenty of inspiration. There's plenty of fuel."

Keenan welcomed the fact that most of their listeners understood Tool on a relatively cerebral level, rather than viewing their heroes merely as a band to headbang to. "All of these people have made us great big rock stars," he reasoned. "We knew if we could get in front of people, they'd see where we were coming from and what we were about. But a lot more people caught on than we thought would, so I think we owe it to them to keep playing... I do know that compared to a lot of the bands that we get lumped in with, I have a more open nature than most of my so-called peers. This totally male, angst-filled energy is coming off of a lot of these guys... I listen to Joni Mitchell, so draw your own conclusions. Most hard-rock or hard-alternative bands have a very masculine, linear approach, while I think there's more of a feminine balance to our point of view. I think that our softer, more compassionate edge is missed a lot of the time, that people think we're all about hate or something. That's not it, you know? The songs are very angry, but anger is a constructive emotion – hate is not. We're not about hate, we're about anger and emotion and intense releases of feelings, and working through those feelings. With some bands the cornerstone of the music is that rage and hate, and you've got to relive it on stage every night. How is it constructive for you to be hateful every night?"

By 1996 and '97 the wave of alternative metal spearheaded by Tool in the wake of grunge was beginning to evolve into nu-metal. Keenan saw this coming and was quick to separate himself from that movement. "I'm sick of that whole attitude," he said, "the one that puts Tool in with metal bands. Not that there is anything wrong with metal bands, but we're not metal. We have a hard edge but we're not metal, the press... can't seem to distinguish between alternative and metal. Take *Metal Hammer* for instance. I mean, what is so metal about it? It's so hard doing this and trying to keep your integrity, everyone wants to sum up your music in terms of whichever band is most popular at the time. I mean, we're getting compared to Marilyn Manson, what the fuck is going on? I think they're a great band, really entertaining, very scary – but Tool are nothing like them. When we first released *Opiate* the press were comparing us to Nirvana, then they were comparing us to Nine Inch Nails... I just don't understand it, it's like we're not allowed to be Tool?"

Of music listeners' tendency to categorise Tool alongside Korn and the rest of the nu-metallers, Jones was more optimistic, saying: "I think it's about as big as it's going to get and then it's going to taper off. A lot of the young kids are going to realise [that] we're not just about fucking and moshing – it's more about sounds, and so I think a lot of them are going to move on... There's people that would get into watching me do a card trick, because there's a mathematics behind it that really intrigues them, and the joker keeps coming back up. And then there's the ones that get really excited to see you shuffling the deck, the noise and the cards flying everywhere. So that's how I see our audience evolving: the ones that are into the technique and the emotion are going to be there – and the ones that are really into the flash of the shuffle are going to move on to some other flash."

Alongside Keenan's more abrasive ideas, Jones was evolving a mellower, more hippie view of the philosophy behind the band. This accompanied the many hints on *Ænima* towards the progressive-rock bands of the Seventies that had so inspired him. Of the album's many long songs, he mused: "I look at each song as a little film. I like to start with an opening shot, and then segue into different scenes. I like to drift off in the middle, go somewhere totally unexpected, and then have everything resolve itself in the end. It's a whole experimental journey... I remember when I was a kid, [the Seventies prog bands would] create their own whole world. The atmosphere around their records and stuff was just so cool. They had a bigger vision than a lot of the bands around now, who just come out with an album and it seems like a bunch of unconnected songs; it just doesn't have a tight, cohesive thing going on. The bands now don't have vision that can transcend putting a bunch of songs out to get played on the radio. It's just so fucking boring... what those progressive bands did [is] a hell of a lot better than anything Pearl Jam or Soundgarden have done. At least they had something artistic in mind, or were trying to get to a higher place."

Ænima was released on October 1 1996 on CD, with a vinyl LP version appearing a week earlier, presumably to encourage sales of the then-declining format. It sold quickly for an alternative-rock album, eventually hitting triple-platinum status seven years later, although that's hardly a world-class performance: it took a particular kind of music fan to appreciate its content thanks to its impenetrable nature. Appropriately, given its philosophical bent, it was dedicated to Bill Hicks.

A tour began in October 1996, only two weeks after *Ænima*'s release. There was a palpable sense that Tool was entering a new era, and taking heavy music along with them.

Chapter 7

1997–1998

"We're not sexually frustrated," said Danny Carey as 1997 dawned. "There's no problems getting laid... We might not get as many girls as some other bands, but most of the girls those guys fuck I wouldn't want anyway."

Adam followed this up with, "Get this, it blew my mind. We went to a porno shop in Las Vegas and I found this fat blow-up doll – if you want to have sex with the fattest blow-up doll possible, you go to this porno shop. I was just blown away by this, so we bought four of them: we used to inflate them and have them hovering over us during the shows in different positions and wearing different things. Now I'm pretty kinky about what I like in sex, but you'd have to be pretty desperate to make it with a fake fat chick..."

A new era had arrived, all right – an era in which the members of Tool were now cult artists, with all the trappings of success this implied. Thanks to two successful albums and a growing reputation as psychedelic shamans of rock, the band members had it all at their feet. It was refreshing, then – and almost unprecedented in the rock arena – that Keenan, Jones, Chancellor and Carey didn't go down the rock-pig route, despite the odd bit of groupie attention referred to above. They seemed

77

to prefer to allude to sexually subversive activity rather than reference it directly, as when Jones explained, "I get a lot of cool guitar sounds out of an Epilady [an electric shaver]... I got the idea from Dave Navarro, whom I once saw perform a solo with a vibrator when he was in Jane's Addiction. I thought that was so cool... It uses a spinning wire – almost like a guitar string – to rip the hair off a woman's legs. I place it over the pickups and control the speed of the motor by keeping my thumb on the coil. And then I started listening to German industrial bands such as Einstürzende Neubauten who use crazy stuff on their instruments to take their sound to another place. So I'll buy a bunch of toys, rip the guts out, and use the motors to make some noises.

"If it's having sex," he went on in his neo-hippie fashion, "[or] reading a book, whatever – as long as my mind is open and I'm expanding my consciousness and I'm aware of my surroundings and I don't take them for granted... that's what it's about, and I think most people don't wanna think about that... [it] makes me sick. They all want answers and they all wanna get wrapped up in stuff, so it slows down our evolution. Bill Hicks said [that] evolution didn't stop at our songs, we can keep going... Spoken language is just one way of communicating, but there's so many other ways."

Communication was a central theme of 1997 for Tool, who played over 60 shows, beginning with an overseas jaunt in the late winter. The band hadn't yet been doing this for so long that touring had become a chore, as Carey explained: "Tool [is] one of the easiest things I have ever had to do. I mean, I spent a lot of my life trying to avoid having to do normal work, so for me Tool was the perfect escape. I could still let out aggressions or explore new territories on a daily basis. There really aren't that many other things that I would rather be doing. Sure, I'd like to be a professional basketball player, but I'd always like to continue playing in Tool....At the beginning of a tour we're all keen to get out on the road and play, but I think it really comes down to the idea that the grass is always greener on the other side. When we're not on the road, we want to tour; and when we've toured for a long time, we can't wait to get back into the studio to record. That's usually the way it goes. Fortunately for us, we're not at the point where we have families... We don't feel as much stress having to go on tour as some other bands might."

Perhaps this relaxed approach came from Tool's policy of allowing themselves time for their own projects – in particular Keenan, who plays in two other bands mentioned later in this book. One of his first guest appearances came in January when he duetted with his friend Tori Amos, the singer-songwriter, on her song 'Muhammad My Friend'. A haunting piano ballad like so much of Amos' material, the song was performed at Madison Square Garden in New York in aid of Tori's charity, the Rape, Abuse & Incest National Network (RAINN).

Asked for her thoughts on Keenan, Amos explained: "First of all he makes the greatest cookies I've ever had. And Maynard's so wonderful. He just really is… he's a good buddy, so I called him up. Maynard's got a lot of interesting ideas about many things… he really is this beautiful guy. And he has a deep spiritual currency, where he believes that you can't separate yourself from what you create. He and I are very close friends and I feel that he's under no illusions that if you put it out there, you cannot separate yourself from it, when the heat gets great, when people disagree or if you stir it up. You can't just collect the publishing cheque and not collect the controversy that you create with it."

She went on, rather gushingly: "We both have a real fascination about comparative religions. And we spend a lot of time talking about that, and what's been hidden. We talk about this one book sometimes, *Bloodline of The Holy Grail: The Hidden Lineage Of Jesus*, and how we've been very manipulated through the ages about the information that's been withheld. I think that if we had the time we'd both be students somewhere… We both believe that whatever you put out there, the phrase, 'Oh I'm just kidding… Oh, I didn't mean that', is fuckin' weak. That is a limp dick if I've ever heard one. 'I don't mean it.' 'You guys are overreacting.' Man, that's child's play. I just don't have a lot of respect for people that don't stand by their work, whatever it is. Then you're a hypocrite… Maynard really stands where he stands. His beliefs aren't something he negotiates with. He doesn't change from one day to another so that he can get along with *Spin* or *Raygun* or whatever else the popular [magazine] that week is. That's why I respect him. There aren't a lot of musicians who are honest enough with their dark side, and humble enough. He knows his shortcomings and that's part of his beauty, and strength."

This view of Keenan – that he is a man of principle, and perhaps even a prophet of sorts – was spreading through Tool's fanbase. Carey, too, was quick to discuss his own esoteric beliefs, saying: "The book I just finished was *Cosmic Trigger Volume III* by Robert Anton Wilson. I really like his view on things, and I think he's got a great sense of humour. I think his attitude toward the scientific community is pretty right on, because I think there's a lot of information withheld just so professors don't lose jobs. I think there's a lot of suppression of information going on, where people are choosing fear over compassion. They get their little niche carved out and they don't want to lose it, so they grab onto these things. It's natural self-preservation, I suppose."

Despite his more outlandish beliefs, like Chancellor, Danny retained a down-to-earth realism that kept the band anchored. He knew, for example, how quickly audiences tire of bands and their endless opinions, musing: "We did lots of interviews with the last record, and you do have to get your name out there somewhat, but we just don't want to be overexposed. There's no reason to make people sick of you. I usually tend to shy away from doing interviews... I mean, it's fine to communicate with people, but then there's also a very valuable thing that I think a lot of bands forget, [which is that] no matter how cool a band is or what their image is, things are usually better in people's imaginations than in reality. I think that the less you go out and exploit yourself, the better an image you have in people's minds... It's easy for people to get sick of you if you're shovelled down their throats in the wrong way. As long as we keep control over our advertising plans and things like that, it makes it easier for us to maintain control. That's one of the things we were lucky enough to have stipulated in our record deal. We got approval over our artwork and our advertisements and everything. We have complete creative control, and I think a lot of bands don't have that luxury."

As Tool's profile grew, so they began to attract attention from other well-known music-industry movers and shakers. One of these was the DJ Howard Stern, whose mildly offensive radio show was huge at the time. He had often proclaimed his support for Tool on the air, but this soured when a disagreement flared up about the use of one of their songs – the cover of Led Zeppelin's 'No Quarter'. Stern had asked for the song to appear on the soundtrack of *Private Parts*, his semi-fictionalised autobiography movie, and Tool's label, Zoo, agreed to it. However, the label had failed to check with the band first, who refused permission – not, it seems, because of any antipathy to Stern or his movie, but because they refuse in principle to allow their work to appear on film soundtracks, this being a relinquishment of control over their work that is against their values. Stern took this the wrong way and, according to *Circus* magazine, said during live ads on his show, "Fuck 'em… Fuck Tool and fuck Zoo, and I don't care if you print that. They're assholes," before instructing his producer to remove Tool's music from all parts of his broadcasts.

Another vociferous opponent of Tool emerged in the form of Courtney Love, the always-fatiguing singer of alternative-rock band Hole and the widow of Kurt Cobain, who had allegedly made some uncomplimentary comments about Keenan. As Maynard told Kurt Loder at MTV, "Courtney hates me. She called me a media whore once. Isn't that great? I have the distinction of being called a media whore by Courtney Love," before explaining that he had launched a typically uncompromising counterattack: "Everybody at that time was trying to get us to do all these benefit shows – you know, like 'Free Tibet'. And I was like, 'I'm gonna have my own platform: 'Free Frances Bean'. Because just watching the tornado that is her mother, my first thought was, 'Oh my God, how is [Love and Cobain's daughter] Frances Bean gonna survive this insanity?' Because artists can be extremely eccentric and insane, and unfortunately, the people they hurt the most are the people that are closest to them. The [T-shirt bearing the slogan] was kind of a flippant joke, and then it just spiralled out of control – everyone wanted them, and I was giving them away."

Despite these scuffles, Keenan retained his dignity, with his explanations of the themes of *Ænima* somehow in tune with the storm of flux through which Tool were passing. "It's certainly a metaphor for change… on several levels," he said. "It's about actual physical changes in the Earth that will result in spiritual growth, depending how you look at it. You can choose to see it as an apocalyptic scenario, or look at it like global awareness and realise [that] changes in the Earth are inevitable. The refrain of the song ['Aenema'] is kind of a joke. 'Learn to swim' is rather than just, 'The shit's hitting the fan, [you'd] better learn how to swim,' but it can also be looked at as involving the whole collective environment, and how all of us as individuals need to learn how to go into the deep dark waters."

Meanwhile, what he said about 'Hooker With A Penis' seemed to sum up Tool's own ascent. "'Selling out' is a silly term," he pondered. "That's the point of the song. It's a silly, empty set of words because we are all the driving force, all of us, of the economy. We are part of that, every one of us. You can't sell out because you have sold out... To make a judgment on how someone has decided to walk their path is kind of condescending. So, that's where I'm coming at with that term. It doesn't mean anything, so when a little kid clips off about Tool selling out, this song is a way to remind him in a subtle way that we're all in this together. This is a song about unity, not cutting myself down. It's about me already being down and bringing this kid back down to where we all are. He's not above it, he's down here with us."

As well as the Tori Amos duet (released on her album *Live In NY*), Keenan recorded guest vocals on an album by drummers Tim Alexander of Primus and Mike Bordin of Faith No More called *Flyin' Traps*. Carey also lent his drumming talents to songs by Paul D'Amour's new project, Lusk, which released an album that year called *Free Mars*, also on Zoo. Recalling the split two years before, Carey explained: "Paul just got more into doing his own thing and he had a bigger desire to be more melodically experimental. With Tool, we have good melodies going on – especially from Maynard's end – but it's more rhythmic and percussive. He was just leaning towards playing lighter music that wasn't so heavy, and he's always loved to play guitar too. I remember, even when we first got the band together, there was a time when Paul had suggested that maybe we could get another bass player so that we could have two guitars, but I was like, 'There's no way we're getting another asshole in this band'. That's just the way his music was evolving, and he's always been really sonically experimental too; you could see some of that show through in his bass playing... Of course it was a little intense when it was all going down, but I played on three songs on Paul's new project, Lusk, which has an album coming out on Zoo in January... they just finished it: it sounds really good."

Tool's major activity in 1997 was their touring schedule, however, and after a trip through Holland, Belgium, France, Germany and the UK, they swung from the US East Coast via the Midwest and Deep South to California. Australia and New Zealand followed, although a slight panic was felt among the fanbase on April 1 when the 'semi-official' Tool website, www.toolshed.down.net, ran a spoof story about a supposed tour-bus crash. The webmaster, Kabir Akhtar, is alleged to have written firstly that "at least three of the band are listed in critical condition", and later an apology for the stunt that read, "[the site] will not indulge itself in such outlandish pranks in the future".

On their return to the USA, Tool headlined Lollapalooza '97 at a crucial time for alternative music. The scene had become diffuse by the mid-Nineties, with Kurt Cobain's death in 1994 the beginning of the end for the term 'alternative': as the fans grew older, many felt (cynically but justifiably) that popular music could not be anything other than a product of the industrial elite, an attitude shared by Tool and many other bands. "It's pretty grim in general the way the big companies control all of it," said Carey. "When it comes down to it, we're really just making ads for Bertelsmann Music Group [Zoo owners BMG], they're the ones that are controlling all this shit. They make a lot more money out of our records than we do, so you've just got to have a sense of humour about it."

This tour was the last Lollapalooza until its return in 2003, although at the time it was feared that it would never come back. Nu-metal was beginning an assault on the charts that would last about six years: in 1997, the rap-metal groove of bands like Korn seemed like the future, with Marilyn Manson, Coal Chamber and many others joined by Linkin Park, and soon after Slipknot and Limp Bizkit. You only have to take a look at the 'final' Lollapalooza line-up to see how few bands survived the nu-metal wave: Tool shared the main stage with Orbital, Snoop Dogg, Tricky, Korn, James and the Marley Brothers, while Beck and Porno For Pyros dominated the second stage – otherwise occupied by entirely forgotten names. A lounge-music version of 'Hooker With A Penis', remixed by Tool's guitar tech Billy Howerdel, played between sets and, by all accounts, Keenan et al were the only truly memorable act on the bill, with their set accompanied by video clips on a large screen.

When Carey looked back at the event, he obviously didn't share some fans' gut feeling that it had been taken over by the record industry, musing: "I never hooked the Lollapalooza thing in with a big corporate nightmare-type situation. It's becoming more and more like that, of course; it grows and grows every year, and it's turning into this big beast I suppose. But when we did it, we were playing with bands we enjoyed. I liked Alice In Chains and Primus and Fishbone and Rage Against The Machine... Three or four of the bands were LA bands that we knew, so we were like, 'Yeah! We get to do 40 shows with our friends and have a good time all summer'. And it did kind of launch our careers in a lot of ways, because of the media coverage that MTV gave that: they noticed who we were and then picked up our video and things took off from there."

Still, the festival's trademark blend of electronica, hip-hop and rock was beginning to seem a little tame compared with the ferocious bellows of the nu-metal crowd, especially when the summer circuit gave way in 1998 to a newcomer with which Lollapalooza couldn't hope to compete – the Ozzfest, created by Ozzy Osbourne's wife and manager, Sharon, as a middle-finger response to the Lollapalooza organisers (they'd refused to let Ozzy on the bill a few years previously). Times were a-changing.

Lollapalooza was a major success for Tool, as it had been in 1993 – but trouble lay ahead for them in the form of a disagreement with their record label. Zoo had gone bust and been taken over by Volcano Records, with whom the band had signed a contract permitting the label to renew its contract with them when the agreement came to an end. Once the agreement did in fact cease, Tool and their management began courting offers from other record companies after a certain period, arguing that the period required for Volcano to renew had lapsed. In a predictable escalation, the label disagreed and sued the band, with court proceedings forbidding Tool from recording while the case dragged out. Tool then countersued, and an out-of-court decision was eventually reached three years later.

It emerged that Tool had been dissatisfied with their label for some time, despite the initially positive state of play at the start of the agreement. Even after a million sales of *Ænima*, royalties were slow to come in, with the first payment to the band a paltry amount. "It was for something really insulting, like ten grand," said Keenan. "That's where it all started. When we discovered that they forgot to pick up the option on our contract, we said, 'That's it. We're out of here'... All the stuff from the royalty companies is so far backlogged, we still haven't even gotten anything from *Opiate*. I expected to at least get a cheque for like 50 cents or something. I suppose it will be a big thrill if I get a gold record, then I can send it to my mom so she can go, 'I don't have to feed my son any more!'"

Volcano, which had renamed itself Freeworld in the interim, was bullish about its actions, with founder Kevin Czinger reported by MTV as saying, "[Tool] have left us with no other choice but to protect our company and artists by filing this suit... Tool has taken what was a creatively and financially successful relationship and has recklessly abandoned it... We will do what is necessary to preserve this relationship." The ensuing legal shenanigans sapped the band so much that they seriously wondered whether they could continue to work together. "We were ready to bail because we weren't making music together any more," said Carey. "We'd just get together to talk about what we're gonna do with this lawyer or that lawyer – all this business shit."

"We didn't get together to open up an office and send each other faxes or become lawyers," added Keenan. "When you're forced to do that with each other, you're in an awkward position... you start to really resent each other because you don't wanna be doing it, that's not why we're here. Once that stuff gets out of the way and you get back to making music, it's like, 'Oh yeah, that's why I'm here'. It can be a very taxing process, all the business, and I think that's why we have prevailed where our peers failed, in that we established that communication and really put our compassion to the test, learned a lot about each other, not really compromising, but just accepting each other."

Much later, when the dust had settled, Keenan looked back on the episode with bitter humour, explaining: "I think they just gave up. At one point they probably were trying to gain complete control, but they just went, 'Oh, fuck it, we can't. We can't fuck with these guys, cos they'll stop doing things until we go away'."

Jones, the least businesslike of the four members, added: "Zoo became Volcano Entertainment and was sold to this jackass, who renamed the label Freeworld Entertainment before changing the name back to Zoo.

At that time, he was supposed to pick up our contract option, but he forgot to. And since we weren't too happy with him in the first place, we informed the label that they forgot to pick up our option and, therefore, we were out of our contract. Of course, they freaked out and tried to sue us for every reason they could think of, just to make it all messy. They hoped that they could at least sell the company to someone else and then let them settle with us. Which is exactly what happened."

Of the falling-out, Jones explained: "They offered us a larger amount of control in exchange for a smaller amount of money, which seemed like a fine trade to us. And we did have control, to a point. But there was the issue of us being promoted as a metal band. And they were supposed to check with us before doing anything that would affect the band. Of course, they'd call us when they knew we were out, and then say, 'Well, we tried to get hold of you'. That sort of shit happened all the time."

Eventually, a deal was brokered between Zoo, Tool and a third party, a label set up by Peter Mensch and Cliff Burnstein of management giants Q-Prime named Volcano II. Tool set up their own label, Tool Dissectional, and formed a partnership with Volcano II for future releases. Jones described the new setup as "a joint company, where we're supposed to make decisions together. I thought it would be good, and it is – to a point. But the guys who own it are managers and it's still just a business. They have their perspective on how things work and we have ours. No one's wrong, but no one agrees either."

Better a slightly tense working relationship than none at all, however, and at the time of writing all new Tool releases are still handled by the Tool Dissectional/Volcano Entertainment II venture. It's interesting to note that the band have gained a little caution over the years: where they seemed relatively happy to discuss the details of their first, 1993 deal with Zoo, little if anything is known about the balance of power behind the new arrangement.

1998 was a quieter year for Tool while they finalised their legal situation, although dates filled up most of March, July and August. While the behind-the-scenes power struggle raged, the band simply went out and did what they do best, which was put on complex, disturbing shows with increasing levels of extravagance. The venues they were now able to fill were bigger than any they had played before, thanks to the success of

Tool pictured in 1993 in Cleveland, Ohio. This bunch of longhairs were about to redefine the heavy music scene in ways that no-one could have expected. *(EDDIE MALLUK)*

Maynard James Keenan performing at the New York Lollapalooza date in 1991. The devil-horns gesture was meant to be ironic. *[EDDIE MALLUK]*

Adam Jones at Tool's first album launch release party at Club Lingerie in Hollywood in 1991. *[MARTY TEMME ARCHIVES]*

Keenan and D'Amour at the launch at Club Lingerie. Paul later described his surname as the perfect rock sobriquet – 'Of Love'. *[MARTY TEMME ARCHIVES]*

Danny Carey, whose love for the simple things in life (basketball among them) masks a profound interest in the occult. *[MARTY TEMME ARCHIVES]*

Carey's old band Green Jelly at the Limelight in New York City in 1993: you could get away with dressing like this on stage back then. *[STEVE EICHNER/PHOTOWEB/WIREIMAGE.COM]*

Keenan (right) with Tim Commerford and Zack de la Rocha of Rage Against The Machine at Lollapalooza in New Jersey, 1993. Tool and Rage shared a musical heritage but explored radically different themes. *[FX IMAGES]*

Adam Jones with one of his beloved silverburst Gibson Les Pauls in 1993. The quiet one of the band, Jones is also a visual artist and video director. *[FX IMAGES]*

D'Amour in 1993, before he and the rest of Tool parted ways due to musical differences. *[FX IMAGES]*

Tool taking a break at their studio in Hollywood in 1995. *[MARTY TEMME ARCHIVES]*

Richard Patrick (brother of *Terminator* actor Robert) and Brian Liesegang of Filter, backstage with Keenan at the American Legion Hall in Hollywood in 1996. *[MARTY TEMME ARCHIVES]*

A vision in blue: Maynard James Keenan live at Roseland in 1996. *[PATTI OUDERKIRK/WIREIMAGE.COM]*

Maynard on stage at the Shoreline Amphitheater in 1997: the lingerie and ponytail sent out a clear message that this was no run-of-the-mill rock band. *[TIM MOSENFELDER/CONTRIBUTOR/GETTY IMAGES]*

British bassist Justin Chancellor, who replaced D'Amour in time for the *Ænima* album. He later became the voice of the band in interviews. *[MARTY TEMME ARCHIVES]*

Maynard (although you'd never know it was him) live on stage at the last old-school Lollapalooza in Devore in 1997.
[VAUGHN YOUTZ/GETTY IMAGES]

A Perfect Circle in March 1999: in this band, Keenan (far left) embraced a lighter, more political style of music than the complex textures of Tool. *[BOB BERG/CONTRIBUTOR/GETTY IMAGES]*

Keenan performing at the Ozzfest in Holland in June 2002. *[PAUL BERGEN/REDFERNS]*

Ænima, and the band were able to expand their vision accordingly. Looking back at this pivotal period in Tool's career, Carey recalled: "We realised that, for a band like ours, this was going to be a very strange experience. The idea of getting on stage in front of 30,000 or 40,000 people every night was a little intimidating, but we really welcomed that chance. It was quite exciting. It was our opportunity to see if we could communicate with a crowd that size on the level we wanted – to reach them on a deeper level than mere superficial entertainment… that was certainly a challenge, but I think we accomplished our goal, at least for the most part."

As ever, communication was key – but the Tool organisation seemed to have been temporarily stalled. Fans waited anxiously to see if they would recover.

Chapter 8

1999

Despite Tool's sporadic touring activity in 1998, the band's drive seemed to be less than it had been in the four, highly productive years beforehand. The world continued to turn without them, however, and the rock and metal music scene was now firmly in the grasp of rappers like Limp Bizkit's Fred Durst and Linkin Park's Chester Bennington. Millions of metal fans all over the world bought into the nu-metal craze (and even a few authors…), with many assuming that the shiny sound of the future would be made by a detuned seven-string guitar, accompanied by a DJ making wicky-wack noises on a turntable and accessorised with a red baseball cap.

Like most people, Tool were repelled by elements of the nu-metal sound and attracted by others. As Maynard observed, "I think the Deftones do a pretty good job. I really like the *White Pony* record. I think that Chino [Moreno] is one of the few singers out there that can actually sing, so it's nice that he doesn't get caught up in the things that some of the other bands get caught up in, like thinking that they're not allowed to. It's good cos it's a vulnerable side that you don't see in most of the popular rock, alternative, rock-rap bands. They don't show their ass."

On the other hand, Keenan had nothing but spite for Limp Bizkit, the biggest and dumbest of the nu-metal acts. More than a few fans were shocked when Bizkit frontman Fred Durst, the Paris Hilton-squiring posterboy for the genre, told MTV (apparently in all seriousness): "Tool's probably the best band I think on the planet… I can't even put them in the field. There's something wrong with those guys. They're too good… They know something that the rest of the world doesn't know… There's something severely intense about that band. You can't get better. You can't think of one way you would have done something different. Their ride they take you on is Tool. You know, it's insane. That band, I can't even be in a category with that band. You know that band is on the highest pedestal for me."

However, more still were left open-mouthed and speechless when Keenan responded: "Sounds like something a fuckin' stoned kid at a fuckin' monster truck rally would say. Let's talk about somebody else… It's like getting an endorsement from the woman who serves Jello in the fuckin' high-school food line. It doesn't mean anything. Just cos she won the lottery doesn't mean you have to listen to what she says."

Informed that Durst had said of Tool, "They know something the rest of the world doesn't know," Keenan retorted: "That's not true, either. We don't know anything that can't be learned. If we had some secret we'd certainly be fuckin' millionaires by now – and we're not… By no stretch of the imagination are we millionaires. I've never had a million dollars in my bank account, ever. Let's clear that one up right away. It's just not the case." Elsewhere, he said: "We shouldn't be on the same chart. Bands like Limp Bizkit should be on a marketing chart. Like, look what McDonald's did with McNuggets this week".

He explained his rather ungrateful wrath as follows: "If you look at Iggy Pop and Henry Rollins, for example, those are guys who completely kicked ass and ended up inspiring a whole new generation of bands like Nine Inch Nails and Butthole Surfers. Then suddenly shitty band A turned up and was taking up their space. Then shitty band B came along and replaced shitty band A. By the time shitty band C came out, people were like: 'Oh, shitty band B are shit, but not half as shitty as shitty band C'… The standards had already been lowered to the point where you're saying the original turd isn't half as bad as the recent turd. The standards continue to lower, so now we're in a climate where we have to try and coax people back into listening to good music, and that sucks."

Finally, he ranted: "We are totally at odds with the current musical climate. Do you really think people are impressed by Nickelback? Or Limp Dickshit? How could you be impressed by Fred Durst? When they come to see something that has more substance, it is a moving experience – there's more heart. There is intent. Going to see Nirvana, Nine Inch Nails or Rage Against The Machine, there is heart. It breathes. You have to be affected by that."

It seemed that the anger within Tool was fuelled nowadays not merely by societal ills such as organised religion, but also by the general ineptitude of their contemporaries. Carey reasoned: "A lot of our songs are just fuelled by the frustrations of daily existence... We are, I suppose, a product of our environment. We just try to be as honest with ourselves as possible at all times. I mean, we don't try to put on an act like some of the metal bands do. It's all very real to us, and we try to keep it that way. I think it eliminates barriers between us and the people. Our music, and the moods of our music, translate a little better."

In 1999, Tool were still stuck in a hiatus. Perhaps their collective energies were at a low; perhaps they'd simply decided to take some time off; perhaps the ongoing legal issues with Freeworld Entertainment had numbed them temporarily. However, this didn't mean that the individual members' drive to make music was completely dead: Keenan was said to be providing guest vocals to an all-star alt.rock project called Tapeworm, masterminded by Nine Inch Nails' frontman, Trent Reznor. From this year onwards, the status of the band was the subject of constant conjecture. Reznor wrote on the NIN website in the autumn of this year that: "We've got some things done, and there are millions of tracks waiting for vocals from a few different people from Maynard from Tool, to Page [Hamilton] from Helmet, from Phil [Anselmo] from Pantera to myself. Danny [Lohner] and Charlie [Clouser] are the main musical force behind that."

While fans awaited the outcome of the Tapeworm project, word came that Keenan had actually joined a whole new band. Not merely a side project or a guest slot, but an actual, touring outfit that required real commitment. This was, it was revealed, called A Perfect Circle.

To this day, many Tool fans don't really know why Keenan did this. It wasn't a logical move, in retrospect: Tool should have been gearing up for a new album, not separating off in other directions. However, Maynard has explained on many occasions that he needed to participate in this other group to come back and commit more fully to his day-job band. As he put it: "We're simply five friends who knew each other for a long time and we always knew that we'd like to perform with each other, play in a band one day, and it was something that was bound to happen sooner or later. We're five people, five individuals who came together to create something, to make music and to complete each other musically, to form a perfect circle. A circle is the reflection of eternity. It has no beginning and it has no end – and if you put several circles over each other, then you get a spiral."

So who were the other four members? A Perfect Circle was founded by Billy Howerdel, Tool's guitar tech. Born and raised in New Jersey, Howerdel had studied TV and audio production and worked with Faith No More, Fishbone, David Bowie, Smashing Pumpkins, Nine Inch Nails, Guns N'Roses and held other high-ranking guitar-tech positions before winding up with Tool in 1992. He played Keenan some of his songs and the singer was impressed enough to offer his services, in the event of Howerdel ever forming a band. When the tech mentioned that he was finally doing so, Maynard came on board, even though it was Howerdel's first real experience of a group. "I had a little three-piece cover band when [I'd been] playing guitar for six months," Billy said, adding: "Other than that, which is barely notable, this is my first band, for sure."

Although Howerdel had originally planned to recruit a female singer for A Perfect Circle, the opportunity to work professionally with Keenan was too good to turn down, as he said. "[APC] was something I mentioned early on and people ran with it. When Maynard presented the idea of us working together, I thought it was a great idea. I think he's a great singer – I was a big fan of his before we worked together – so it was an easy thing to discard the female vocal part."

Initially, A Perfect Circle also included Paz Lenchantin, an Argentina-born bassist and cellist who has guested with various American rock acts over the last decade, including the post-Smashing Pumpkins project

Zwan, Queens Of The Stone Age and Melissa Auf Der Maur. Guitarist Troy Van Leeuwen also played with the band before finding a long-time gig with Queens Of The Stone Age. Tim Alexander of Primus, whose path crossed that of the Tool members several times in ensuing years, played drums with A Perfect Circle's first line-up, which changed frequently over the years.

Despite the high profile of Keenan and Alexander, A Perfect Circle wasn't taken particularly seriously on their formation in 1999, although the release of their debut album the following year helped gain some mainstream attention. As Howerdel recalled, nothing was made easier for them because of their well-known singer – and the idea that APC were some kind of 'supergroup' was hard for him to swallow: "When we started out, we were playing 200-seat venues and not selling [them] out... it takes time to get your name into people's brains and get on the radar of people out there... the whole supergroup thing, I never know how to take that. Is that like a stab, or is that like a compliment? Probably on paper as a classification it makes sense, you know. These guys have been in a lot of bands, but at the end of the day... the chemistry is there, and it's been there from the first couple of weeks we've been together. The word 'supergroup', when you say that word, some horrible Eighties band comes up... something like that. It's probably not something that would be helpful in any way to us. I would never go ahead and initiate that categorisation, but if someone says it, we just go 'OK', nod and continue on. We always joke about it."

Although the other members of the band, Keenan in particular, had plenty of experience of life in a band, Howerdel's previous career had been confined to the back of the stage, tuning guitars and checking speaker connections. The intensity of being in the spotlight took him by surprise, he said: "When we first started out, I had no idea how much press you would do for a tour, and especially getting a band up and going... Bands that have been around for a long time would practise for years and then get a break, and then it would kind of trickle in and then they'd be swamped with it, but we were really swamped with it right off the bat. Maynard and I had decided, 'Let's put out a record by Christmas 1999', which was completely unrealistic, but it really did kick us in the ass to get going... Doing all the press in the beginning made it so you couldn't focus on even taking a breath into going, 'This is great, OK what's next? What's next? What's next?' And little sleep and all work, and from there, it was hard to reflect on it till later."

A Perfect Circle worked on songwriting until the end of 1999, having signed a deal with Virgin, which outbid Volcano. Maynard explained: "Volcano had matching rights. Virgin expressed interest to [Volcano] that this was a serious thing. I think [Volcano] thought that I was just going to be off gallivanting for a weekend. When we realised there was a label that genuinely understood what it was about, that helped us decide to go to Virgin." The singer was also very clear that the band would be a different proposition in every way from his much more abrasive main group: "Tool is far more brutal vocally. I don't think I could do two sets [in] one night. There's too much emotional dynamic. I'd be physically and emotionally exhausted in a week."

Tool fans were, of course, intrigued by this new development: the formation of A Perfect Circle was announced in the autumn of 1999, song fragments were available online by the end of the year and an album release was said to be in the offing by the following spring. It all happened very quickly, and mystified more than a few long-time Tool followers, whose minds had been blown by the behemoth that was *Ænima* and wanted to see what the band would do next. After all, three years had passed since that album's release, and *Ænima* itself had appeared three years after *Undertow*; surely it was time for a new Tool album?

Apparently not. Keenan issued upbeat press releases from time to time, explaining how pleased he was with the progress of A Perfect Circle and that the chance for him to do something musically different was highly enjoyable. "One of my biggest heroes in music has been David Bowie," he remarked. "He's said, 'I'm going to be a painter now, or I'm going to do some films', and his audience is very forgiving, because they understand him as an artist. Whether you agree or like the result, you respect that he's expressing his artistic feelings. This is like that."

Many of Tool's fans wanted to know what Adam, Justin and Danny were up to while Maynard was enjoying his side project (although it was a point of principle for him to label it as a full band, rather than merely a diversion). Jones had had a busy year, marrying the singer Camella

Grace (he had been briefly married to his high-school girlfriend Antonia Jones, née Antonia Benyovszky, as a younger man) and playing with Melvins guitarist Buzz Osborne. Danny Carey played with Jello Biafra of the Dead Kennedys, but Justin Chancellor, it seemed, was still getting used to life in the American rock world, saying: "It feels like I've been away from England for years now. It's weird, because all of my friends are doing the same thing that they were doing before, and I feel like I'm in space or something. Tool is the only band that I would have left what I was doing to join. They are my favourite band. It is just now getting really comfortable. There is that immediate kind of fear that you're not going to be worthy. If you are a fan of someone else's music, then when you're suddenly expected to help write it… there is a bit of apprehension… Maynard is an intense personality. I remember when I first saw Tool, it was kind of the same thing. I didn't take it as being scary. I took it as being totally intense – something that really sucked me in, watching him. I always looked up to him a bit before, because he was so cool with my last band, being very supportive. He has his moments, but now we've all learned each other's personality traits and got used to each other."

Keenan himself paid little attention to the rumours that spread – in particular those that accused him of causing Tool to split by focusing on A Perfect Circle. Asked if there was any tension between the band members as a result of his absence, he later said: "Only the kind of tension that would arise between brothers who've agreed to go to a movie and one of them decides not to [go] until a later showing. We're all brothers, so it's like, 'Hey, I'm gonna do this thing for a little while'. And they go, 'OK, well it takes us a long time to write a record anyway, so it's no big deal'. They [are] working as if I was there anyway. So I didn't put a skip in our step at all, really."

In any case, he explained, the shift in focus was necessary for him to come back and give Tool his all at a later date. "Another thing that helps me get back to what [I'm] supposed to be doing, artistically, with Tool [is] going off and doing A Perfect Circle. That was great because, once again, we as Tool – or at least I as part of Tool, I being an extension of that – proved that the industry doesn't want you to be anything other than that thing they know you as. So I proved that if you have a solid audience, if you have people who appreciate what you do as an artist, then they're not going to pre-judge what it is you're trying to do… We put a band together, went out and toured it and now it has a complete life of its own, in and of itself. And it's almost a completely separate audience. When we do A Perfect Circle shows, the kids are outside holding their A Perfect Circle CDs and it's those they want signing, not *Undertow* or *Opiate*. I think it's Tool fans – mostly guys, if I'm being honest – telling their sister, who they've been trying to get to listen to Tool forever, to now listen to A Perfect Circle. So now we as artists have proven, once again, that you can break the boundaries. You just have to really want to do it."

With or without Tool, however, Maynard was still fighting his old battles, in particular his straitjacketed religious background. "I got this questionnaire once," he said, "one of those ones from 'strongly disagree' all the way to 'strongly agree'. This was the question: 'When you get married, are you going to do it in a Catholic church or a Christian [ie Protestant] church?' How do I answer that? Already there's a point of departure that has nothing to do with where I'm coming from. If the lyrics already have a point of departure that's unfamiliar to a person in the Midwest or South Central [Los Angeles], that's going to cause them to go, 'Wait a minute, where's this guy coming from? I never thought like that'."

It's interesting to note that Maynard's earlier, generally unfocused resentment of the religious nonsense he'd endured as a child had now crystallised into a specific, point-by-point attack on church dogma and administration. He illustrated this with statements such as: "The religious upbringing that most people go through, and its association with Western religion, is all based on lies. At some point you either wake up and realise [that] they are lies, or you continue in a fog. I realised I had been lied to and wanted to know the truth. There is a big difference between religion and spirituality. If you're walking a spiritual path, it is because you're trying to help yourself or others for the greater good. You're trying to become a more conscious being through your actions and by understanding what motivates you. Religion, on the other hand, is basically a marketing plan. There is a middleman involved, and somewhere along the line someone is going to ask you for your credit-card number. They're going to pass a plate in front of you, trick you into giving ten per cent of your income to some child-molesting fuckhead, or worse, trick you into giving up your civil rights over some storybook."

A Perfect Circle addressed these issues (as we shall see) with as much power but perhaps more subtlety than Tool, aided by Keenan's extracurricular activities in the mass media. At one point, for example, he performed a role on *The Ben Stiller Show* as the incarcerated murderer Charles Manson, causing some consternation in doing so because of the silent intensity he brought to the part. "We didn't glamourise him in any way," he explained. "We made fun of his image as a psychopath... I think the media made Manson, turned him into some larger-than-life figure and surrounded him with mystery and some shady glamour. I don't even think that he was really a psychopath, that he had any form of mysterious power. He was just a frustrated guy who wanted to be a rock star. He dreamed about having groupies, getting laid and the whole [way that] people imagine rock stars live. The kind of stuff you read in the tabloids. Nobody gave him a record deal and he latched on to some drugged-out people who were so spaced out on acid that they did what he told them, and went and killed some people like he told them. I can't believe that the media didn't see that part of him and turned him into this larger-than-life figure, almost a living legend... Of course, he was a monster. It's his fault that terrible crimes were committed, but I think there's nothing great about him. For 35 years people treated him like dirt, and then he freaked out."

And yet so much of Keenan's persona was just that – a projected façade that wasn't really him. He was open about this, shrugging: "It's said that when Michael Keaton was contemplating playing Batman [in the 1989 film], and wondering how he was going to do it, Jack Nicholson told him, 'Sometimes you have to let the costume do the acting for you'. That is kind of where I am with that... The ideas come from the music, and you do it and it either works or it doesn't, in which case you abandon it and go on to the next thing." He was equally candid about the fact that his music was his saviour: "Things happen to you as a child and they might damage you in some way, and that can make you see the world in a strange light. If you allow that damage to run your life, you could end up being a guy on a building with a rifle. Alternately, you could channel your damage in a different way and become a sculptor instead. Art provided me with an outlet."

A significant opportunity to expand that outlet was already being offered to him via A Perfect Circle's forthcoming support slot with none other than Nine Inch Nails. Keenan was realistic about APC's chances, but hopeful that the new band would make an impression with the industrial-metal monsters' crowd, observing: "I would expect that we're going to have a rough road because, of course, everybody wants to hear Nine Inch Nails. They're not there to see us. But [APC] played about a month of shows back in August, and the wonderful thing about that was rarely did anyone in the audience demand to hear Tool songs, which I thought was great. That makes me feel like I was successful, that we attracted an audience that is forgiving and open-minded and will allow me to do this. So hopefully those people will be showing up at the Nails show, because we'll certainly need their support."

By the end of 1999, with no sign of public Tool activity and only the untested music of A Perfect Circle to look forward to, fans were getting restless – and with the nu-metal scene beckoning rock fans with the promise of easily digestible music and attitude, our story could well have ended here. It was that close...

Chapter 9

2000

Once millennial fever had died down and people resumed what passes for normal thinking in the modern era, the Tool fanbase refocused its collective attention on Maynard James Keenan and A Perfect Circle. While Adam Jones, Justin Chancellor and Danny Carey soldiered away on new music behind the scenes, the frontman was preparing for the Nine Inch Nails support slot and the release of a debut APC album.

Before that, the members of Tool parted company with their manager, Ted Gardner. Not much is known about why the two parties fell out, but Gardner brought a lawsuit against the band later that year. *CDNow/Allstar* later reported: "Larrikin Management's Ted Gardner, co-founder of Lollapalooza and Tool's manager of eight years, filed a $5 million-plus lawsuit against Tool... in Los Angeles Superior Court. The suit is for rescission of the management contract between the band and Gardner, fraud, negligent misrepresentation [and other charges]. Gardner claims that he was not paid his 20 per cent commission on, among other things, the lucrative multi-million dollar joint venture deal the band made with Volcano, formerly Zoo, in 1998... Gardner claims that the band said they would not pay him his commissions unless he signed a new 'extremely onerous' management contract, which 'substantially reduced the commission rate of, and limited the time for, the continuing commissions,' according to the suit."

The report went on: "Gardner, who 'was in financial dire straits by the end of 1999 as a result of defendants' actions', signed the new deal this March and the band fired him shortly thereafter, around May 23. According to the suit, '[Tool] would conceal from Gardner their intention to fire him and to deprive him of his continuing commissions. [Tool] would falsely represent that they wanted Gardner to be their manager... [Tool] would withhold the commissions they owed Gardner... thereby putting him in a precarious financial condition, until he signed a new, substantially less favourable management contract, which would specifically provide that [Tool] had no obligation to pay continuing commissions if they terminated his employment for 'cause'. And, once Gardner signed the new agreement, [Tool] would immediately fire him, without any basis, and then assert that it was for 'cause'.' Gardner is asking in excess of $5 million to be determined at trial."

The outcome of the dispute remains undisclosed, but the media found an amusing way of spinning the story when they reported that Keenan had been seen deep in conversation with the porn star Ron Jeremy, who had become something of a cult figure in recent years, even outside the adult-entertainment world. Many plays on the word 'tool' were printed once an unfounded and frankly hilarious rumour began to circulate of Jeremy's potential as the band's new manager.

Ignoring the chattering of the press, Keenan focused his attentions on A Perfect Circle, which was touring in support of Nine Inch Nails in the spring of 2000. NIN had released *The Fragile*, their first album in six years, which was a huge success, topping charts in several countries and being lauded by *Spin* as the album of the year. Fans of Maynard's other band might well disagree, especially after the release in May of APC's debut album, *Mer De Noms* ('sea of names' in French), which made number four on the *Billboard* chart and sold close to 200,000 copies in its first week on sale. Fans flocked to the NIN shows, at which Keenan wore a long wig on his bald head (according to some, to distinguish himself from his Tool persona) while delivering the softer, much more art-rock-oriented material from the album.

Mer De Noms was a world away from any Tool album, not least because of its gentler, more emotional feel and its less aggressive tone. Virgin released three singles from it – 'Judith', '3 Libras' and 'The Hollow' – of which the first was the most striking. Its chorus of "Fuck your God, fuck your Christ" reads on paper like the ranting of a satanic death metal band, but in fact the song has more in common with Led Zeppelin or the less contrived end of U2, a fact emphasised by its riff-heavy performance video. The name Judith is a reference to Keenan's mother, still partially paralysed from her stroke in the Seventies.

"Many of the song titles on *Mer De Noms* are actually names of real or mythological people," he said. "A lot of the names of the songs are actually people I know in real life, and some elements of their lives seem to be the same as elements in the lives or stories of mythological figures. A lot of names in America and Europe have their roots in Latin and Greek words. A lot of them go back to archetypes and their stories. It's amazing, isn't it? If you take different mythologies from different cultures, the names may change and the storylines may vary but there is always something in common... Most religious stories and mythologies have some sort of similar root, some sort of global archetype. There are hundreds of myths that are talking about virgin births or murder. It's really hard to find out what happened first: was it something that happened to people in their lives and it got turned into a myth, or was there a myth and people tried to copy it somehow?"

Keenan was open about the fact that A Perfect Circle allowed him to explore more sensitive territory than Tool, so much of which (band name included) was focused on masculinity. "I think people who listen to A Perfect Circle hear something totally different from me," he explained. "It's much more like The Cure. It's more ethereal and accessible. Also, I think a lot of Tool fans weren't aware that I could sing... I think bands like Queen and Judas Priest ended up shining out of the crowd [in the Seventies]... The vulnerability and emotional aspect in their heavy music was recognisable because it was genuine... You figure, Rob Halford and Freddie Mercury, being gay, and they can't say it out loud, that's a lot of genuine frustration, genuine passion."

The rest of Tool were hard at work on new music. Danny's aforementioned project with Dead Kennedys frontman Jello Biafra had evolved into a full band, Pigface, which also included Martin Atkins of Killing Joke, Paul Barker of Ministry and grunge producer and Shellac frontman Steve Albini, but this didn't stop him focusing on the next step for Tool in Keenan's absence. "We write when we're all together in one room, so it really needs everyone's head to be in the same space at the same time," he said. "It doesn't really work, writing on tour. We've tried it a little bit but it's kind of a lengthy process when we're writing. It's kind of introverted as far as the four of us go: we need to be detached from everything."

Keenan himself was also answering the press' questions about Tool as well as APC. Of a potential next album, he observed: "We can't really say even a tentative date at this point. We're still writing songs and letting them progress naturally. What can end up happening is the powers that be jump in, and all of a sudden we're working under the confines of some deadline or window. We're not obligated to have the record out by a certain time: there've been hot spots where we end up getting really creative and we'll pump three or four songs out in a couple of weeks, and then there are times where it's harder and you just work through it."

He added: "I don't really like recordings. As for making them, it's kinda fun playing around in the studio, hearing back the sounds. But it really just doesn't compare to a live show. So much of our stuff is about moments... a combination of a whole lifetime of moments. It's hard to find that in the studio. It's all about takes and retakes. Live there are moments and energy and that's what it's all about. I kinda like The Grateful Dead's approach of just letting people record shows and circulate the stuff themselves."

After the long hiatus, Tool fans were finally rewarded with new material. As A Perfect Circle completed their first recording and touring cycle and the band members returned to other activities, Tool made the shock announcement that a new album was on its way in December 2000 – but that it would be a combination of live and video tracks, in a departure from the usual format. Tool – always a band who stressed the importance of combining visual and audio material – were immediately faced with bemusement from some quarters, although most of their fans understood what they were trying to do. Danny chuckled, "I heard people saying like, oh, we were selling out by putting out a DVD with film clips on it. And it's like, 'Fuck man, so what – you think aural art is the only thing that is genuine or worthy?' The visual aspect of it is just another element of what we do, and we want that seen."

Chancellor added; "Unconventional maybe, but we were always gonna release the videos – that's been a long time coming, just to make them available. Then we decided to add a bit of live stuff to make it a nicer package. It's been a while since anything's been out, and we really didn't see the harm in it. It's a very different thing to what our [next] album's going to be like."

The title of the live CD/DVD package, set for release on December 12, was *Salival*, an instantly recognisable addition to the list of Tool song titles thanks to its evocations of sex and anatomy. The band soon regretted placing the name so squarely on the record, however, when websites began selling bootleg material based on the title. "After the release of *Salival*," said Carey, "people were selling bootlegged merchandise – really shitty-looking designs with lame artwork. And they were pawning it off as if it were [from] the real *Salival* website, like we were responsible for that. So [next time we'll] throw something out there just so they waste their money on domain names and T-shirts that have no meaning."

Other sites leaked the nature of the content long before the release date. "I had to yell at a few websites," said Keenan, "because we had a few surprises in the *Salival* box set and they posted them on their website as soon as they heard a rumour about them. Whatever happened to being surprised? Whatever happened to a kid going and buying a thing, and taking it home and going, 'Wow! There's extra in here for me that I didn't expect'. If you read these websites, your presents are open before Christmas comes. It's fucked."

When *Salival* was released, it came as a CD plus a DVD or VHS video-cassette, this being at the beginning of the DVD era when players for the home market were still expensive items. The video element made *Salival* an essential purchase in the days before YouTube or enhanced CDs, containing four videos ('Ænema', 'Stinkfist', 'Prison Sex' and 'Sober') or five (with 'Hush') on the DVD. The live CD was equally interesting, featuring nine songs including three new tracks – 'Merkaba', 'Maynard's Dick' and 'L.A.M.C. (Los Angeles Municipal Court)' plus a cover of 'You Lied' by Chancellor's previous band Peach, Tool's cover of Led Zeppelin's 'No

Quarter', and four old Tool songs with different arrangements ('Third Eye', 'Part Of Me', 'Pushit' and 'Message To Harry Manback'). "We don't really wanna put out a greatest hits record with live tracks," said Maynard. "We wanted more to put out some various versions of the tracks... different arrangements [and] different approaches."

This explains the multifarious nature of the *Salival* content, which seemed to be intended as a stopgap release before a full new album, as well as a chance to get the videos out to the fans now that they were no longer current staples on the MTV playlist. The set's other useful function was to stall the many rumours of Tool's split in the wake of their long absence and Maynard's perceived defection to A Perfect Circle.

Of some of the new content, Keenan explained: "'LA Municipal Court' is definitely a tribute to life in Los Angeles. If you've ever been in LA trying to go down and take care of a parking ticket, or call and try to get some information as to how to take care of a parking ticket, or a jay-walking ticket, or something as ridiculous as that, you really realise how sick the red tape is out here. It's retarded. Most people who've ever been in that situation can relate to that song, and I think we did a pretty good job of capturing the tedium that goes along with that, to the point where people go, 'That was a great song. It really summed up that feeling, and I never want to hear that song again'."

However, he didn't reveal much about 'Maynard's Dick', an old song from the *Opiate* EP days. Despite this, the song received a reasonable amount of airplay on radio, although DJs were usually forced to retitle it 'Maynard's Dead'. The song, the first that referenced a member of Tool (indeed, the member of a member of Tool), was a sign of the times: a revealing symbol of the celebrity of the band. Slowly but surely, Keenan and, to a lesser extent, the other three musicians had become names to conjure with on showbiz TV and radio, a process they seemed to resent. "We're not doing this to become famous," said Maynard. "We're doing this because it's what we do. It's a natural extension of who we are and what we are. If people find that a little different or mysterious, then I guess that's good."

Despite his protestations, his personal life had become interesting enough for the press to ask questions about it. "I have two dogs, an African grey parrot [and] a red lord Amazon parrot," he informed the world. "I've got some koi in a pond that I built out back, three water dragons, and three Jackson chameleons. I had a turkey, but I gave it to a friend to put on his ranch and his goose pecked a hole in it and killed it…" Asked about his love of martial arts, and specifically Brazilian jiu-jitsu, he described the sport as "pretty hard, but it's a good way to get in shape and it's a good way to learn about yourself and what you can take. Plus I'm small, so for me it's more of a matter of learning to protect myself, you know? I'm never going to be a tournament fighter, I'm just not big enough [or] aggressive enough."

Adam, too, was affected, complaining: "We've been told by people that we're going to have to start to embrace fame and celebrity a little bit. They say that with the position we're getting into that it's going to be unavoidable. But we're going to try and hang on to what we've got for as long as we can." Like Keenan, however, he was physically more iden-tifiable than either Carey or Chancellor (both of whom are basically tall long-haired dudes with generically musician-like looks), as Maynard once revealed in high amusement: "Once, Adam and I were leaving the Hollywood Palladium after seeing a show. And after we said goodnight and split to go to our cars, some kid runs up to me, frantic – 'Oh my God, oh my God, oh my God, were you just talking to Adam Jones from Tool?' I was like, 'Yeah, he's cool, you should go talk to him. He might take you out to dinner'." He knew that the cult of celebrity is meaning-less, though, adding: "Ninety per cent of the articles tell us how awe-some we are. And 100 per cent of the letters. And after a while a person starts believing that bullshit. You believe you can do no wrong, then you start putting out little side projects of your acoustic set. Yeah, I can bab-ble to a drum machine and somebody's going to think I'm a genius. You lose touch with being a creative listener, and you start being more of an obnoxious babbler."

Apart from Carey's occasional participation in the deliberately celeb-oriented 'NBA Entertainment' basketball squad alongside actors Ray Liotta and Michael Rapaport, the band generally stay away from main-stream exposure. As Jones put it, "We try to push the music first. If you look at someone like Jon Bon Jovi, he was a rock star before he was a rock star. You know, those type of people think the only way to appeal to people is to be like, 'Dig me'. I think Jon Bon Jovi's gonna be real embarrassed about being Jon Bon Jovi one day. He's gonna wake up and feel like a fool."

On the subject of abject fandom, Keen recalled an incident in New York: "I had a chance once to walk up to Kiss as they were coming out of the backstage area, [but] at the moment where I thought, 'Yeah, it's OK to do that', I turned and thought, 'What the fuck? Why? What am I gonna say?' My appreciation is that I support what they do, I buy their albums, and I listen. After consideration, I didn't really see the point in bothering them."

This self-distancing of Tool from celebrity culture is one of the factors that sets them apart from just about every other major rock and metal act. A slightly more credible endorsement than that of Fred Durst came at one point from Sharon Osbourne, wife of Ozzy, after Tool had played on her Ozzfest: "You can count on one hand how many bands of today have great frontmen... Maynard is definitely one of them. He has one of the best voices out there, and he's just so creative. You don't know what to expect when you see Maynard. He's just amazing."

By 2000, it was much more difficult for journalists to gain access to the members of Tool. As we've seen, this seemed standoffish or arrogant to some writers, but the reality was more subtle: the band didn't feel the need to publicise themselves over and above a certain, efficient limit. "We don't want to be in that category where you're thrown in someone's face and they say, 'OK, I like it,' and the next week something else is thrown in their faces and they say, 'OK, I like it,'" said Jones. "Tool's deeper than that. I'd rather have a small group really respect us for what we're doing and really get it, than a bunch of people only scratch the surface and not get it."

Keenan added: "It's a prying thing, and I think for the most part we're private people and that's why things come off like they do, when we do the art that we do – we're private, individual people. Also, I think the interviewers end up asking similar questions, and they end up getting into a rut with really defining where we're coming from, and I really don't want to define where we're coming from. I'd rather keep it different so that we have the freedom to move about within our artistic forum."

Pretentious? Perhaps. Still, there was always Danny to defuse the tension. Whisper it: Tool were really not that cerebral as people. As he explained: "I think people always thought we were a lot more serious than we really are, but still, we're just guys playing music and we have a good time, and that's what it comes down to. That's why the band's lasted so long; everyone has a good sense of humour, and we spend all our time on the road watching comedians and horrible movies that we find funny. It's not like it's a constant debate about philosophy or meta-physics!"

Jones was more interested in any case in talking about the music than his private life. Although he had become deeply uninterested in per-forming press duties, he still spoke up about his love of Tool's art and his role in executing it in some detail. "Music has always been part of my life, since I was a little kid," he said. "But I think whatever I do, it will be art standing in the shadow of music, or music standing in the shadow of art – that kind of realm. As long as I get to express myself visually and with audio, I'll be really happy. It has really opened doors for us now because now I'm directing our videos, and doing our album artwork, and so I'm getting the release I need. Tool is my life. A lot of people get wrapped up in their bands, but want to do something else, or they want to get away from music. I love this because there are so many different things we can do."

Of the new album's progress, he explained: "We're very comfortable jamming. We bring riffs in, and jam the shit out of them. We take them down every possible path, and then we choose the paths that went well, and start arranging them into a song. That's why it's not like, 'We've got the chorus, now let's get the verse'. It's just how the song went, and maybe one part that felt like a chorus never gets played again."

He was also starting to gain serious recognition for his guitar skills, always a sign that a musician is sinking into the wider consciousness. Of his signature style, he revealed: "I like Frank Zappa, and Ry Cooder and Stevie Ray Vaughan and Jimi Hendrix and all those guys, but after a while the lead guitar thing started boring me. I never really went there, and it wasn't important to me to practise scales. So in that respect, I feel really inadequate. If there's some really good guitarist in the audience, and I know he's watching me, I just go, 'God, he must think I suck!' I play from my gut, and play as passionately as I can, but I'm not a very good guitar player, comparatively. I'm really just into what we do, and I love writing riffs, and I love challenging myself to play in a different time than Danny's playing on drums, and trying to figure out something over the top of it that sounds really cool. But as far as being able to fluidly solo over something, I'm not into it. That's why on some solos I'll pick up an Epilady, one of those things ladies use to rip out their hair. It has this revolving, figure-eight, guitar-like string on it; I keep my finger on it to stop the motor, and it goes, 'rrrrr'... Using delay, and other kinds of effects, it can be really powerful... I got one of those old hand massagers, and I could hold the motor and control it. Buzz from The Melvins showed me you could take a remote from your TV, hold it to your pickup, and make your guitar go 'beep, boop, beep' – you get different tones right from the pickup. Then you put some flange and delay on, and it sounds great."

A year had passed without a single Tool gig, but all this talk of new music seemed to indicate that this was about to change. The fanbase held its collective breath for what would come next.

Chapter 10

2001

What actually came next was a slight division in the ranks between A Perfect Circle and – not Tool, as some had predicted – but Nine Inch Nails, of all bands, with whom APC had toured the previous year. Touring in January and February, the Keenan/Howerdel project included in their set a song called 'Vacant', originally recorded by the oft-rumoured, much-delayed Tapeworm. As you'll recall, this supergroup-style project had been assembling an album for a couple of years under the supervision of NIN supremo Trent Reznor and engineer Danny Lohner (who had also worked on *Mer De Noms*). However, little sign of an actual release date had materialised, and APC debuted the song in their set – to the slight annoyance of Reznor, who wrote on NIN's website: "I have to admit I find it mildly irritating for ['Vacant'] to debut in this fashion before feeling it has been properly realised."

However, this minor difference of opinion was swept aside in late January by the earth-shaking announcement by Tool's management that a new studio album was on its way later in 2001. Titled *Systema Encéphale,* the album was set to contain 12 songs, among them the mysterious 'Riverchrist', 'Musick' and 'Coeliacus'. A few days later, the band announced that this had been a ruse designed to thwart the would-be bootleggers of the album, and informed the relieved fanbase that in fact the new album would be called *Evasion* and feature the songs 'Prescipissed', 'Bindlecup', 'Alcawhorlick', 'Alcaharlot', 'Bushwhacker', 'Munge', 'Poopy The Clown', 'Gullabored', 'Smell Me' and 'Buzz's Revenge'.

Yes, another prank. *Lateralus'* correct title was announced a month later, accompanied by statements from Tool that revealed their disapproval of the illegal file-sharing phenomenon that was beginning to make an impact at the time. "I think there are a lot of other industries out there that might deserve being destroyed," said Keenan in evident annoyance. "The ones who get hurt by MP3s are not so much companies or the business, but the artists, people who are trying to write songs." However, he was buoyant about the sound of the new album, explaining that an old convention had been let go: "On past albums, we felt imprisoned, although that's a little bit strong of a word. We always wanted to be able to play everything live, just like we did on our records... We kind of let go of that [on *Lateralus*]. Adam did more experimenting with his guitar tones and layering, and Maynard did the same... he put a lot more harmonies on here that he wouldn't be able to pull off live. I was really happy that we broke out of that purist thing... it'll wake up a lot of kids to what you can do musically, and still have it work as a song. It doesn't necessarily have to conform to the verse/chorus/verse format, that sort of thing. You can develop structure and mood without having to conform to length and classical structure."

Once again Tool had employed the services of David Bottrill, who had done such a spectacular job on *Ænima*. *Lateralus* was already beginning to sound like another giant leap forward for the band, reinforced by his explanation that "their style is still powerful; it has mystery, but it still invites you in. Whereas prog is all about musicianship, it's all about the esotericness of the piece. It pushes people away a bit more; you have to be studied to understand it. You don't have to be studied to understand Tool."

A promo single was sent to the press in the spring of 2001 of a song from the album. Called 'Schism', it was many rock fans' first experience of the band, as they had been effectively dormant for five years and a new generation of consumers had grown up with nu-metal as their rites-of-passage soundtrack. Educated that metal was often loud, angst-fuelled and accompanied by swearing, hip-hop beats and pimp streetwear, this new demographic would have been shocked to the core by 'Schism', as solid a piece of prog-rock as has been released in recent times.

'Schism' is driven by a superbly dexterous bassline from Justin Chancellor, who had emerged at the forefront of the songwriting as well as the latterday voice of the band when the others had mostly tired of performing press duties. He was still marvelling at his career six years after joining Tool, remarking of a recent video shoot: "I did these three sculptures, where we took a body cast of my girlfriend. I had to pour out these moulds and make them all in different positions. So I had these three sets of different limbs [and] I had to break them up and put them back together. They're like an embryo inside a tank or jar or something, but a full-size body. I would be working all night until morning, to where I ended up being just as focused as Adam. By the end of it, I was like, 'Fuck, I'm doing all this shit that I wouldn't have had a clue about before!'"

The song begins with a soft, understated chord progression before Chancellor's bassline, a rich flurry of hammer-on notes, begins. It's executed with perfect skill in a groove that is picked up by the guitar and drums and has gone on to be a staple in lists of notable heavy metal bass lines. As he explained: "The twiddly 'Schism' riff came from fooling around. I just play as much as possible, and I don't write stuff down – so when I get a good idea, I play it until I can't forget it. My inspiration comes from a place that's mysterious even to me. I pick up my bass, my fingers move, and something happens. I call it the 'mystery ingredient'. We write a lot of songs that way; we'll jam in soundcheck, record it, and work on it later. It's always interesting when other band members react to something I come up with. They might treat it in a way I never really thought of."

The song is complex, especially in its time-signature changes, which have been tabbed as fluctuating from 5/4 via 6/4 to 3/8, 13/8 and 10/8. Other unusual times such as 11/8 and 9/8 occur throughout the song, with the band jokingly explaining that it's in 'six and a half' over eight. Although the shifting time signatures (a prog-rock device, of course) have been endlessly pored over by fans and press, the band themselves don't seem to be too concerned with them. As Carey explained: "There's never any mention of time signatures, ever. There have been times when I played a weird beat and one of the guys wanted to play something over it. Then you have to use a meter metaphor to get the point across, say, 'Play over this meter of five or 15', just so there'll be a meeting point somewhere. It mainly comes in the arranging stages, like when we're trying to find ways to string things together in a subtle way. As far as the riffs the other band members bring in, it's pure feeling. It's pretty organic, picking themes from a jam we've had, until it comes to arranging. That's when the hard work starts. The payoff is having songs that go a journey instead of just verse, chorus, verse, bridge, chorus, out."

Carey's evolution as a musician became obvious when he added: "The main thing I work on now is trying to free myself from time. I still feel like a prisoner of time. Sometimes I catch a glimpse of that freedom, and shed the shackles and knock down the barriers. It's in those moments when I feel so inside of the music that time doesn't exist. That's when I do my best drumming and the flashes of inspiration come. The only way for me to get to that inspirational place is to get myself out of the way and let it come through. And that only comes through discipline and a lot of hard work, keeping clarity of mind and concentration when I'm playing. It's a never-ending thing. That's why I'm still playing the drums after 30 years."

Chancellor explained of the process: "We hear downbeats in different places, so we tap it out to understand the cycle. If someone reads it differently and we take their lead, though, it'll twist the whole thing and we'll be able to hear it from a different perspective. It sounds unnatural to most people when you layer two different times on top of each other. But if you let it breathe and keep playing it over and over, you find places where the two time signatures conflict and where they lock back together. Eventually, you start to see this really interesting relationship between the two… I listen to a lot of classical music, drum'n'bass, and other styles that ignore the beginning and end of a bar, and deal with all the possibilities between those points. When a pattern comes into my head now, I'll sit down and tap it out. It's just a bunch of rhythms in my head."

Although 'Schism' wasn't released until after *Lateralus*, it was already receiving significant airplay by the time the album came out – also thanks to another eyeball-searing video clip – and remains the song most associated with Tool's third full-length album. The twisted, persistent nature of the central bassline and the big, melodic vocal layers (multi-tracked by Bottrill for the first time in the band's career) are the first sounds that come into most fans' minds when they think back to that confused time in Tool's history, along with the regular (but enigmatic) updates written by Keenan every month and posted at www.toolband.com, which became a serious web presence at about this time.

Lateralus itself was released on May 15, 2001 and was another breathtaking step forward for Tool. Of course, you might reasonably expect a biographer to say that, irrespective of its quality, but in their five-year hiatus the band had progressed in their philosophy and songwriting to the point where they were operating on a different plane to most musicians. Check the opening track, 'The Grudge', if you're not convinced. The metal elements are there, notably in the fat guitar tone of Adam Jones' riffs, but the song is made up of several merged sections, including an ethereally beautiful bass arpeggio from Chancellor. Keenan variously advises the listener to let go and be transformed in the lyrics, which are sung in tones varying from subtle and staccato to the full-blown scream that endures for a minute or so at the song's end.

'Eon Blue Apocalypse' follows, a rather beautiful, one-minute solo guitar piece from Adam dedicated to his Great Dane, Eon (or Eon Blue), which had died of cancer some years before. This leads into 'The Patient', a long drone song in which Maynard delivers obscure lyrics devoted to the theme of waiting. It's a true whole-band song, with each musician contributing key parts that are equal in importance to every other element: Jones' guitar is commanding in every area in which it is used, whether clean or overdriven. Chancellor uses a wah effect in the introduction, but without resorting to an effects pedal, remarkably. As he explained: "In the beginning of the song, I hammered on the notes with my left hand and used my bass's tone controls to get a tone sweep for a wah effect. The guitar started out playing my part; we ignored the bass until later on, and then suddenly it made sense... I've never really copied anyone's style – I'm not the kind of person who listens to something and tries to play the exact same line. And when I'm fooling around, accidents happen, and they become part of my style."

'Mantra' is a minute's worth of slow, echoed dolphin or whale noises – or so it seems. In typical can-he-be-serious? mode, Keenan is said to have told a Japanese magazine in 2001 that he was squeezing one of his Siamese cats when the animal started making a moaning noise (presumably in pleasure rather than pain). He fetched a recorder, captured the feline's unusual utterances for posterity and slowed the sound right down in the studio. It's a good story, true or otherwise – and, given that Tool are too sophisticated to resort to New-Age clichés like whale noises – rather convincing.

'Schism' is next, and it's one of the most profound songs on *Lateralus*. That unearthly bassline, followed later in the song by the mesmerising choral layers by Keenan, makes it sound both gripping and extraterrestrial. It was released as a single in August and was accompanied by a typically disturbing video clip. Using a mixture of live action and Claymation, the clip features bald, naked people in body paint performing bizarre, slow-motion acrobatics, levitating and sinking through the floor of a monochrome, sparsely-lit set. A red, tentacle-like plant slowly emerges from the neck of one of them; they walk on all fours, nodding their heads, like strange nightmare creatures. A cubic sector of brain is pulled slowly out of one character's heads, and the camera zooms inside it, revealing that a spidery, predatory biped lurks within. Once released, this Claymation animal – an eyeless human with teeth and spindly limbs – runs across the floor and multiplies, with his offspring biting into the faces of the humans and hanging from them. The clip ends with close-ups of a rotating ball of flames. Heavy stuff.

The song was crucial to Tool behind the scenes. As Keenan later said: "The song 'Schism' is very significant for me. It came out a month before September 11, and the second verse says, 'I know the pieces fit cos I watched them tumble down...'. When Tool was on the brink of breaking up, it was our ability to communicate with each other that saved us."

The soft, droned 'Parabol' – featuring samples of Carey breathing through a tube for a chanting effect – is effectively an understated introduction to 'Parabola', a beefed-up rock anthem with a choir-like effect on some of Keenan's vocals. The singer delivers a human, almost optimistic paean to physical contact, telling a tale of two intertwined bodies whose pain is merely an illusion: the guitars and bass rage around him, with Jones delivering a solo that is the closest he has come to melodic radio-metal to date before breaking down into a huge, doomy riff that is apocalyptic compared with the rest of the song. It shouldn't be forgotten that many of the biggest rock and metal hits of the day featured DJs and rappers, of course – and how refreshing it is from some years' distance that Tool avoided any of that briefly fashionable stuff.

'Ticks And Leeches' is a vengeful song, aimed at the people who (according to Keenan) have sucked his blood. Perhaps he's talking about the band's fans, or maybe he's referring to the leeches of the music industry – but whoever the target is of his attacks, he aims real vitriol at them. The music of the song is appropriately thunderous until a mellow section at about four minutes in, when a guitar is strummed lazily with a background of wind, ambient conversation and slide guitar. There's also some high-register soloing from Justin, before the song builds again to another peak.

The album's title track is one of its most ambitious. As the years have passed, information has been revealed about its structure, which only a reasonably advanced and observant listener would have picked up on first spin. For starters, a large part of it is based on a repeating sequence of time signatures – 9/8, 8/8 and 7/4 – which form 987, the song's original title. Next, the drumbeat played by Carey comes from an unusual source, as Chancellor explains: "On the new album's title track for example, we got Danny to play my bass part on drums. He took the line's rhythm, and I did something completely new. We do that quite a lot, and not just between drums and bass."

Danny added: "Every number has its strike on the subconscious in one way or another, whether we're aware of it or not. The more you can make yourself sensitive to these things, the more it can open you up to other forces that may want to be heard. It's my job to get my ego out of the way enough to be sensitive to these things and let them flow through me. I've always been fascinated with sacred geometry – those are some of the shapes I've drawn on the Simmons pads [electronic drums]. It's about tracing the manifestation of matter into the physical world. Those are little signposts along that journey… I've always preferred equatorial woods for drums, which are higher in density and heavier and tend to reflect solar current… that's the vibe that seems to fit with Tool. The lunar current, rather than solar current, is what Tool is about."

Of this particular song, he explained: "The drum groove, which is prominent, is in five. The beginning is in 9/8, 8/8, and 7/4 repeating, which is kind of fun because you can divide it into groups of three. You can take it to the breakdown, where the guys are in six and I play in five over the top of it. I thought it would be fun to take it in a different direction."

The internal weirdness is just starting. If you examine Maynard's lyrics, which ask the listener to join body and mind, reach out and progress rather then merely exist – he mentions spirals a few times – you'll notice that the number of syllables of the words he sings between pauses are 1, 1, 2, 3, 5, 8 and back down to 1 again, or 1, 1, 2, 3, 5, 8, 13 and back. These are the numbers of the Fibonacci sequence, a series that equates to the proportions of a spiral and that is found on innumerable occasions in nature – from the shape of galaxies to the structure of fern leaves. The old song title, 987, meanwhile, is the 17th Fibonacci number.

It goes on. It's been suggested that a rearrangement of the tracks from 1 to 13 to 6, 7, 5, 8, 4, 9, 13, 1, 12, 2, 11, 3, 10 (five pairings of numbers, each adding up to 13, with 13 in the middle) leads to a more harmonious listening experience (although this has yet to be satisfactorily proved). Finally, Keenan starts singing at one minute and 37 seconds into the song, which equates to 1.618 minutes: 1.618 is the famed 'golden ratio', a mathematical constant based on the relationship between two quantities, which has been the subject of much study since the ancient Greeks.

Left breathless by the phenomenal 'Lateralus' (misspelled 'Lateralis' on a few thousand early CD pressings, leading to some confusion), the listener is then treated to a trilogy of songs – 'Disposition', 'Reflection' and 'Triad'. The first of these is driven by a distant tabla beat and is composed of guitar and bass drones; the second is longer and more electronic in nature, with a Middle Eastern string instrument adding an ethereal atmosphere, along with Keenan's urgings to abandon the ego for wider awareness; and the last is a long, guitar-based instrumental with an insistent bass drone. The trilogy is effectively the end of the album apart from 'Faaip De Oiad', supposedly a phrase in the occult Enochian language meaning 'The Voice Of God'. In this two-minute song, a barrage of industrial noise rises threateningly while a man is heard making a phone call. He claims to be an ex-employee of Area 51, the secret US military site in Nevada, and that his employers were aware of the existence of both extraterrestrial life and of impending large-scale threats to human life.

"That's about all hell breaking loose," said Danny. "That track features a sample of the rantings of a guy who worked at Area 51. Who knows if he was speaking from a rational state, is really panicked, or is a complete schizophrenic who completely lost it? We may never know." In fact, the call was revealed to have been made to an American radio show, *Coast To Coast AM*, hosted by DJ Art Bell, and it's said that the caller admitted that his story was a hoax. As with so much of the Tool mythology, the real truth is not known.

Of these shorter, segue tracks, Carey added – explaining the generous length of the album in doing so – that: "We had more little bits and pieces that we wanted to put in between the songs, but when we went to mastering we had to leave out a lot of those. The manufacturer would only guarantee us up to 79 minutes. So our record is 78 minutes and 58 seconds long. We thought we'd give them two seconds of breathing room."

With its glittering sound (the album was released as an HD – or High Definition – CD) and stunning visuals, *Lateralus* was one of the most impressive releases of 2001 and went straight to number one on the US albums chart as well as in several other countries. A double vinyl version was released four years later boasting holographic images on its sleeve: in the interim, buyers had to make do with the still-impressive art on the CD. This came in a see-through slipcase, with the album track-listing and credits laid out as if on a wiring diagram, and in a booklet made of transparent colourless film with overlaid panels of images. The primary image was created by conceptual artist Alex Grey and was a series of human torsos, with the inner organs revealed in Technicolor detail. One of the images revealed the word 'God' spelled out by the convoluted masses of the character's brain – another statement supporting the album's general theme of self-development and expansion of consciousness.

Lateralus sold a massive 555,000 copies in its first week on sale – a huge number for a band who now resided squarely in prog-rock territory. More than a few Tool fans regarded the album as their idols' first real step into the mainstream, comparing it to Metallica's 'Black Album' and other career-defining releases. When the comparison was mentioned to him in a fan webchat, Adam Jones pondered: "Metallica did their own thing and really held their ground about their approach to music, and their exposure in the world of music, and all their efforts paid off when they made the 'Black Album'. It was like they'd arrived, and their crowd had followed them the whole way... we've been around for quite a while and we've established ourselves on our own terms. A really interesting pairing was watching Metallica and Nine Inch Nails at Woodstock 99... watching the old guard and the new guard exchanging time on the stage... Nine Inch Nails had been the child coming in in the new year, and Metallica had been the old wizard handing the torch over. I think that we're kind of that way... this more established band that's been around and there's gonna be a new... something coming up. Who knows what it's going to be, but it will be something that's influenced by our peers, and a whole new thing."

He added that the recording process of the album had been fraught in parts: "Ron St. Germain, the guy who mixed our album, would mix a song and we'd come in, listen to it, and go, 'OK, sounds good' or 'No, it doesn't sound good, so do this'. He wanted to cut up our songs. He said, 'I like my steak without fat; I like to trim the fat off'. We told him, 'Fuck you, man, you're not touching any of our songs!' He wanted to take little parts out of each song and make them follow the formula of what sells. I don't want to follow formula. We want to have our own formula. But we respect Ron, and he can make suggestions like that. I'm not putting him down, it's just that I don't agree with him. I highly recommend Ron as a mixer and have the utmost respect for him. In the end, we got our way."

The release of *Lateralus* was followed immediately by an extended tour. Kicking off in Atlanta, the jaunt took Tool across to the East Coast and then to a series of dates in Europe, including a show at the UK

Ozzfest at Milton Keynes. Switzerland, Italy, Germany, Holland and France followed before more UK shows and a swing through Eastern Europe. In July, Tool focused on playing gigs in New Zealand, Australia and Japan, boosted by an array of film footage projected onto the back of the stage and a stage show that included Osseus Labyrint, the art-theatre performers who had made the 'Schism' video so unsettling. The film was played in real time during gigs by Adam Jones' wife Camella Grace, of whom Justin Chancellor said: "She's essentially part of the band. She's almost like a DJ. She's jamming to the music, and she can actually synch the video up in perfect time to the music."

"We can't really rely on MTV to play our video," added Maynard, "but we still want our fans to be able to see it. And rather than try and synch ourselves up to it, we just thought it would be good to play it there in the middle of the set. It also gives us a break… because we're not really into doing encores – we're not going to go like 'Goodnight' and then come back out and play three more songs, which seems very Barbra Streisand to me – so the film clip gives us a chance for a break in the show."

The show was often dominated by Adam Jones' pyrotechnic guitar playing, although he was that rare thing – a virtuoso player who chose not to show off. He had a huge crowd of admirers, as he said: "Guys ask me all the time, 'Do you think I should go to the Guitar Institute Of Technology [in LA]?' I ask them, 'Well, what do you want to learn? What do you want to get out of it?' They usually can't answer. I think that if you want to learn theory, how to read music and scales, then GIT's great. But if you want to be in a band and write music, then you should just be in a band and write music. I think people like Steve Vai are so boring."

Of the band's huge success, Adam shrugged and said, "We've established ourselves in what we do. It's great if it keeps on growing. But there's certain sacrifices that need to be made beyond the level we are. We're pretty content where we are, not having to plaster our faces all over TV shows and magazines everywhere. We're pretty discreet about that, and by doing that, we've been able to keep a quality of life that is high. We can still go to most of our shows and walk into the crowd and watch the support band play, and people will not bother us. It's not as easy for Maynard, as he's much more of a focal point, but for us three, we can still get away with that – and that's a pretty rare thing in this business. So I'm fine with the way progress is going right now. If it gets bigger, that's fine, but we don't want to sacrifice our integrity in any way."

Maynard was even more nonchalant, saying: "It's difficult to tread that line between having your finger on the pulse of what's going on in the world – as far as where we are in our development – and maintaining the integrity and the purity of what's going to come out of your work. Focusing on what other people are saying about it, or what they want to know… that might shift your focus if you listen to that. Just don't read your press. Let it go and don't even worry about it. We have a vision; we have the four people in a room trying to come together and create this baby in the centre, and if we start listening to other people's ideas about what the baby should be, it's gonna be born with flippers."

The tour had descended into a degree of anarchy by this stage. Jones recounted a tale that would be enough to make most potential stage-invaders blanch in fear, related to the band's occasional habit of bringing a cage with them. "We'd ask for a volunteer from the audience to go into the cage," he laughed. "Usually, Maynard would pick a girl and we'd just leave them there during the whole show. But the best was in San Francisco – we got a guy to come up on stage. The whole idea was to put this guy in front of my amp, a 100-watt amp, and just pummel him. We just wanted to see him crawl out and say, 'I've had enough' and leave. So Maynard said, 'I'm going to get this guy to leave tonight, no matter what I have to do'. So we put the cage behind Maynard this time, right in the centre of the stage… Sometimes when he sings 'Prison Sex' he sticks his dick between his legs so it looks like he has a vagina. So 'Prison Sex' came around and he did this standing over the cage, and the guy was kinda looking up at him and laughing. The crowd was laughing, and Maynard grabs a bottle of water and pours some on this guy when he's not looking. The guy freaks out, but sees Maynard drinking it and realises it's water and laughs. Then Maynard reaches behind and grabs his tea, which is lukewarm by now, and pours it on the guy. And he just broke the cage wide open and dove back into the audience. He thought he was being pissed on. We were laughing so hard, we fucked up the song. It was hilarious."

The tour rolled on, with Maynard sometimes lending a hand by playing second guitar. "I use the guitar mostly as another voice," he said. "Because I can't sing all my parts at the same time, I use simple guitar lines live to approximate the vocals on the album. Most of the time you can't even hear it – all the guitar playing you notice out front is still mostly Adam – but it helps to fill out the sound."

The band passed through the centre of the US and then to the West Coast, packing out venues in their home states, before circling back east and north. As the tour rolled on into September, Tool were as stunned as everybody else by the events of 9/11 – but it wasn't long before they made it clear that their views on the matter might not coincide with the rest of America. Once George W. Bush's War On Terror had started, a few weeks after the World Trade Center attacks, Keenan in particular found himself in something of a quandary.

"I can't say anything right now," he told one reporter. "No matter what you say, it's construed by someone as an anti-American statement – even when it's the same thing you've said all along [in Tool], which is: 'Think for yourself, and question authority'... The more we'll talk about this, the more I'll shoot off my mouth and end up in [trouble]. Every now and then, you get people who tend to forget what this country is about, which is a melting pot of races and cultures and freedom of speech. And as soon as you open your mouth and speak freely, [criticism] gets thrown at you... I just don't think that murder is an option to fig-ure out a way to punish the guilty... I was in the Army for three years. I received an appointment to West Point; I'm probably the only musician in my peer group who can say that. So 'anti-American' is not a label you can put on me. I received a distinguished graduate certificate from my basic training and advanced training. And if I'm 'the model soldier', then we have problems... You learn how to co-exist in the Army, how to sur-vive, and how it's all about relationships. You walk into a situation with prejudices and unjustified hatred, and then, when you sit in a tent with someone in the middle of the desert, doing training, you learn about each other and learn you're all in this together."

During one song at a show in Toronto, an audience member threw an American flag on stage – perhaps assuming that Tool would wave it in a gesture of down-home solidarity. Instead, Chancellor kicked it to a roadie, who removed it. As Keenan explained: "I wanted to piss on it. The audacity that some people would assume that we're going to wave the flag and turn what we believe is a spiritual endeavour focusing on self-reflection and discovery into some kind of cheesy American propagandist movement, was the furthest thing from our minds... The people who have been touched most are the families of the victims. But I'm not sure about the guys in Iowa, Montana or Arizona who get their information filtered through CNN. Because to them, information is coming in... thick with propaganda... all these media guys have hard-ons because of this war. They can sell more papers, magazines, keep us glued to the TV longer."

He added, more sombrely: "This so-called new world order has been very effective in undermining the creative process, to the point where it is run by actors and businessmen with marketing plans. It is no longer about music. I mean, when was the last time you had three CDs come across your desk in a month that really impressed you?... I know very creative people who are considering putting their process on the back burner so that they can make money with some horrible, horrible band, one with no artistic integrity. What they don't realise is that as soon as they do that, the band will use their name to undermine anything credible they could possibly do in the future. They are completely selling out their credibility for the money. It happens at so many levels here that people pretty much accept it as the process, and it has completely undermined everything."

The tour continued until the end of 2001 – a year in which Tool had experienced a triumphant return to the public's affections. Times were changing, though, and the music industry was beginning to consume its own young at an alarming rate. Tool's survival depended on their focus, as Carey put it: "It got to the point of panic a few times, when we had to lock ourselves in a room with each other and hash it out. There was a point where everybody was crying and hugging and laughing, you know, all at the same time... there were some pretty intense moments. When I think about it now: no, I don't think we would've broken up. But you never know how far things can explode. If we hadn't have been able to express ourselves to each other and keep the lines of communication open, we would have definitely broken up."

Chapter 11

2002

Several years after the rock-consuming public had accepted, along with Fred Durst, that Tool was a unique musical phenomenon that might well go on to change the world, the record industry woke up and smelled the coffee. Tool was awarded the Grammy Award for Best Metal Performance for 'Schism' in January 2002, the most obviously compelling – but not, perhaps, the best – song from the gobsmacking *Lateralus*, which had still not given up its complex secrets for most people even nine months after its release. The band won their category against serious competition from four much better-known bands – Black Sabbath, Slayer, Slipknot and System Of A Down.

Fans awaited Tool's response. Would they turn up to the Grammy ceremony and pick up the award, or would they ignore it roundly, like the lords of doom their albums seemed to indicate they were? In the event, the band arrived and clowned around, with Justin Chancellor using his acceptance speech to state, "I want to thank my dad for doing my mom" (his conversion to Californiaspeak was, it seemed, well underway) and Danny Carey namechecking Satan.

Perhaps it was time for the band to reveal their human sides, after three frankly terrifying albums, a clutch of videos that brought grown men to their knees and enough New-Age philosophy to stun a cow. As Adam Jones laughed, "We're geeks. Danny and I watch *Star Trek*. Maynard loves watching cartoons and doing stupid stuff, and watching the same movie over [and] we love *Caddyshack*... we're a bunch of friends who are all geeks. That's why it's not about what we look like, and how we 'rock out' or whatever the fuck... A guy in an interview the other day was complaining what a shoegazer I was onstage, and [he missed] the point. Because you can barely see me onstage to begin with. We have all these projections, we have lights, we have a really atmospheric, emotional, trippy, dreamy presentation with our music which completely stimulates each other, and they totally missed out on it. Because I wasn't rocking out, swishing my hair."

The band's keen sense of humour came out more and more these days, now that they had gained sufficient power to be able to refuse most press requests and people actually understood what they were trying to achieve.

The fans didn't escape the razor-sharp Tool wit. "I saw Ted Nugent play a little while ago. It was him and Tired Skynyrd," sniggered Keenan. "We were in Nashville, we got the night off. Danny was having the best time, because it was like 20,000 rednecks with stars and bars, all drunk as shit... real small teeth and eyes real close together... There would be two dudes duking it out and Danny's getting in there with the people that were watching, taking pictures. I'm waiting for the film to come back, all these rednecks all going, 'Hit 'im! He's drunker'n you!'... it was out of control. I mean, we saw that show and we thought, 'I hope this isn't the same element that's gonna come to our show'. Well, basically it was their kids."

He went on, incredulously: "This guy brought us a dead animal on a stick. A big railroad tie, with a skinned snake nailed to it – 'Here!' 'Oh cool, a dead animal on a stick! I've got one of these at home, I'll just put it on the other side.' So when we played, right before the encore, there's this little dead silence before Danny clicks into the song, and out of the crowd, you hear, 'What about that snake, boy?' I just dropped the mike and shook my head, and Adam is fucking up the lead cos he's like, 'How bizarre!'"

Maynard recalled another fan who had taken things a little too far, saying: "There's one that kept sending me paintings, and somehow, I met her over in France. We didn't even do anything, even go out, and all of a sudden, I was her lover or something. I had my address tag on my bag, and so she got my address and I kept getting these letters at my house – not the PO box, my house – every other day or so for a while. Then she stopped. She sent a final letter saying, 'You're an insensitive bastard!'"

As for Jones, he occasionally revealed unusual facts about his past in interviews – perhaps because he'd gained more confidence as the years had passed. "The whole point, man, is being happy," he mused, "and if you're happy right now. Because most people aren't happy, and I've learned that people make their own hells... People say, 'Oh, this happened and this happened and I can't get things together' and I'm like, 'You do this to yourself, man'. I've always been successful in what I was doing because I do things for me... I had some friends die during grade school and high school. Then my uncle killed himself. That really freaked me out... He lived in Washington DC, and... there were a bunch of rumours about why he killed himself, but I think it was something to do with the government. The trains there are over a hundred miles an hour... he laid down on the tracks. It was really funny, because the guy who found him had chased him away the day before because he had tried it. They were setting up his wake and I was just a kid – pretty young, 14 or 15 – and I opened the coffin up and there was just this big blue bag in there, so I touched it."

The lecherous old music industry bothered Jones at times. He fumed: "We totally make our own rules. We're constantly fighting with the record company, because they want us to do it this way because that's the way it's done, or market it this way because that's the way it's done, or edit the song this way because that's the way it's done. It's bullshit, man, just let me do what I'm doing... I think a lot of bands start worrying about how they can double a dollar from their last event. They tend to pare it down – perhaps water it down is a better way of putting it – on their next release. Or they try to second-guess what they feel their audience will want. If you've had enough success on one record that your rent is paid, then I would say that you've afforded yourself the luxury of going a little crazier, of going off at the deep end, or just exploring. I think it's unfortunate that most bands don't do that, that they just kind of play it safe."

In 2002, Tool was reeling from the success of *Lateralus*, as were many of the reporters they dealt with on a daily basis. Asked repeatedly why he thought the band had met with so much success, Carey pondered: "I think the reason that people seem to have such a loyalty to us is that the commodity they are searching for is really rare. Maybe these people need something above and beyond the pop songs that are everywhere and are inescapable. We offer something that's not that. Our music is an alternative to that, and it's harder to find. It's harder for me to find something that I really like, and if I find a band that I really dig and who sound new and who make me have flashes of inspiration, then I become fanatical towards them also. I think it goes along with being a little more selective, you know, how rabid your fans are."

On the same subject, Chancellor chipped in: "The people who are into us are intensely loyal. They stay with us, and if anything, we get new fans, so we're incredibly fortunate that way. We're this word-of-mouth sensation... We make music that has many levels to it. That's what we're about. When we make an album, we want it to live and breathe for a long time. It should be something that a listener can grab hold of and experience for a long time. Fame in so many ways is a distraction. It's self-destructive for a lot of our peers. We don't need that... We just want our fans to focus on our music. That's what we're most proud of, not our haircuts."

The music came to the forefront once again when Tool issued a video clip for 'Parabola' to the press. Rather than releasing a physical single at this stage, the band chose to produce a clip to promote *Lateralus* that was their most detailed video yet – thanks in part to the song's ten-minute-plus length, made up as it was of the two songs 'Parabol' and 'Parabola' segued together. Jones directed the clip, made up of two distinct scenes. The first portrays three strange humans (yes, more of them) with block-shaped heads, animal faces and fat, porcine hands, meeting around a table. One chops an apple in half, revealing a six-pointed star inside. The three characters then levitate and lean forward over the table, opening their mouths to vomit a thick, tar-like substance onto it. They then float sideways, leaving trails of the black material that join to form (pun presumably intentional) a perfect circle.

The second and longer scene is more involved and tonally different, with intricate Claymation and special effects. The British rapper Adrian 'Tricky' Thaws acts the role of a semi-alien man who has two thin tentacles sprouting from the sides of his head. Accompanied by a knee-high, metallic humanoid with teeth and a detachable face, Tricky smashes a marble block, places his head in a glass box, banishes a malevolent zygote after it crushes his robotic companion, dissects said friend with a knife to reveal the detailed organs within, enters an enchanted forest, picks up a leaf and is horrified when it bursts into a flame with a mystic eye at its centre, is transformed into a glowing, digital human anatomy model straight from the Alex Grey canon, is surrounded by a universe of eyes, opens a third eye at the site of his pineal gland and finally merges with a scintillating grid of energy before fading into a blinding field of white. Not your standard rock video, in content or duration – but a work of visceral genius from start to finish.

The 'Parabola' video distils everything we've learned about Tool's philosophical trajectory to date into a single, ten-minute trip. The themes of transformation and immersion in the universe are apparent. The band's fascination with the workings of the human body – elegant, nauseating and otherwise – is apparent, as is the idea that those workings can combine with the processes of the mind to access a higher plane. The three (or four, if you include the zygote) types of creature in the clip all interact as they move towards a common goal – and the overarching message that evolution is everything couldn't be clearer. It's all a long way from the mere headbangers who had released the *Opiate* EP a decade before.

Whether the nuances of the song, and the others like it from *Lateralus*, would translate to a live audience was another matter. Tool were set to play the 2002 Ozzfest, or at least its nine European dates, with only Ozzy Osbourne himself above them and various bands of the day preceding their set. These ranged from the good (Slayer, System Of A Down) to the average (Lostprophets, Cradle Of Filth) to the mundane (Drowning Pool, Millencolin), and perfectly represented the confusing period through which heavy metal was passing at the time. It's interesting to note that the normally consistent Keenan had once bad-mouthed the event: when his band were playing on the final Lollapalooza tour in

1997, he said: "This year takes it to a whole new level. There's not the two or three bands on the bill that everybody likes. There's completely different flavours, and that's a little unfortunate in some instances, because the kids… aren't open enough to allow the music to move them, because they're putting labels on things. Like the Marley brothers: 'They're reggae, and I'm not into reggae, so I'm not going to listen'. When in actuality they're a solid band, and who better to play Bob [Marley's] tunes but his kids?… This Lollapalooza demands that you get involved. If you sit down and get into that headspace where you're there to really listen and feel and experience what's going on, you're going to enjoy this tour. If you're there because it's a hip thing to do and you're there to mosh, or whatever – go to the Ozzfest."

Despite their dabblings with the big industry players, Tool were gaining something of a reputation for their integrity when it came to playing live, specifically in their choice of support act. A series of shows this year were opened by Tomahawk, the new band of ex-Faith No More singer Mike Patton. Perhaps implicitly acknowledging that alternative-rock bands such as Tool would have had a far more difficult time of it without pioneers such as Faith No More, Tool took Tomahawk on the road, even though Patton's band were both untested and resolutely uncommercial. "[Tool] are friends of ours, and I guess they like our band," said Patton. "God bless them that they have the balls to follow through with their instincts. I'm sure that there were a billion and one people trying to talk them out of it, because we don't sell a lot of records and we're not going to pay them to play with them. Basically, us being on this bill is not doing anyone any favours, industry-wise."

A little later, it was announced that the opening slot for a leg of Tool's ongoing US tour would be filled by the Swedish quintet Meshuggah, the most experimental extreme metal band yet formed (with the possible exception of their countrymen Opeth). This act were at the beginning of a long and fruitful career in 2002, with the Tool dates gaining them valuable exposure to the correct audience – which is to say, a crowd made up of people who were accustomed to investing considerable time and thought into complex music. Without the help of the much bigger band, Meshuggah might never have made it to their current position.

Carey, whose complex drumming style shares certain elements with the practically octopus-like playing of Meshuggah's Tomas Haake, said of the Swedes: "Meshuggah has been a constant source of inspiration for me from the very first time I heard them until today. They are true pioneers who have consistently broken new ground with each album. *Nothing*, which is my favourite record of 2002, is another prime example of their musical expertise and unique compositional style, which continues to evolve and change the way people listen to music."

Maynard, much less of a music geek than the other three, observed of Tool's support acts: "Over the years, we've taken out people that we liked, and as time goes on, of course, all of our musical tastes have gone in different directions. Now we've kind of got it down to where as long as two guys vote for it, we'll take that one. Don't get me wrong: I like Isis and Mastodon, but I would much prefer to take out Peaches or Autolux or the Yeah Yeah Yeahs; just something that's out of the ordinary, but it's not heavier or darker than Tool. But that's the beauty of our band: we're all such diverse thinkers. So now I get to tour with Mastodon and Isis, and I would have never made that decision. It's great for me, cos now I've been exposed to music that I wouldn't have otherwise been exposed to… You know, I grew up listening to Joni Mitchell. The melody is what I gravitate to – and it's my job to listen to what's happening when those guys go down these staccato, rhythmic, insane mathematical paths. It's my job to soften it and bring it back to the centre, so you can listen to it without having an eye-ache."

The year was shaping up to be another hectic one for Tool, with the Tapeworm project making its presence felt as well as a new A Perfect Circle album, which was scheduled for release some months into 2003. In August '02 Nine Inch Nails frontman Trent Reznor explained of Tapeworm, "[The songs] started as one idea, and have mutated and grown into another altogether. Musically, the results are becoming much more song-oriented than I would have thought… It has been an interesting experiment for Maynard and I to peek around in each other's heads, shining flashlights in some shadowy corners. We've realised we're each in somewhat similar places in our respective lives and outlooks, so it's been great to collaborate on that level." He added, in slightly ostentatious tones, "Tapeworm provides me the opportunity to work with some people I respect immensely in a democratic environment."

From all these weighty announcements, you'd think that the most important music ever heard was about to be released. In fact, Tapeworm has never released anything, with the project still under wraps as this book went to press, despite the weight of expectation that has accompanied it. Times were hard for everyone in the record industry, then as now, so it's perhaps understandable that a project such as this was forced to remain in obscurity. The members of Tool were aware that alternative rock as we knew it back in 1993 was now well past its peak, with Keenan explaining: "You have to figure that the beautiful thing that Tool and Nirvana and Soundgarden and the Melvins and Rage Against The Machine and Nine Inch Nails and all those bands brought to the table was an 'indie' sensibility. All of a sudden, you didn't have to listen to corporate America, where record companies and radio stations told you what you had to do. In fact, you should go against what these interests tell you, because it's your responsibility as an artist to defy them. I think what happened was that all of those bands got caught up in that sensibility of not doing anything to take a stand. But the quarterly numbers have to be kept up, so the record companies and businessmen went and found themselves the chumps and the clowns who would allow them to keep those numbers up, the chumps and the clowns who would jump through whatever hoops the record companies and businessmen asked them to jump through…"

In a sentiment shared by more than a few of his contemporaries – notably Billy Corgan of the Smashing Pumpkins, who made the same point on several occasions – Keenan blamed the fall of alt-rock on the bands' lack of application. "Nirvana, Nine Inch Nails, Rage, Soundgarden… all of us," he added. "If we'd have been a bit more diligent about our mission and had filled up the spaces a little more, then there would have been a little less of them and a little bit more of us. There's a finite number of magazine covers and there's a finite number of hours in the day for radio stations to play music, so all we need to do is create from the heart in order to offer our contribution as to what should fill up those spaces. And people will respond from the heart… But I don't want to be so pretentious as to suggest we were responsible for the downfall of music, or anything. I don't think our role is that important. I do worry that it might now be a little too late. I thought that the Nine Inch Nails record *The Fragile* was an incredible record, I loved it – but nobody heard it. It didn't have any singles on it, and all this other stuff was clogging up the pipe, so people missed it. The Rage record *The Battle of Los Angeles* did OK, but it didn't do as great as it should have done… I like this new Tool record, but we might have waited too long. Who knows?"

Despite Maynard's misgivings about the future of Tool's place in the market, fans flooded to the dates the band played during the 2002 leg of the *Lateralus* tour. On stage, Keenan had morphed into a cross between a drag queen and an extraterrestrial, confounding the frat-boy element of Tool's crowd with his body paint and a black leather bodice while crouching in front of the video screen, back to the audience. Occasionally he would strip down to a skimpy Speedo and leather boots, delivering the vocals bent over the microphone: there was literally no other frontman who would dare perform like this at the time.

The huge tour passed from Japan to New Zealand and Australia before jumping to Europe for dates in Holland, France, the UK, Germany and many other countries and then across to the States for almost six months of dates in their home country without significant incident, although there was some drama at a November 12 show in San Antonio when a fire broke out in Keenan's dressing room. As the Tool webmaster described the incident, "Maynard heads for the dressing room. As he is about to enter, he sniffs, turns to our recording engineer in the nearby booth and says, 'Mike, can you smell that?'… The door opens, and smoke billows out, engulfing the room. A candle put there to mask the smell of old hockey pads and jock straps. Nice… Anyway, flames everywhere, and the room is full of smoke, swirling and spreading. The alarm raised, Maynard wanders off to soundcheck, nonchalantly stating…'My dressing room is on fire. What song should we start with tonight?'" After the fire had been doused, it emerged that the candle which he had placed in the room had ignited a curtain: the band were required to pay "a few thousand" dollars to cover the damage, and the tour moved on.

Finally, the band stopped moving at the end of November and gathered to collect their thoughts. All agreed that a high point of the tour, and of their careers so far, had been a short string of dates they had played the previous summer with their heroes King Crimson in support. The embarrassing nature of headlining over a band whose heritage is so much more impressive than one's own was highlighted when Keenan announced on stage: "For me, being on stage with King Crimson is like Lenny Kravitz playing with Led Zeppelin, or Britney Spears onstage with Debbie Gibson."

Carey added: "It was a surreal experience… it's the only way I can describe it. But it was one of the most educational tours I've ever been on, that's for sure. Just being exposed to Robert [Fripp] and Adrian [Belew]… all four of those guys are such fantastic players that it can't help but rub off. Robert's been such a legend, such a brilliant role model for any rock player to follow, that the experience is hard to describe. To look over your cymbals and see him smile at you is beyond words… I'm sure I was grinning from ear to ear… plus, it was really cool, they let me play 'Frame By Frame', which is one of my all-time favourite King Crimson songs."

King Crimson prime mover Robert Fripp had a rather different angle when asked about the similarities between the two bands. "Do you hear the influence?" he said. "There's just one figure where I hear an influence, just one. It was a piece we were developing that we dropped. And it's almost exactly the same figure: [a] three-note arpeggio with a particular accent from the guitar. So I don't think you could have heard it. That's the only thing… I happen to be a Tool fan. The members of Tool have been generous enough to suggest that Crimson has been an influence on them. Adam Jones asked me if I could detect it in their music, and I said I couldn't. I can detect more Tool influence in King Crimson than I can hear King Crimson in Tool."

"It's terrifying and it's an honour at the same time," Keenan added. "Robert Fripp is definitely a musician to be reckoned with. He said he's been writing a lot heavier stuff lately, just in response to what he's heard from us… [it's] terrifying to have him go out and open for us, because he's the master. And of course we've always said that we're very much influenced by King Crimson and bands of that ilk, and to have them play ahead of us… I have a feeling kids are going to come and hear King Crimson and go, 'Fuck, Tool ripped these guys off blind!', because it'll be right there for you to see. But we've said that all along that we were definitely influenced by this band, there's no mystery."

As 2002 ended, Keenan made one more appearance in the public eye before retreating to his personal life and A Perfect Circle's rehearsal studio. This was an acting role in a movie called *Bikini Bandits Go To Hell*, a deliberately schlocky exploitation film in the vein of Seventies Russ Meyer, which was a faintly amusing tale of scantily clad, well-endowed females shooting people. On their arrival in hell, the Bikini Bandits are welcomed by Satan (Keenan) in full red body-paint and prosthetic codpiece, hamming it up with obvious relish. The film also featured Dee Dee Ramone, Jello Biafra, *Howard Stern Show* associates Hank The Angry Drunken Dwarf and Gary The Retard and, in a touch of cutting-edge irony, the Eighties heart-throb has-been Corey Feldman. Director Steve Grasse was quoted as saying: "Satan plays a major role in the film, and Maynard is a really good actor. He's a natural. If he wants to be an actor, he could be huge."

It could be argued that, like all performers, Keenan was used to acting out a role – in which case, with Tool on ice from the end of 2002, it was time for him to switch to another character. A Perfect Circle were calling.

Chapter 12

2003

Like all great albums, *Lateralus* took a couple of years for people to really get into after its initial success. The members of Tool, recuperating after the long tour cycle, were fully aware of this and didn't try too hard to push the album, allowing it to settle into its natural position among their fanbase.

"It's a lot to take in right away," laughed Danny Carey. "But those are the kinds of records I always loved as a kid. When I first heard them they would baffle me in places, like the old Yes and King Crimson records. You couldn't 'hear' them all at once, but those would be the ones that would grow to become a part of me. That's my goal for *Lateralus*." He added that after 11 years as a touring band, Tool had outlived more than a few musical trends: "When we got signed, Nirvana's album came out a month later, so everyone went, 'You're grunge!' They went from calling us 'grunge' to 'heavy metal' to 'industrial'. Now they don't know what the hell to call us. I think putting labels on people is just an easy way of marketing something you don't understand. As far as the grunge thing, there are three bands from Seattle that I would call true grunge. I seriously do not think Nirvana [was] grunge. The Melvins are grunge. But they invented it, you know? It's just silly. It became popular, and the music industry made it more popular by hyping it; they sold more albums. It's all about money... I think we let a lot of people down, because when they heard *Opiate*, everyone thought, 'Oh, they're a metal band!' Many of the songs on *Undertow* were written at the time *Opiate* came out. But we picked our hardest-sounding songs, thinking that that was the kind of edge we wanted our EP to have. When *Undertow* came out, I think a lot of people who like metal got bummed. But I don't really care!"

Keenan had much to say on the subject of Tool's relative longevity. "We've proven that we're survivors," he said. "We've had to face a great deal over the last four years, but we've come through all of it in a very positive manner. In fact, a lot of the emotional turmoil that was caused by what went on around us proved to be of some benefit – that emotion was what was behind the writing of a lot of the new material. It really helped give shape to the whole album."

"One of our big goals on this album was to expand the audience that might hear it," he added. "It's not that we've gone out of our way to change what we do to try to acquire a wider audience, but I think that there's no way we can be viewed as one of the metal bands that's out there today. We'll always be a four-piece rock band, but we haven't been afraid to throw a few things in there this time to shake things up a little... Making great music isn't about running around in limos and having your face plastered all over *Entertainment Tonight*... I think there was something of a void created in music at a certain point in the late Nineties, when a lot of interesting, challenging bands seemed to take some time off. Because of that, other bands managed to get noticed – for good or for bad. Most of that stuff wasn't very good, and it became popular mainly because there was a demand out there that needed to be fed. Hopefully, with our help, bands that have a somewhat different way of doing things – and a different perspective on the world – can start making an impact again. I think that's important."

Sad news awaited the singer. On June 18, his mother, Judith, died of undisclosed causes: he placed a statement online that simply read, 'November 22, 1943 – June 18, 2003... Pillar of faith and determination. You will be missed' alongside a picture of her. Tool and A Perfect Circle fans asked where they could send tributes, to which the singer provided the address of a funeral home in Dover, Ohio. His bereavement occurred as he was preparing for the release of A Perfect Circle's second album, *Thirteenth Step*, issued by Virgin on September 16.

A Perfect Circle looked rather different these days. Bassist Paz Lenchantin had left after the release of *Mer De Noms* to join Billy Corgan's new band, Zwan, while Troy Van Leeuwen was now a touring guitarist in Queens Of The Stone Age, then at their commercial peak. The former was replaced by Jeordie White, who was best known by the stage name Twiggy Ramirez, which he had used while playing in Marilyn Manson's band for the previous nine years. The nature of the itinerant Californian music scene was revealed here: it emerged that White had also tried out for QOTSA (losing out to Van Leeuwen) and also for Metallica, as depicted in the film *Some Kind Of Monster*. Sometime Smashing Pumpkin guitarist James Iha joined APC in place of Van Leeuwen, with the new band a more experienced line-up as a result.

Thirteenth Step was a lighter, more expressive album than *Mer De Noms*, with more emphasis on subtle textures than riffs, despite Keenan's recent loss. The album title suggested a reference to the 12-step programme used by Alcoholics Anonymous, although Keenan denied this: "I don't think the album is specifically for people who are going through recovery, although that metaphor is absolutely present. Many of the songs are sung from the perspectives of recovery: from the perspective of a person who is in denial about a loved one, and from the drug perspective itself – the perspective of a person who is starting to realise that there is an issue, and of a person who is ready to deal with it. This was a very difficult task for me, because I don't know what [addiction] is like. I drew on the experiences of friends who have gone through recovery, and friends who will never go through recovery. Layne Staley, for example, who was an old friend."

The reference to Alice In Chains singer Staley, who had overdosed on a speedball the previous year after years of addiction, was telling. Alternative rock was losing its icons one by one, a fact that must have been in the back of Keenan's mind when he said: "There was nothing you could do, and it's very difficult to understand. Being a friend to someone like Layne, it really kind of does your head in. I don't

understand it, but I do want to help other people who are on that bor-
derline, who might hear [a song] and go, 'You know what, I think I want
to try to live'… I've experimented, absolutely. I've definitely [walked]
that fine line. But I've never gotten so down into [drugs] that I couldn't
dig my way back out, luckily. There's that voice in there somewhere –
which some people don't have – that says, 'Hang on, come back'.

A Perfect Circle planned to spend the rest of 2003 on tour, as demand
for their music was high in all territories. This meant that the media
spotlight was almost exclusively on Keenan rather than on Carey,
Chancellor and Jones, who retreated into their own private spaces for
the duration – probably a chance for recuperation that they welcomed
after the previous couple of years. Still, the Tool spark wasn't completely
extinguished during this period: the three musicians recorded some fan-
club-only music and issued it to the faithful.

Asked, as he always was when A Perfect Circle re-activated, if it meant
the death of Tool, Keenan replied: "I'm sure that crossed all of our minds.
There was a point when the industry thing [the lawsuits] got me so
down that our communication dropped to zero, and I just said, 'Well, I'm
gonna go do something else for a while'. I'm sure once I took off to do
A Perfect Circle, the other guys [in Tool] were saying, 'Well, it's over.
We're breaking up'. But that wasn't the case. It was just a matter of taking a break and reminding ourselves who we are, what we want, and
what we bring to each other's table… [The bands are] both a priority,
and there's equal space for both of them. To say I should focus on one or
the other is like going up to a mother and saying, 'Your first kid was
great, but your second kid was so much cooler than your first baby. You
should focus on that one. Fuck the first baby'. It's just a weird argument.
I've given birth to some words in different forms and reacted to different musicians. I want it all to succeed. I want people to hear all of it."

As always, the themes of Keenan's music were various and complex.
He was now intimidatingly well-versed in occult philosophy, explaining:
"There are some life stories going on that yield resolutions of sorts. A lot
of things happen when you turn 30. There are major life choices and
major changes in orientation. The entire celebration of Easter is about
that kind of orientation. Easter is like the equinox, and the sun and
moon are on opposite horizons. If you're standing in the right place at

the right time, you can't tell one from the other. They're of equal intensity. Metaphorically, that's kind of the rebirthing, the mid-life statement, where the moon has gone through its progression from youth, of a crescent into the full moon. And at that moment [as] the fullest, brightest that it can be, there's the realisation that it's not its own light. There's a higher source it has been reflected [from]."

Statements like this would seem horrendously pretentious from any other hard-rock musician. Somehow, however, Keenan manages to get away with them and retain his dignity, perhaps because he also says chilling but pragmatic things like: "That's the big thing about education. People can be book-smart, but not really intelligent about anything else. A lot of times they're just taking in all this information and regurgitate it. It's much more important to process it and personalise it. To apply it to your world, to your life. You have to walk the walk, or you can't really report about it honestly… Jung used to talk about staring into that shadow in the corner. Just stepping into that shadow and going, 'OK, what is it that I fear the most? What is it that freezes me up like a doe in the headlights?' And then go and do that and see what happens. The worst thing that'll happen is you'll die."

Technology was also his passion, and especially its impact on society. In line with one of Tool's implicit themes – the fusion of machine and human, as depicted in many of their video clips – he was fascinated by a rumoured new development (although five years later it is yet to go into production): "Have you seen the new phones the Japanese have developed? It's basically a watch, and there's a microphone in the wristband and a little contact that pushes against a bone on your finger. You talk into your wrist, stick your finger in your ear, and your finger acts as the speaker. It resonates on the bones of your ear and you listen through your finger."

On the same subject, he added: "I think the internet is definitely a metaphor for the collective unconscious. There's the old master saying that if you meditate long enough with focus, you can tap into the collective unconscious. Well, what the fuck do you think people are doing every day when they sit in front of the computer? Pretty soon, we're gonna get to the point technologically where you're not gonna even need the external apparatus to do that. Eventually, quantum physics will develop some kind of orientation where you'll just be sitting there talking to your friends on the East Cost with nothing – just with your focus."

Most of this could be dismissed by cynics as the kind of talk that everyone indulged in, back when the internet was new (or at least, not yet old) and people were still excited about concepts such as virtual reality. However, Keenan was capable of crystallising these modish ideas into coherent thoughts that continue to resonate, such as: "We're dealing with the chaos of life, and we're rubbing it down. The deeper you rub, the more patterns you can see, until you realise that it's really an organised chaos. There isn't really ever any chance to understand it all, but we're here to keep rubbing... I truly believe that we're not living in a time when we should be looking to someone or something else at all for guidance. We all really need to be moving on our own accord, finding the messiah within ourselves that's going to lead us to the promised land, whatever the hell that may be. But I don't think that a lot of people are doing that. They're turning to other things, when all they gotta do is turn toward themselves and realise that everything that they need to know is right [inside their head], and the more you listen to the voices outside your head, the farther you are from understanding who you really are, where you come from, and where you're going."

As far back as the mid-Nineties, the idea of evolution and progression had been at the core of Tool's music. Keenan once said that Tool were all about "evolution. Drastic change and evolution. I think our society has slowed down and become numb, and a lot of people don't want to think. I think a lot of people are scared, they don't want to think about their existence, they want to take things for granted because they're gonna die, and no one knows what happens when you die. As far as I'm concerned, you die. That's it. It's a pretty scary thought. You need security. So a lot of [our] songs are dealing with that."

All this heavy stuff was familiar to anyone who had been a fan of psychedelic and progressive music in previous decades, of course – but Maynard is about more than merely old music. "We do have a connection with some of the progressive stuff – Crimson, Yes, and Pink Floyd," he admitted. "But a lot of those bands aren't very emotional. They're more about the head and the technical stuff. I think we've progressed that kind of rock to a point where we've now integrated the emotional element. I love King Crimson and Rush, but there comes a point where you just have to go and listen to Billie Holiday."

This explained why, despite advances in technology, so much new music still disgusted him: it was just too clinical and categorised. "Back when Nirvana opened a door, a lot of the bands got popular that had a more idealistic view of the way things should be for music," he reasoned. "'No, you don't have to do this, and you don't have to do that'... And they stuck to their guns about it. Pearl Jam, Soundgarden, Nine Inch Nails, Rage [Against The Machine] and Tool – all did things their way. The only downside to that was that they didn't fill in the space – 'No, you don't need to do a record every year'. Well, Limp Bizkit and those kinds of bands are willing to do that, so they've filled up the space, and because we weren't around and because people's attention spans are short, they kind of took over. It's all mediocre, and they're all willing to do things that have nothing to do with art – all posturing and shaking hands and hanging out at the Playboy Mansion. It has nothing to do with art or music or anything, but it doesn't matter because they're filling up space. There are so many slots on a radio station for a song; there are so many magazine covers per year. And they need somebody on the cover, so if they're willing to do the goofy poses and flip off the camera and wear funny hats – do all that kind of stuff to get on the cover – they'll fill up the space and sell magazines."

He went on, clearly on something of a roll: "It would be a flattering thing if I heard that PJ Harvey was influenced by something we did, or Massive Attack, I would go, 'Great!', because I feel the deeper movements to this music. When I hear these loud, goofy posturing idiots jumping up and down, more concerned about their hairdos than their music... what am I missing? There's nothing to the music that moves me, or compels me to want to sit down and listen to it, which is unfortunate. Maybe I'm just a cynical old bastard."

But here's the thing. In no way did Maynard James Keenan rest on his laurels at this point in his career. While the spotlight was on him and him alone, because in 2003 he was engaged in his side project rather than his main band, he took risks, saying things that were unpalatable to the mainstream and possibly commercially threatening to his livelihood. Specifically, he launched into several attacks on the ongoing war in Iraq and Afghanistan, even claiming that he had been silenced in the past when he had spoken out on the subject. As he told one reporter, "Artists everywhere are up against a brick wall when it comes to speaking their minds. After the World Trade Center disaster, I made a point to encourage everyone at our shows to investigate on their own. Ask questions. Don't rely on the media (especially Fox News) to fill in the blanks for you. For this simple position, the position of a free thinker and a responsible citizen, I was silenced. Radio stations throughout the Midwest labelled me anti-American, which I find amusing. The censorship continued. Almost every interview I've done in the last four years was censored. I've been more active in encouraging our fanbase to register to vote ever since 9/11. I've been very vocal about my positions regarding our rights, as citizens, to ask questions of those people whom we've chosen to represent us. And yet most of these topics never made it into print. All the newspapers and press wanted was gossip and road stories. Even pre-taped radio interviews were hacked to pieces."

His central theme, as had increasingly been the case in recent years, was the control of information by the authorities. "There's a great film out called *Outfoxed*," he said. "Of course, it's a very biased film, but it's worth a look, because I think most people get their information from watching TV. And if stations like Fox News present twisted facts, like they do, and I've witnessed it first-hand, people are not going to have enough information in their laps to make an informed decision about the world around them. If they don't have the facts, how can they make an informed choice or have an opinion one way or the other? Watch Fox News, read all the major newspapers, but also read all the independent papers, read international papers. Go to international news sites and international news networks, rather than just sticking to the ones that are run by the people who would have you accept their agenda, and then decide for yourself. Look at that Pentagon website and say for yourself, 'That's bullshit'. But certainly there's a question, so let's ask some questions. It's worth asking the questions, I think. You have to be a conscious being that's asking these questions, you have to be a conscious being that's seeking out truth. If you really want to find out the truth, it's out there, and you just have to have the balls to go out there and look and find out."

America was due to hold a presidential election the following year, and Keenan had strong opinions about the core issues that would drive it, perhaps informed in part by his military past: "It's a multitude of things. It's personal freedoms, Patriot Act issues, censorship, and… yes, our role in Iraq. People are really, really, really having a brain-fart, since Vietnam didn't happen that long ago. I think we're very close to that situation. It could go that way. Is our role in Iraq the same as our role in Vietnam right now? No. Could it go that way if left unchecked and left up to morons? Yeah. That's the whole point. Focus on this so it doesn't turn into another Vietnam."

Reading Keenan's comments, it would be understandable if Tool were lumped in by a large number of people with super-political bands like Rage Against The Machine, their friends and contemporaries. There's certainly an overlap between the way that the members of both acts view the world in general, and modern America in particular; but there are some stark differences, too. For example, a famous animal-rights show that Tool was once asked to play: as Jones recalled, "We were asked to do an anti-vivisection show and we're not anti-vivisection. If using an animal will help solve AIDS or any other disease that kills people, then go for it. Anyway, it was supposed to be an acoustic show, and lots of different bands like Alice In Chains, Rage Against The Machine and Porno For Pyros played. We got out and Maynard just sang [the line from 'Disgustipated'], 'This is necessary', while us and the Rollins Band smashed 30 guitars and played these tribal beats and Maynard shot off a shotgun. We just felt like doing a studio version of it. We'd never even rehearsed it before. We just got up and went for it. No one really got it, you know what I mean? It was anti-*anti*-vivisection. When we did it live it went for 20 minutes. It seemed like two. It was really fun. We have it on videotape."

Keenan, whose borrowed shotgun from Carey was, of course, loaded with blanks, sighed: "It was music. It was an acoustic show, and that was one of the instruments. Nobody gives Blixa [Bargeld] any shit for taking a chainsaw to a Chevy with sparks flying everywhere when Einstürzende Neubauten plays!"

Being unfashionably against animal rights marks Tool out as individualists – and then there are statements from Chancellor such as: "Our drug experiences are more to do with our personal lives, our personal growths, but all of us have in common that when we've had a drug experience it's been for the purpose of drawing something out of it. Tool isn't a band that will become trapped by heroin or anything like that, it's not like that – it's not a habit, they're just tools that are here on the planet. Psychedelics are a good way of exploring the unknown, because everyone is essentially confused about what we are doing here, and psychedelic [art] has always been free-flowing or stream-of-consciousness, and it's a good way of exploring the chaos aesthetically." A far cry from anything said by the new wave of straight-edge hardcore bands that had arisen in recent years – and who made a political point about their abstinence from stimulants, legal or otherwise.

Then there's Tool's androgynous approach to sex in their music, as they told none other than *Penthouse* magazine. "Tool is a house built on a foundation of sexuality," said Jones. "I don't think that's the key to everything, but it's underneath there. It's not cock-rock. It's passionate, but it's not something where we go, 'Well, let's write a song about fucking'." Carey added: "You don't have to be vulgar or crass... You can watch dry-humping videos all day on MTV, and it's boring. We're trying to offer something a little subtler, with slightly higher aspirations in mind. But we're all sexual people, so that element has to be there."

Next, of course, there were the many assertions that the members made about their image – or rather, the lack of one. Few other metal bands would keep a straight face while saying, "We don't want to look and act like typical rock stars, because that's what people have had shoved down their throat for years," as Adam said at this time. "Anyway, we're not celebrities, we're just geeks. I go to comic-book conventions and I like toys. I'd much rather have someone listen to our music and look at a cool visual to help them understand where we're coming from than look at us."

Finally, success didn't seem to mean that much to Tool (Keenan: "When you hear about all the bands who claim to be influenced by us, selling ten times as many records as we are, no, I don't think we're selling that many records. If you just look at how many people are in a city, we're not selling that many records. McDonald's sells more happy meals in a day than we do records"), and nor did the right to free music through illegal file sharing, a practice that bands such as Limp Bizkit actively endorsed by accepting sponsorship money from Napster. Maynard reasoned: "Nobody is communicating to these kids who are taking music off of Napster. The implications and the repercussions of their actions on the artist... they just don't know. It's not that they're doing it vindictively, they just don't understand. They don't understand how little a band makes on a record. In average-case scenarios, a band makes about a dollar a record – and that's after they've paid back everything that they spent making the record, and doing the video and promotions and tour support and all that. It's quite overwhelming."

However, like all visionaries – and make no mistake, Tool had become exactly that by now – the band knew that they would only progress if they focused inward. Danny put this well when he summed up their musical evolution, saying: "People have been victimised by the media over the last couple of years, because [songs] keep getting shorter and shorter. I like albums [by] Yes, Jethro Tull and Todd Rundgren in which one song would take up a whole side of an album. Those would be, like, 30-minute songs. Those are the kinds of records that I always wanted to make. And with *Lateralus*, [we came] closer to that... I think we got a lot more emotional depth translated into the music and lyrics this time. I think the listener will see it, too. And that's what it's all about: hearing something new and discovering an emotion that you didn't know you had before."

After so long in the business, Tool had reached a peak of sorts. They had recorded, released and toured their best album yet, on top of a series of stunning releases. With no need to tour for a living and under no pressure to record more music, how would they avoid sacrificing their talent on the altar of success?

Chapter 13

2004

Answering that question was impossible as 2004 began. For one thing, the Tapeworm project was now officially dead, according to Trent Reznor. "Let me try to explain as honestly as possible," said the Nine Inch Nails frontman at www.nin.com. "Tapeworm wound up being about Maynard, Danny [Lohner], Atticus [Ross] and me working collaboratively together. I provided some music I'd been working on as a starting point and we began. Atticus and I would work on music, Maynard and Danny would show up when Maynard could around Tool's tour. We worked on a number of tracks and had Josh Freese [later of A Perfect Circle] play drums. Eventually, however, things got in the way. Managers, lawyers, record companies, [A Perfect Circle's] needs and frankly my own enthusiasm for the material came into play to work against the project seeing the light of day. The bottom line is this: if the music had been great, all of this probably could have been worked out."

He concluded: "Maynard is a dear friend and a great singer and writer. I'm sure we will work together in some capacity, but the planets were not aligned for that project. My apologies for getting people excited about it – but I was, too."

This explanation was interpreted by most people as the various parties being too busy to get their collective act together – and as there's nothing less interesting than a band that doesn't release any music, Tapeworm was largely forgotten, although it does crop up from time to time in 'Great Lost Music' lists in magazines.

While Keenan toured with A Perfect Circle, the other members of Tool were working on new music. Carey told the press that it would be a little heavier than the songs on *Lateralus*, which had been as much about atmosphere as riffage. The songs, he explained, were "very much in the infant stage, where we have all these different jams and we start piecing them together. There are no true arrangements yet. We like to develop ideas, but we don't want to solidify anything too much until Maynard gets involved… There seems to be a little more brute force going on in the music, rather than being lighter and more intricate like some of the stuff on the last record. It still has quirky time changes, but so far we've been working on really heavy stuff."

Some of this might have been due to the recent tours that Tool had put in with Meshuggah, who play complex death metal, and Fantômas, whose drummer Dave Lombardo was between stints with the always-powerful Slayer at the time. "Mike Patton and Dave Lombardo – those guys are a good, heavy influence," Carey added. "And we did most of the dates on our last tour with Meshuggah. They're incredibly heavy, so it was a good kick in the teeth playing with them."

However, 2004 was destined to be another year devoted to A Perfect Circle – but don't let that put you off if (like many fans) you regard Tool as a much more significant entity than APC. This year, their final as a serious business proposition, A Perfect Circle stepped up to a previously unthought-of level and fulfilled an important function as political commentators. It so happened that the 2004 election, which was won by the Republicans by the slightest of margins amid much controversy, came at a time when the majority of the more outspoken rock bands of recent years were on hiatus and thus unable to make a suitably audible comment on the process. Rage Against The Machine, who had split in 2000, were still three years away from their current reformation, and the only other band with a comparably significant approach and platform, Marilyn Manson, was neither at their creative nor their commercial peak. It was left to cult acts such as A Perfect Circle to deliver a coherent commentary on the events of the day, which they did as best they could, given their position from several steps outside the mainstream.

"First of all," said Keenan, "our disdain for this particular administration should come as no surprise for anyone who has been listening to me for the last 14 years. We [Tool] were very vocal about George Bush Sr. back when he was buying and selling bombs and oil. Anyone who bothered to listen to the Bill Hicks CDs would know this. I've been very clear about this, and have been since before most of you could even reach the keyboard to type your complaints... The fear and absurdity I've witnessed across this country post-9/11 breaks my heart. I have stories so ridiculous you would belly-laugh until you shit yourself."

As always, he advocated a healthy cynicism when it came to the mass media: "If you start looking at international press, you'll start to see different points of view coming out, and that starts to paint a picture. When you read ten articles on the same subject, but two articles were written in Canada, one article was written in Australia, one article was written in Britain, a couple are translated from German and French and Italian, and the other couple of articles are, say, one from Texas and one from California, you read that same article about that same subject, and you'll see what each territory has in terms of an agenda, and you can sort through those agendas and say, 'Oh, clearly these guys think this way, and clearly these guys think that way,' and somewhere in the middle is the truth."

This message was amplified in the summer by the new APC video, recorded for the song 'Counting Bodies Like Sheep To The Rhythm Of The War Drums'. The music itself was more of a collage of beats, distorted ambient noise and vocal effects than an actual song, but it was clear that the visuals were the more important message anyway. Animated in 2-D with an industrial, almost *South Park* feel, the video follows a caricature of George W. Bush as he walks into a school, replacing the students' books with a TV that the horse he rides has excreted, walks a path made of televisions thrown before him by members of the public, and shepherds flocks of sheep over a cliff into the flames of hell. Symbols of a rising and falling oil derrick and a collapsing peace sign appear. Along the way, dissenting sheep are shot and hung on walls with the white flags of traitors, and the final minute of the video is a close-up of Bush's cartoon face, hypnotic eyes swirling, against a background of white noise.

The 'Counting…' video preceded the release of a full A Perfect Circle album, released on November 1, the day scheduled for voting in the election. *Emotive* was an album of covers of political songs from artists as diverse as Elvis Costello, Depeche Mode, Black Flag, Devo and Joni Mitchell. There were also two new songs, although these were in fact covers too: the first, 'Passive', was a version of the old Tapeworm song 'Vacant', while 'Counting Bodies…' itself was a remake of the A Perfect Circle song 'Pet' from the previous year's *Thirteenth Step* album. Both 'Passive' and a version of John Lennon's song 'Imagine' were released as singles, and the album reached number two in the US and Canada.

An issue-linked release such as this one was bound by definition to have a relatively short shelf-life, and in fact Keenan himself didn't try to amplify its status beyond reasonable bounds, saying: "Look, clearly I'm supporting anyone but Bush in this upcoming election, but I'm not telling anyone who to vote for with this new album. I'm still just trying to encourage people to think for themselves… to stop buying into this absurdity and rampant fear. But even that message has been somehow edited over the last four fucking years and it pisses me off. How can a simple message of 'Get off your ass and educate yourself' be turned into a reason to dismiss our efforts? We're speaking our minds. We're following our hearts."

When the result of the 2004 election was announced in Bush's favour, delayed a couple of weeks after wrangling in Florida over recounts and court judgements, one of Maynard's responses was to point out how the result could have been different if a few more of the kids had made the effort to vote. When it was put to him that the government might have deliberately convinced voters that their voices were insignificant, he shrugged: "I'm not sure how they went about doing that, but it's a baffling phenomenon. Take Florida, for example. I think I've played six or seven shows in the last year in Florida, to an average of four thousand to five thousand kids. Any one of those shows that I've played there, if all the kids from that show voted, we would have a different president right now. Just one show!"

The new era of Bush began with a new – and, as it emerged, final –

Danny Carey, whose ear for an arrangement and spiritual philosophies make him one of Tool's secret weapons.
[ROBERT KNIGHT/REDFERNS]

Maynard embraces the '80s roadie' look in
June 2002 at the Ozzfest. *[FX IMAGES]*

Keenan and wig on stage with A Perfect Circle at
Lollapalooza in 2003, as the War On Terror (about
which he would often comment) hit its stride.
[TIM MOSENFELDER/CORBIS]

Danny Carey, now regarded as one of the world's most accomplished drummers, live in LA in 2003.
[ROBERT KNIGHT/REDFERNS]

Keenan, who had become a wine producer by 2004, at a wine-tasting event in Birmingham, England in January that year.
(ANDY CANTILLON/RETNA UK)

Maynard in full pimp regalia for the launch of A Perfect Circle's *Lost In The Bermuda Triangle* DVD in May 2004.
[KMAZUR/WIREIMAGE FOR VIRGIN RECORDS/GETTY IMAGES]

Keenan with his then-fiancée Jennifer Brena Ferguson at the premiere of *Constantine* in Hollywood in 2005: normally he shuns such events.
[FREDERICK M. BROWN/STRINGER/GETTY IMAGES]

Maynard live on stage with Tool at Coachella in April 2006. The cowboy hat is a nod towards Puscifer's 'Cuntry Boner', perhaps? [LUCAS JACKSON/REUTERS/CORBIS]

Adam Jones at the Download festival in June 2006. *[REDFERNS/REDFERNS]*

Tool's eyeball-searing live show at Roskilde in July 2006. [SEAN SMITH/WIREIMAGE.COM]

Keenan rocking the punk look at Australia's
Big Day Out festival in 2007.
[MARC GRIMWADE/CONTRIBUTOR/WIREIMAGE.COM]

Justin Chancellor bringing the groove
in 2007 as only he can. [RETNA UK]

Keenan (second from left) with sushi chef Nozawa, his wife Yumiko (with some of Keenan's wine) and Nine Inch Nails' Danny Lohner in California, June 2008. [JESSE GRANT/CONTRIBUTOR/WIREIMAGE.COM]

Danny Carey and Maynard James Keenan at the Grammy Awards in LA in 2008. Don't they look pleased to be there? [DAN MACMEDAN/CONTRIBUTOR/WIREIMAGE.COM]

Carey giving some love to industry legend Clive Davis at the Grammy afterparty. [L. BUSACCA/WIREIMAGE.COM]

Keenan, doing what he does best – inspiring fear and devotion in equal measure.
He is that rare thing: a truly unique performer. [MYRIAM SANTOS KAYDA/RETNA LTD]

release from A Perfect Circle in the form of the *aMotion* DVD and CD set, which gathered all the APC videos to date and also offered the fans a set of remixes of audio tracks. The DVD also contained trailers for *Bikini Bandits Go To Hell* from a couple of years previously – an appropriate inclusion as Keenan was about to make an appearance in the sequel, *Bikini Bandits 2: Golden Rod*, reprising his role as Satan.

A Perfect Circle's future has never been fully clarified since then, with Keenan making the occasional comment to the effect that a song might continue to appear here and there, but that a full album or tour would be impossible to manage given the conflicting schedules of the members' other bands. He returned to Tool, of course; Billy Howerdel formed a new band called Ashes Divide, which featured cello-playing from Keenan's son Devo; Josh Freese moved to Nine Inch Nails; and to top off the game of alt-rock musical chairs, Jeordie White rechristened himself Twiggy Ramirez and returned to Marilyn Manson.

Once back in the Tool fold, Keenan had time to reflect on the political situation – and although he was no longer in an explicitly political band, he had plenty to say on the subject. "I think we are here to create a new world order," he declared. "George W. Bush is an extremely evil person, and what he is doing is going to bring us down. He is going to make it very difficult for me to travel around the world because I am an American, and people will look at me in exactly the same way they used to look at the Germans when they were travelling in the Fifties, right after World War II. We are living in McCarthyism, the Third Reich, and people don't realise it. Look at the events of September 11. The person who profited from that was the President of the United States – the same man who was not elected by the people but instead by a fault in the electoral system. His public opinion was at an all-time low, so he benefited from it. His family's oil, war and weapons interests all benefited. And everyone was so scared that they willingly gave up their civil rights, so that if anyone discovers how evil this guy is, they can't do anything about it. It really amazes me that the American people are just blindly letting this go on. They are not even considering the possibility that their government could be lying to them. It is absolutely nauseating."

He added, with prophetic confidence: "We're heading towards some big changes, definitely – combined with technology, computers and the internet advancing exponentially. It's pretty incredible. We're in a differ-ent mind-set now. We're in a mind-set where we're not so sure what tomorrow's gonna bring, because there's such an increased rate of ideas coming into fruition, coming to light and physically appearing for us. A hundred years ago, somebody had the idea of talking down a phone line to somebody else, and it was just an idea and it kinda evolved slowly. But the idea that a hundred years ago somebody saying, 'I'm gonna make this thing that you talk into, and you can talk to somebody on the other side of the globe, which is round, by the way, not flat, you know?' Those would just be crazy ideas."

Danny Carey also chimed in at this point with his own views about the authorities: "The government doesn't want people thinking for themselves – no one who's in a position of power wants that, because it makes people more uncontrollable. It's because they're afraid, but there really isn't anything for people to be afraid of. As long as you have com-passion and move forward, you can't go wrong. Drugs are fine for some people, but for some people they do damage. Everybody that I know who's a good musician uses drugs. I've never heard a band that spoke out against drugs that sounded good, honestly... it's a sad state that it's like that, but it's because the government has made them illegal. Now you have all these people on these hardcore anti-drug kicks."

He added, of the 'right' way to use drugs: "I don't think the rules change or anything just because people do drugs. You're either in con-trol or you're not in control. I don't want to lean towards anything that I think I might become addicted to. You have to know yourself to know where your weak points are, and if you don't, you have to go through things and learn from them... I would never condemn anyone for using psychedelics, even if they did have their most creative moments doing them. I don't see any problem with that. If you're doing good work and people are becoming inspired by it, that's the bottom line."

The occasional press interview executed by the band while new music was being assembled usually revolved around their future when it wasn't about the government. Carey and the others were ebullient about the next Tool album, and Maynard too showed signs of being excited by it and what it offered in place of the usual pop fare. "I think in light of what's out there right now, people need something," Keenan predicted.

"Something they can sink their teeth into, something that they know they can come back to and rediscover more in it as they go... This band is definitely for somebody where we make these pieces that are something that you can come back to, and whatever issues you're going through in your personal life, you might find a song on the record that is very much suited to that particular struggle. Most bands that are out nowadays, they're not really making movies – they're more like commercials. Their heart isn't really in it... Speaking in terms of what would be considered progressive rock, say Pink Floyd or King Crimson, or bands like Yes, I think we're picking up where they left off. Their music is very much in the head and very much [from the] left brain. I think what Tool brings to this kind of music is more heart, more emotional aspects to the intellectualised music – so it's a wide spectrum that involves the heart and the head, and that way we've evolved where they've left off."

Behind the scenes, away from the public persona that Maynard presented to the press and fans, he was evolving as a songwriter. The music that Tool was now making was more personal in nature, an inevitable result of the passing of the years (the band were all now aged between 33 and 44) and, in the singer's case, due also to personal traumas such as the recent death of his mother. Not that he let any of this show: as he declared, "What I wear, how I walk, who I'm fucking, what I eat, what time I go to bed, has nothing to do with what we're doing. Presenting those things as somehow being part of Tool is deceptive. It's not honest. I don't embrace anybody. I want my space, my distance. I'm not a very warm person. I'm sure that most of the people whose music I love are assholes. Where I met them is at their music. That inspired me to do something for myself."

As time passed, the band's viewpoint of both their past and future work expanded, so they began to see the full picture of what they had done and what was left for them to achieve in a clearer light, even if the public were still some way away from sharing this perception. To apply a very Tool-like idea, the continuum of musical style they had traversed over the previous decade and a half had lengthened, to the point where Adam Jones could ponder of the next record, "The fact that so many of our heavier songs appeared on our first album was something of an aberration. It just happened that was the direction we chose to follow. It was something that kind of developed when we were in the studio. But we [don't] feel limited this time… Some of our other sides have reared their ugly heads this time around, and I believe people will find that to be very interesting."

Jones also knew that good music needs a long time to find its place in the popular consciousness, saying: "It's a slow process. Ten years from now we'll look back and see if anyone actually stepped up to the plate… one thing you'll learn as you grow older, is that the sooner you don't give a fuck what your heroes think, the better off you are. So when you hit that point where you just move forward and just do what you do, you've come to an amazing spot in your life. The big thing is that you've got to do it for you, for something that really moves you… MTV got behind us last time, but who knows what will happen next? Quite often those same media people who love you one year turn against you the next. Who knows why? It's just a fact of life. So why should we spend even one second worrying about it? We just proceed like always, just the way we've been doing it for the last four years."

People were still unaccustomed to Tool taking so long between albums, whatever the band said in mitigation. The musicians had different ways of explaining their methods: for example, Justin observed that Tool was simply lucky to have fans who would wait around so long. "It's really reassuring that the people that are into it are in for the long ride and have the patience to let us do our own thing," he said. "It's nice to know that you can keep your focus and not have people wander off and get distracted… [Some bands] underestimate people and they're going to do things however it works easiest for them. You get what you get and there's not a lot of choice, because they pick the stuff that works best for them. If you've got something good going, you need to keep focused on that and just ignore what everyone else is doing."

Adam viewed the hiatus as a necessary evil required for the band to handle their demons, saying: "I feel like everything that's happened to our band in the last three years has just been a huge test. Let's just say that I like the outcome of the test – I think it's good. It was a healing process. David Bowie said something in an interview that got me really excited: 'I had to become a better businessman to become a better artist'. I thought it was beautiful because it's so true. When some bands become too big, they start fighting about money and control. Then other parties get involved and everything starts to disintegrate. That's why you hear about great bands breaking up. When we started out, we decided to split everything four ways. We didn't want to be one of those bands that fought over this song, that song, the single or who gets what put on the album."

Carey saw the gap as a chance for personal growth, explaining: "I think it could do a lot of bands some good to take a sabbatical and try to expand their horizons in one way or another, and then they could come out with something that their fans would really appreciate. If you just keep cranking out things, you don't give yourself a chance to grow as individuals. That's one thing that's good. It's allowed us a little time off from each other too, to explore our own ways a little bit. It's kinda been good for everyone."

Keenan, of course, had a metaphysical approach to all this, explaining that time is circular: "If you're into astrology or any of that kind of stuff, there's a process called the Saturn Return – your 30-year cycle. It's something like a mid-life crisis, where you step back and re-evaluate... I'm not that fluent in astrology or hocus-pocus, but it's a 28- to 30-year cycle, where when you're born Saturn is in one position and it takes approximately 29 years to come all the way back around. It just so happens that it coincides with the majority of people's re-evaluation of their lives. It's kind of a traumatic time, because you're trying to figure out who you are and what the hell you've been doing for 30 years, and recognising patterns. Like, 'Why do I keep ending up with these same people in my life?' – that kind of stuff."

Of the next Tool album, Keenan explained his role as a mediator: "Think of it in terms of metaphor. I'm the translator between what happens in our rehearsal space with the music and the listener... here I am, translating one position to another. These people come into a position and they're gonna try to get a thought, or a bomb, across to somebody else. There has to be some kind of middleman to figure out where you are in reference to where you're going – in essence, a translator... When you get to a certain age, you start to get a better perspective. You get more hindsight and you write from that place, and it's certainly going to be a different place, but a natural progression… Because blotter acid can't be downloaded, we figured we're gonna do the whole cover as a big blotter acid, and if you eat the cover, something strange will happen."

Keenan's famous sense of humour had obviously not deserted him, and in fact he once defined the band as humorists to the core. "We're just, you know, shit-talkers, and we're definitely into comedy," he laughed. "We're just a band that requires you to become involved, to show up ready to experience this with us… and if you don't know that we have a sense of humour, then you aren't listening."

His fellow musicians agreed. "We never set out to be mysterious," added Jones. "We just didn't want to worry about image. 'How does the band look? What are they wearing? Are they cute?' We just said, 'Let's allow the music to be the star'. And you know what? I'm comfortable with the fact that I can go watch the opening band at one of our sold-out shows and never be recognised."

One interesting, and slightly unnerving, theory proposed by Keenan didn't bode well for Tool's career. He posited that all bands go into a decline in quality after a surprisingly short space of time. "For the most part, most of your favourite records are the first three records of a band's career. So, here we are on our fourth record. Do we evolve past where we came from and make it better, or do we fall under the same pattern that all of our peers have and make the disappointing fourth record?… Look at it, it's just generally true. The first three Devo records, the first three Psychedelic Furs records, in general. The only bands that transcended that process have been bands like Led Zeppelin or The Beatles or the Stones… Especially in the light of everything else that's happening with our evolution, with the internet and Napster and all that, it's a scary prospect. Even if we do make a good record, perhaps in a year it'll be irrelevant. People will just be able to download it in its entirety."

He was certainly right about the march of file-sharing technology. As for whether Tool could break the three-good-albums trend, the answer was coming steadily closer.

Chapter 14

2005

As always, life seemed to get in the way of a new Tool album: when you're a platinum-selling international rock band, people keep asking you to do things.

In February 2005 Maynard James Keenan stepped up to sing with three-quarters of the cult rock band Alice In Chains, taking the place of singer Layne Staley, who had succumbed to his drug habit in April, 2002. Invited to headline an alternative-rock bill at a fundraiser for the victims of the Boxing Day tsunami two months before, the band hadn't played together in six years, and the venue (a club in Seattle, spiritual home of all things alternative) was packed. Compered by sometime Nirvana bassist Krist Novoselic, the show also featured Heart, Sir Mix-A-Lot and Children Of The Revolution, but was most notable for the parade of singers who sang with AIC. Wes Scantlin of the then-fêted rock band Puddle Of Mudd, Pat Lachman of the recently dissolved Damageplan (whose guitarist 'Dimebag' Darrell Abbott had been shot dead on stage three months before) and finally Keenan strolled through the Alice In Chains catalogue. They ended with a unison version of the song 'Rooster'. The verdict was that Maynard would be a good fit in the band, should they ever reform.

The year started relatively sanely, then, but as always things took a turn for the surreal on April 1 when a statement was posted on Tool's website saying that "Maynard has found Jesus", and that he had withdrawn from the new album. Kurt Loder of MTV is said to have emailed Keenan for clarification and received a confirmation of the news, and that on contacting the singer a second time he was sent a simple "Heh heh" in response. As the members of Tool well knew it would, the news caused a sensation in the media, with Launch Radio Networks reporting even four days later: "Keenan himself emailed the webmaster of Tool fansite ToolShed.down.net, saying, 'I thought it only fair to inform you first, before you hear it second- or third-hand. Some recent events have led me to the rediscovery of Jesus. Tool will need to take the back seat. This may come as a shock. I just thought you should know considering all the support you have given us over the years'."

Two days later Keenan posted on the official site, "Good news, April Fool's fans. The writing and recording is back under way. When approached for comment on his recent encounter with the Son of God, Maynard said, 'That guy's a punk!... Turns out he was here the whole time, and not that difficult to find if you know where to look... Every time our Lord goes to get a glass of water, it transforms into a generic grocery-store Merlot. Because the alcoholic is the Son of God and an all-knowing being, he knew of Maynard's extensive interest in collecting wine. So he went to work trying to get his lips on it. Maynard caught J.C. in his cellar transforming his precious wine collection into urine, then pissing it into the empty 'sparkling holy water' bottles for the eventual sale to all those people who bought, read, and embraced *The Celestine Prophecy...* Truth be told, I wasn't feeling top notch when I found him. The evening prior to the day in question I had over-indulged in a series of bad Molotov shrimp cocktails with a side of Maker's Mark and twin strippers. So after an entire night of G.I. Blowouts, hot/cold sweats, and blurred vision, it's very possible that the guy I met wasn't even Jesus at all. For all I know, it was Willem Dafoe.'"

You can imagine the amusement that Tool felt at muddying the waters once again. Fans had just got over the fact that Keenan was in two parallel bands, a difficult situation to understand on its own, without more doubt being cast on the future of his more established act. However, in the summer Tool did announce with no ambiguity that a new album was under way, stating online: "For various reasons, the album is being recorded in relative secrecy... even more so than past recording sessions and related Tool projects. When [Tool] release certain details pertaining to the recording process, as well as any projected timetables, etc., it will most certainly be posted on the band's official website... this could be tomorrow, or two days from now, or in a couple of weeks or even a month from now... the members of the band are working hard and, as the saying goes, there is light at the end of the tunnel."

However, before fans heard any new music they were reminded of the epic *Lateralus* with the long-awaited vinyl edition of the album, which came out in August as a luxurious double picture-disc LP. A limited, autographed edition was made available to the fan club before the wider release. More unusually, two songs from that album – 'Schism' and 'Parabola' – were scheduled for release as DVD singles later in the year, eventually appearing in December. Each contained both the audio and video files as well as remixes by the experimental Welsh musician Lustmord. The crowning feature of each disc was a 'dual audio' commentary, with two tracks recorded by Jello Biafra and The Jesus Lizard's David Yow on either audio channel, for the user to switch between at will.

All this retrogressive action was a little odd given that a new Tool album was obviously under way, but you'll recall that the band have rarely taken the most obvious route throughout their career. In any case, they were still keen to emphasise that their best work still lay ahead of them. As Keenan put it: "For me to have done *Lateralus* and then come out with another Tool album within a year wouldn't have been a good step forward. We've always subscribed to the idea that you have to process life experiences and go through your natural progression as an artist to let the [music] come out, rather than forcing it out. We're just the kind of band where it takes a long time for us to process. Meanwhile [with A Perfect Circle], I'm processing other things while Tool's going on. I have another outlet... But I think now they realise the benefit of [APC]. It allows us to do what we set out to do, which is to take the time that the music needs to take before you present it."

Of the fans who wanted more from Tool, he explained: "I just hope that our fans are people who are inspired by music, and use our music as a background or inspiration for whatever it is they do. I would hope they would be our fellow artists, rather than trying to emulate or idolise clowns like us… It's obvious there are people that have come around, and that's inspiring to know, 'Oh, yeah, you guys are getting it'. But then it starts to get to that weird Holy Grail level where at some point you go, 'Dude, we were just having fun. They were just songs. We inserted some codes in there just as a joke, but we weren't serious. We're not wearing masks in some basement chanting, nothing to do with any of that stuff. It's just us having fun'. And so when it becomes familiar, like most of my peers, we take off in different directions, and do something else to just have more fun in a different way."

'Fun' entailed more side projects for the band while new songs took shape. In 2005 alone, a Jello Biafra collaboration with the Melvins called *Sieg Howdy!* was released with Adam Jones playing guitar on five songs; Adrian Belew of King Crimson released *Side One*, a solo album with Danny Carey playing drums and tabla on three tracks; and Carey also composed and released the music for an independent movie, *Tweeked*, as well as exec-producing an album by the highly regarded tabla player Aloke Dutta called *Sinuosity*.

Perhaps the most unexpected news from Tool's battery of extracurricular activity came when Keenan announced that he had established a winemaking business near his home in Sedona, Arizona, where he and his son Devo (who alternated homes with his mother in LA) had been living since 1995. Already a co-owner of a restaurant in LA called Cobras And Matadors and a produce market in Cornville, Arizona, Keenan had expanded his business interests to encompass a ten-acre vineyard and winery, named Merkin (the Shakespearean name for a pubic wig) and Caduceus (an ancient staff symbolising commerce) respectively. He was under no illusions about how much work it would require for him to be taken seriously as a winemaker, or how much scepticism he would face on all sides, saying with his usual dry resolve: "[People] immediately just shrug and go, 'OK'. They think I'm [Mötley Crüe singer] Vince Neil coming in with a bottle of vinegar. Initially people go, 'Oh, you're in a band. It'll sell just because you're in a band'. Yeah, but it doesn't mean that people are going to take it seriously. So I have to try three times harder, work three times harder, and have three times as good a product for them to take it seriously."

Proof of Maynard's commitment to the Caduceus brand came when he even promised to arrange Tool around the business's needs. "The guys know that I've gotta be in Arizona for the harvesting and processing, and then I'll need to be back there again for the bottling. We'll be working our touring schedule around it," he said, to many fans' disbelief. It seemed that a new concern had come into Keenan's life that matched Tool in priority, or even outweighed it.

However, the singer explained that the business was integral to him. "Wine is in my blood," he said. "I'm just a creative, restless person, and I like to challenge myself, and winemaking definitely takes patience, so this is teaching me patience. And the payoff when you open up the wine is immense. I have a history of winemaking; apparently my great-grand-father made wine in northern Italy. So because I'm a person who believes in that intuition, that thing that brought me here, I want to believe on some level that history in my family was somehow speaking in my ear and brought me here to start this industry here, to pioneer this with Eric in this area." 'Eric' is Eric Glomski, the owner of Page Springs Cellars, where Caduceus is based: like Keenan, he had a vision for rein-troducing viniculture into Arizona, where wine was produced centuries ago but which had become overshadowed by neighbouring California in winemaking terms over recent decades. Glomski told a visiting writer from *Spin* magazine that: "When we first met Maynard, none of us had even heard of him. We certainly weren't fans of his music. He could have turned out to be a prima donna, but he's been the opposite... At this point, I think he's more a winemaker than a musician."

Of his move to the desert a decade before, Keenan explained: "My friend Tim Alexander [the drummer with Primus] used to live in this area and I told him that I had this [dream that meant that] I was sup-posed to be in Arizona. That was in the early Nineties. And then having met Bill Hicks and him talking about his *Arizona Bay* record, that kind of cinched it for me. I then came out for a visit in '95 to see Tim, and I told him about the so-called dream, [which] was more like passing thoughts and daydreams, and he said, 'Well, I have to show you this area'. And he brought me up here, and I immediately went to the Motor

Vehicle Department, changed over my licence, got a PO Box and registered to vote all in the same day."

The Caduceus business had been under wraps since 2000, it emerged, when Keenan took his first steps into winemaking. The first bottles, with the signature 'M. Keenan, Winemaker' on their labels, sold for around $100 per bottle and gradually increased in output to 1,200 cases a year by 2005, which Keenan described as "super-low volume". Diarising the progress of the business at regular intervals at the Wine Spectator website, he built the profile of the brand until it had reached a respectable level. By now he was also living with a long-term partner, a woman whose name (like that of Devo's mother) has never been revealed. "For the first time in my life," he said, "I have someone who's taking care of me, rather than the other way around."

It seemed as if Keenan had reached a plateau of contentment after all these years, with his only worry being the occasional overzealous Tool disciple who tracked him down. As Tim Alexander, his friend and fellow Arizona resident, said: "He's definitely gotta watch it. We get weirdos up here looking for him, trying to find out where he lives so they can have a séance on his doorstep or something." Alexander added that Keenan has sometimes chased off visitors with a paintball rifle. Of the obsessive fans, Maynard cursed: "Get out of the nest, for fuck's sake!... What the fuck have you done with [the music] that you need me to keep doing it?... I don't have any talent. I'm just a dumbass. I mean, I can put a couple of words together, but I'm not Stephen Hawking; it's not that kind of stuff. But people are treating it like it is."

Keenan had reached a turning-point in his life that many Tool fans would have seen coming over the previous few years – a point at which his life's ambition began to rival the importance of Tool in his view. In late 2005 the soundtrack to the torture-porn film *Saw II* was released, containing a song called 'Rev 22:20 (Rev 4:20 Mix)', credited to a band called Puscifer (pronounced, it was later reported, somewhere between 'Lucifer' and 'pussy fur'). This, it emerged, was Maynard's new side project, but not in the format that anyone would have predicted. Puscifer also contributed a song to the feeble horror film *Underworld: Evolution* the same year.

The name 'Puscifer' had been heard before, notably when Keenan played a role as the singer of a band of the same name for the *Mr Show* TV slot in the previous decade. This time, he had used it for real, making music under that name with various collaborators and designing a range of clothes and accessories for sale under the Puscifer brand name. In various interviews he gave the impression that he was building an independent business based on the same mindset as the one behind Caduceus and Merkin – perhaps the tangible personification of the message he had been sending to listeners of Tool and A Perfect Circle for years.

Keenan was putting his neck on the line with these ventures, financing them from his own funds and becoming an adept businessman in doing so. "I'm not going to be making the money I'm making now forever," he remarked astutely, adding: "Tool and A Perfect Circle... are very much aware, on many levels, what goes on with our business. We were much older than most people are when we got involved in it, and we knew that with the difficult-to-navigate material that we were presenting, we would have to survive on our own for quite a while before someone actually caught on. With that in mind, we had to really buckle down and gut it out to get to where we are now. And in '96, '97, when we already had two platinum records, I was still living on 500 bucks a month. People go, 'No, no, you were a millionaire back then when I saw you on Lollapalooza '97'. 'No, dude. Credit card with a limit'."

Keenan appeared to have found a concept that meant everything to him. Of his attempts to found a business in hick-town Arizona, he explained: "It's like looking at that hill and saying, 'I think there's a little mug of gold coins buried there. I had a dream, and I can see it'. So you make this long trek, and after searching and searching, you find it... All the shit you had to go through? It's about embracing your intuition. And being right."

The new musical project, he insisted, might be different in platform but still gave consumers what they wanted – good tunes. "One thing that's not going to change is [that] people like music," he said. "Digital downloading [has] actually made it a lot more accessible to people who might not have heard stuff before, because you had to buy the CD with this mysterious cover, you don't know what it's about. Well, now a lot of people are just passing around MP3s. 'Check this world music out, check out this country song, check out the Gypsy Kings' – stuff you wouldn't normally have been exposed to, because radio stations have pigeonholed themselves. They're not going to be diverse in what they're playing on their format."

As an artist, Keenan explained that he needed different stimuli to function – and, as he'd done before with A Perfect Circle, the ability to switch characters as he wished. "When I'm doing something I'm looking for truth in some way," he said. "Hopefully people who pay attention to what I'm doing get that there's an idea in mind. There's a method to the madness, and I'm looking for something." He cited David Bowie's chameleon-like persona as an example: "All the theatrics and the changes he did… even the *Let's Dance* era I thought was great, because it was him going, 'I'm going to try this now. I'm going to see where I can take this'… he made the choice to look for something and seek something out: as an artist, I respect that. So I guess that's always been my choice."

This time around, Keenan was neither performing abrasive prog-metal nor textural art-rock, but rhythmic, semi-electronic music that defied categorisation. "I started listening to old James Brown, Aretha Franklin, Jackson Five stuff," he said, "and I remembered, 'Oh, yeah, back when I was younger, there were these songs that I didn't care who was doing them. I just liked the feeling that I was getting hearing them'. And there was nothing that demanded that I get involved. There was just a feeling and a rhythm that I liked. I didn't know what they were talking about. I didn't have to do acid and put on headphones to enjoy it. It could just be there while I was making cookies and I could enjoy it. So that was the goal with this project, on top of trying to navigate this whole new world for an individual artist trying to make music in a very network fashion. I have friends helping me make this music with every little piece they can bring to the table. And the goal is then next year [to] help those guys do their music. I'll perform on their projects and it'll be their thing, their vision. They'll be telling me what to do and what they have in mind for their thing."

Which brings us, of course to Tool. What did Puscifer, Maynard's second side band in a period of just six years, say about his relationship with his best-known act? He now described Tool as a "very small part of my life, it just happens to take up the most of it. My main focus is our relationships with each other and dealing with life and the shit it throws at us. At the moment, I'm thinking about how I want to build a wine cellar in my house, and I've wanted to do it for a while. So while I'm out here, I'm just daydreaming about my wine cellar."

The clearest signs that Keenan was suffering from Tool fatigue came when he said, "I'm not that person any more. I wrote the songs for them to be cathartic. You exorcise the demon… and then you move on. But the way we're doing it, I have to keep bringing it up again. It's destructive – physically and emotionally destructive…. Pavarotti [used] to say that one of the only things that got him through was solid sleep, a familiar bed, and not singing… periods of not singing."

"We'll make music together until one of us is dead," Maynard promised of Tool, but he added, "I don't have the energy to come from those places any more. I just can't do it. It's like picking scabs at this point."

Not the most positive of moods, you might correctly think. Away from his self-made retreat in Arizona, Keenan seemed to regard the rest of America as fundamentally out to get him. This could have been partially the result of the roasting the last A Perfect Circle album, *Emotive*, had received from the fanbase. As he said: "I tested the water with the political album A Perfect Circle did. I didn't even write those songs; I was just letting people hear what was said before me, the things that inspired me as a child, and things that were said during various turbulent times. And I was fucking crucified. If you go back and listen to that album and just forget that it's covers, it's a good album, but I was crucified because of its content, because there's an army of little fucking brats out there just going into every little chat-room, talking shit and undermining anybody who has anything to say. It's like this insane, 1984/Big Brother infrastructure… I'm not an educated man. I only know what I'm told, and I'm not told that much; I have no frame of reference for how to place things in history [that would let me] be a responsible leader. All I can do is be an artist, and basically waffle on about my feelings – which helps people, you know, get through a root canal, but it doesn't really help them deal with political stuff. All I can do is say I smell a rat. I don't know where it is or what kind of rat it is, but as an artist, I can express how [I feel about it]. But I couldn't responsibly stand up and tell people which way to go, because then I'm just as guilty as the people who are telling everybody else what to do and where to go."

Politically, too, things were depressing him. Keenan saw nothing good in the US administration a year into George W. Bush's second term: "The people that have been duped are embarrassed, but they're not going to do anything about it. They're going to toe the line just to see if it pans out in their direction, so they can say, 'See, I was right'. It really is imploding; it's getting nuts everywhere – and it's this crazy nationwide, if not global, push for this polarising religious fanaticism that's just infecting everything… it's the kind of thing that only ends in bloodshed. You know what I mean? It's so polarised that there is no grey area, and it comes down to a religious war… I don't know what the solution is, other than just hoping that we can weather the storm, and then looking to places like Europe, post-World War I and II, where the communities that survived were the ones that were already surviving. They had their own little localised economy and farmers and trade, just to get through the winter. They're the ones that survived, and have survived, and will survive. So that's the positive. That's my silver lining in the cloud: starting a wine community in Arizona, hoping that the United States [will go] through an entire saturation of winemaking, and then level out to where it ends up being a cottage industry and people are just surviving locally, no matter what happens with the clowns running things."

Add to this the idiocies of the press, which constantly dogged him, and it becomes understandable that Keenan was more than a little repelled by life in general at this time. "We don't suffer fools lightly… we're artists, and we really work hard at what we do, and we just assume that when we go to talk to a journalist, they're as passionate about their art as we are about ours. And then you end up talking to this buffoon who has no business managing a Starbucks. So we just got into this funk right away, doing interviews – we were like, 'You know what? Fuck this. I'm not doing this shit'. We'd just go out and do what we do, and the people would come one by one and then tell a friend, and they'd tell a friend, and they'd start coming out and seeing what we're about. Eventually, that may catch up to where we have people showing up knowing what we're about, and knowing that this is a conversation between two humans who are passionate about what they do. When that happens, then I'm willing to talk to the guy."

Finally, it seems that he had even lost touch with Tool's fanbase. Keenan's disgust was evident when he spat: "[You play] heavy music, and your record company, which has never owned an album anything like what you're doing, immediately markets you to the obvious stinky kid with the dreadlocks and the BO and the urine on his shoes because he's been sleeping in his own filth in a festival in the middle of the rain. They basically market right to that guy. And then you realise the only people showing up to your shows are those primates – these weird, cretin people... Then, let's say you're at a coffee shop, and you've got a friend sitting next to you, and you've been reading some Noam Chomsky, or you're reading *The Onion*, and you look over and see a bunch of kids [who] look like they could be made of cheese, because there are flies everywhere. And you go, 'Hey, you want to go where they're going?' and everybody goes, 'Fuck no'. And they're wearing Tool shirts. Why would you want to go there? Why would anybody other than those kids wanna go see Tool if that's our representative in that area? So it ends up being a no-win situation."

Maynard James Keenan had always been a reserved character with a refreshingly no-prisoners attitude, but until now he had at least engaged with the wider world. Was this the end of an era?

Chapter 15

2006

Having acquired a healthy paranoia about the joys of illegal file shar-ing, Tool elected once again to release some misleading fake titles before the release of the new album, just to unnerve any potential pirates. Fans were well aware of the band's fondness for such tricks, and when the title of *Teleincision* was announced, few really believed it. Inevitably, when the album's real title – *10,000 Days* – was announced on March 3, 2006, exactly the same scepticism prevailed and most peo-ple simply waited for Tool to announce a third title... in vain.

After a couple of years out of the public eye, the band seemed more willing than usual to talk to the press, and judging from the content of their pre-release interviews, *10,000 Days* seemed set to be another com-plex, multilayered work that would cause fans yet more philosophical headaches. Sonically, it would be heavy, said Adam: "We've all been lis-tening to a lot of Meshuggah: I see a lot of them in us and us in them, and they really have a very experimental prog side to them. I don't think it was like, 'OK, right here we're going to play like Meshuggah,' but more, 'Oh my God, that's come out a Meshuggah moment'."

Carey spoke of his political disillusionment, explaining: "We have the most retarded president we've ever had, and we're frustrated, and that's the reason it's a little heavier this time. That level of frustration [is] like when we first got the band together: we were products of that fucking Reagan thing, we were pissed off and bummed out, we had that angst, and now it's coming forth again: like it or not, we're products of our environment. We're pissed off again."

Keenan, in contrast, had reached inward for inspiration. "The last few years have really been crushing," he said. "For me, as an artist, I needed to see, on some level, if speaking my mind would actually inspire people – you see the sky falling and you feel like you've got to say something. I think of *Ænima* and *Lateralus*: lyrically, I had this idea of trying to share things and push some kind of higher purpose – enlightenment, this global consciousness thing – and everything that's going on nowadays has kind of left me a little disappointed, a little bummed… So I think on this album I've talked more about my personal stuff, things that I needed to get off my chest. It's a little cynical and it's almost like coming from a sad place. There's some hope in it, but it's more back to rock'n'roll basics, just expressing some very big sadness that's from the gut."

Justin Chancellor added that the recording process had been smoother this time than it had been with *Lateralus*, "because everyone was getting on much better this time, and the attention to detail was a little more involved on everyone's part. I think we worked a lot more with Maynard during much of the process, so there's a lot of interaction between the music and the vocals. It was a more positive experience on my end. The last album was a real hard road and a little like pulling teeth at times. These sessions were more enjoyable… We had a lot of ideas that were left over from [the *Lateralus* sessions], and all of us worked on coming up with riffs and ideas. We just made a big pile of ideas in the middle of the room, and you start playing around with them and jamming. It's kind of a process of exploration and discovery. And at some point, the ideas started coming together in groups and they become songs."

The title of the new album was explained a little further down the line. Ten thousand days add up to approximately 27 years: the length of time between Keenan's mother, Judith's, aneurysm when he was a child, and her death three years before the album's release.

10,000 Days wasn't all introspective, though. The first single, 'Vicarious', was released on April 17 and featured as its theme a vitriolic rant from Keenan on the subject of the public's fascination with media reports of human suffering. He invokes images of dying children and murdered adults, all projected back at a society that refuses to admit how much it enjoys them. Asking the listener to admit that he or she enjoys it too, Keenan calls for an end to hypocrisy over a complex, riff-heavy song that extends across several different sections. The video didn't refer directly to any of this, simply offering up an intertwining set of computer-generated visuals (a world away from the gritty Claymation of the *Undertow* singles) that resolved into more of the expansive, psychedelic imagery of the mind generated by Alex Grey, Tool's collaborator on some of the *Lateralus* artwork. The video clip's first half follows a semi-transparent human figure who stands in a desert, close to a floating glass cube, while a maggot-like creature and a giant flea fly over him: the latter seems to suck one of his eyeballs from his face, which then grows octopus-like tentacles, expands and floats into the air like a hot-air balloon. Like *2001: A Space Odyssey*, the clip breaks away into an entirely different dimension in its latter few minutes, diving inside a cave made up of Technicolor fractals in a symmetry of eyeballs and statues. The maggot from earlier dives, spermatozoon-like, in and out of the eyes and the occasional floating fireball – a combination of the creative minds of Jones, Grey and conceptual artist Chet Zar.

The tone of the video may be similar to a head-spinning clip such as 'Parabola' from four years previously, but the riffage of the song is heavier and more industrial and the lyrics are, for the first time in Tool's history, relatively easy to interpret. The single made number two on the *Billboard* Modern Rock Tracks chart but didn't make much of an impact on the main *Billboard* singles list, although it did receive a nomination for Best Hard Rock Performance at the Grammy Awards the following year.

At last, *10,000 Days* – the album's real title, to many sceptics' surprise – was released on May 2. Although it went straight to the top of the US albums chart, Tool was disappointed to discover that a version had been leaked a week before its release and distributed through file-sharing programs. "We were really bummed out about [the album leaking]," said Chancellor. "We took a lot of precautions to stop that from happening. But you can pretty much guarantee it'll leak as soon as the finished packaging and CDs are put in the trucks to be shipped to Alaska, or whatever... We expected it, and we were pretty pleased that it managed to last that long without getting out there, and even happier that people wanted to go out and buy it anyway."

Fortunately, the physical album was such an elaborate release that few, if any, of those who downloaded and enjoyed it would have failed to buy the artefact itself when it became available. For the first time in the 20-year history of the compact disc, the *10,000 Days* release was a viewing device as well as an audio carrier. The thick cardboard case extended beyond the usual double flap with an additional section that contained two durable plastic lenses, as far apart as human eyes. When held close to the viewer's face, the lenses revealed a three-dimensional view of the images in the CD's inlay booklet – a series of beautiful, complex pictures that caused enormous debate among Tool's fanbase.

The first image was the title of the album, seen floating above its background in three dimensions. Panels with the track listing and a pair of eyes followed before more artistic elements, including a close-up of a skull inside a glass bell-jar on a table with some daggers, books and a pack of cards. Stereoscopic portraits follow of Carey (seated at the same table, lifting the lid from a chalice and allowing a white plume of smoke to escape), Chancellor (an eagle perched on his wrist, surrounded by candles), Keenan (holding a glass of red wine to the viewer, with his reflection in a mirror behind him) and Jones (surrounded by pickled animal organs, a ghostly skeleton and scientific specimens). Each of these is preceded by figurative or photographic images taken from the 'Vicarious' video or of individual items in the solo portraits. A warning from SonyBMG, the album's distributor, asks the owner to use the lenses safely with a legal disclaimer, although what damage anyone could inflict with them is hard to imagine.

The packaging is stunning for a mainstream CD release, and even more so given that the retail price of the product was standard. By the end of the year it had sold over three million copies, a triumph in the age of file sharing – and due at least in part to its luxurious presentation. Musically it's no less stunning, beginning with 'Vicarious' (see above) and moving to 'Jambi', one of the album's most enduring songs in the three years since its release. Stuffed full of staccato riffs and the expansive textures for which Tool had become famous, the song manages to be both clever (it's largely in 9/8) and musically digestible, with Keenan's intense, barked choruses a high point. Begging for peace of mind and (according to rumours) narrating the tale of the sultan of Jambi in Sumatra, Keenan tells a story of corruption and regret that is perfectly in synch with the thunderous music, which may also be titled after the iambic pentameter. A notable feature of the song is Adam's talk-box solo, in which he delivers the perfect synthesis of weird vocalising and guitar tone for which the instrument is famous: keen to achieve the same effect achieved by (of all bands) The Eagles, who often used talk-boxes, he asked that band's Joe Walsh for advice. As engineer Joe Barresi recalled, "Adam would always reference The Eagles and Joe Walsh for the sound of the talk-box. Bob Heil, who invented [it], came down when we did the talk-box stuff... Joe Walsh actually called to give us some insight on how to record the talk-box."

After these two heavy songs (the beefed-up sound inspired by Meshuggah to which Carey referred earlier), *10,000 Days* enters more subtle territory with Keenan's tribute to his late mother, Judith Marie Garrison. Funereal in sound and sentiment, 'Wings For Marie (Pt. 1)' begins with a simple repeated bass tone before flights of delayed guitar fade in, alongside Keenan's near-inaudible lament. He intones that he was barely worthy of her, likens her to an angel and allows the music, a hypnotic drone that ends with the ominous clang of a drum (a coffin lid slamming shut?), to convey his message. In parts the song is more like the recent work of British hip-hop duo Massive Attack than Tool, other than a ferociously heavy riff that briefly breaks loose in the midsection.

'10,000 Days (Wings, Pt. 2)' is more direct. Keenan addresses his mother, telling her to demand her dues from God should she meet him in heaven. Alongside a one-note drone from Chancellor over a gentle, cymbal-heavy beat from Carey that combine for a mesmerising, 'Riders On The Storm' effect, his impassioned words help the song build to a mighty climax after 11 minutes. An anarchic feedback solo from Jones adds a streak of vitriol to the atmosphere, while Keenan's shouted invocations at the end make it clear that this is an elegy with a difference: the quintessentially 'Tool' ingredient that so many people had responded to over the years. Two minutes of restrained drone end the song.

'The Pot', which Jones told more than one reporter was a reference to the term 'pot calling the kettle black', was scheduled to be the album's second single, released in early 2007. Perhaps embittered by the experiences of the last few years, Keenan addresses the second song on *10,000 Days* on the subject of hypocrisy to an unnamed target. The song is all Chancellor's, whose busy, semi-funky bassline is matched occasionally by Jones' guitar part but drives 'The Pot' along on its own for most of the song's duration.

After 'Lipan Conjuring', a one-minute *a cappella* verse of Native American chant, we come to 'Lost Keys (Blame Hofmann)', a short song that appears to refer to the plight of a patient who has been admitted to hospital after taking LSD. We can infer this because of the spoken-word content – a doctor and nurse, who briefly discuss why the man has been admitted – and the title, a reference later posted on Tool's website to Albert Hofmann, the scientist who first synthesised the drug in 1938. Jones' wife, Camella Grace, credited on the Tool website as one of the inner coterie who help the band with their various activities, provides the voice of the nurse. Musically, the song is a slow guitar drone, one of many on the album so far.

After the two 'interlude' songs, the 11-minute 'Rosetta Stoned' returns to strong riffs and a long, almost stream-of-consciousness narration from Keenan in which he remembers an encounter with aliens, invoking L. Ron Hubbard, 'Bob' (possibly the Church Of The Subgenius' icon J. R. 'Bob' Dobbs, a man beloved of bands such as Devo), and The Grateful Dead. Meandering and unfocused rather than coherent, the song doesn't add much to the album, at least lyrically. Musically, however, it's more proof that the members of Tool had become master performers and arrangers – and note the reference to the Rosetta Stone in the title, the ancient tablet that resides in the British Museum in London and without which Egyptian hieroglyphics would be less understood.

'Intension' and 'Right In Two' blend together to make a long, ambient soundscape that takes up almost a quarter of the album's total running time. Both songs focus on the space between the sounds, taking the listener deep within themselves, but 'Intension' has endless fan appeal thanks to a reversed message inside the track. Play the song backwards and you'll hear Keenan whisper, "Work hard... Stay in school... Listen to your mother... Your father was right."

Of the two songs, 'Right In Two' is the deeper – an unhurried nine-minute exploration of atmospheres and near-silent breakdowns in which each musician is allowed the chance to expand his palette. The song is full of Carey's electronic and acoustic percussion, as well as tablas, of which engineer Barresi laughed: "When I first showed up to their rehearsal, I thought there were eight guys inside playing. I was like, 'Who's playing percussion in there?' And it turns out that it's all Dan. He has Mandala electronic pads that his friend Vince De Franco designed for him. He plays the Mandala pads, and they trigger sounds that he has sampled himself. It sounds like he has eight limbs." Singing in soft, ballad-like terms of the violent evolution of the human primate, while subtle guitar and bass figures spiral around him, Keenan addresses the pointlessness of life in what seem to be saddened tones. When the emotional high point of the song comes, it's epic: a radio anthem for some alternative world.

The last track on the album is 'Viginti Tres' (the mythical number 23 in Latin), and although it's an ambient electronic instrumental, any awareness of what the number means on the listener's part gives the song great meaning. Read Robert Anton Wilson's *Illuminatus!* trilogy for a fuller explanation than we have space for here, but, in brief, the number 23 occurs at several key points in world history, as well as cropping up in occult literature with a greater frequency than could be accounted for by mere coincidence. As a result, it's beloved of conspiracy theorists, vigilantes, UFO-watchers and followers of Nostradamus and Satan: perfect fodder for Tool.

There's even said to be another hidden message in the deep, slowed-down Latin speech that appears in the middle of the song, which translates as, "One infinity / The horror begins in autumn / This is your trial, which tries your power / Twenty-three steps to total power". Fans have also posited that 'Intension' and 'Viginti Tres' make a whole, 'complete' song when played on top of each other, but this is hard to prove in the absence of any confirmation from the band – and Keenan's repeated (and plausible) protests that such devices are merely the sound of Tool messing around with their fans' preconceptions.

The album sold an astounding 564,000 copies in its first week on sale in the USA. Some of its appeal must have come from the band's decision to take their sound into their own hands, bid an amicable farewell to David Bottrill and produce *10,000 Days* themselves, although engineer Barresi played a crucial role in deciding its shape. Having honed his chops with bands such as Queens Of The Stone Age, Kyuss and the Melvins, and being eager to try more complex projects, he said: "I'd always been a fan, and I had always wanted to work on their records just cos I thought it'd be an interesting combination – what I do and what they do. What really sticks out is their amazing musicianship. They are just ridiculous." With his stated aim to make the album sound like "*Undertow* on steroids", he recorded most of it at Grandmaster Recorders in Hollywood because *Undertow* had been recorded there. "They're a great combination of heaviness and huge dynamic range," he added. "They're one band that came in, and I think Danny said, 'We don't care if we're the loudest thing on the radio. We just want you to maintain our dynamics'. You have to really respect that in a band."

Needless to say, Tool was still refusing to print their lyrics, and on this album – their most mysterious to date – the decision made a lot of sense. "All the lyrics are meant to be for each individual to interpret; that's the reason we leave a lot of the subject matter wide open," said Danny. "That's one of the whole points to the band; that way, people can be drawn into it and get something out of it, let their own mind work a little bit. Lyrics were always a secondary thing for me too – like most of my records I listen to, I didn't know what half the people are saying. I'm listening to their phrasing and the way they sing it and the emotions more, so I always looked at the voice more like an instrument, I guess."

"There's nothing being hidden," shrugged Maynard. "I think it gives a person more: giving them less is giving them more. They can experience it for themselves. There's certain images that I think come up for people if they don't have everything spelled out for them. Eventually, they'll have two different songs, they'll have what they heard, and I'll give them a new one that might take them farther, [but] might not have taken them as far as they went. If it takes them farther, that's great, but I'd much [prefer] the idea of them having gone farther than the song went. I'd rather take that risk that they're gonna be mad at me for not seeing the lyrics."

It emerged, reasonably enough, that Tool thought that reading lyrics detracts from the appreciation of music. As Keenan put it: "Reading is more of a left-brain process, and listening to music is a right-brain function. And the right-brain function is far more emotional and has softer edges, so when you first hear the album, you should hear it and feel it. When you start 'reading' it, then you're thinking it, and you rob yourself of that initial impression of how the sounds affect you. I believe that when you go into a gallery or a museum, the most powerful pieces are the ones that don't have the words in the corner that distract you from the larger piece. You know, if the Mona Lisa had 'Eat At Joe's' in the corner, that's all you would remember."

Still, for all his miserablism, Keenan was pleased with the impact that *10,000 Days* – his most confessional record to date – had made on the charts. "Believe me, I'm absolutely delighted," he said. "I'm absolutely surprised and grateful that there's a lot of people out there that get what's going on. But you know, I'm the negative-Nancy, curmudgeon, glass-half-empty-with-a-leak-in-it guy – which is basically the fuel that fires me up anyway. Without that, we wouldn't have me."

Chancellor added: "You never quite know if anyone's going to care any more when it's been so long, so it's nice to know people are still into it. With it being five years since the last one, you don't really know what's going to happen. None of us are complete experts on the industry, but we were happily surprised – [although] we were hoping for number one."

After a set at that year's Coachella festival at the end of April, Tool was set to be on tour for the next four months, taking a week off here and there according to Keenan's requirements at Merkin Vineyards. As befitted a band at a mature stage in their career, Tool's live show was even more extravagant than before, with awe-inspiring live visuals derived from the work of Alex Grey and operated from the desk in synch with the music. Despite the logistical issues that accompanied moving a set of this nature around the country, the tour progressed smoothly, although a surge in the crowd at an August 7 show in San Diego left several fans with crush-related injuries. "Step back so you don't get trampled. It's just rock," said Keenan when the surge first occurred near the start of the set, adding after a few minutes: "If you all take a few steps back, we can keep playing". His words probably saved other fans from being injured: an official had come on stage to talk with him, possibly even warning

Keenan that the show would be stopped if he didn't speak to the crowd.

On August 18 Tool was joined on stage by guitarist Kirk Hammett of Metallica when they played in Honolulu, Hawaii. Hammett, clearly blown away by the experience, said the next day: "Having just had an incredible experience jamming with my friends in Tool, I have this to report – it was one of the most profound jamming experiences I have ever encountered! We all played a show together in Korea and I was bummed that I was missing the show as I was getting ready for our own set. I knew they were on the same flight as I was to Hawaii, so I talked to Adam [Jones] and told him that I was going to check them out. I gave him my number and we had dinner the next night. He also invited me to come out on stage and play 'Sober' with them and I instantly said yes. He mentioned that the band even worked out a new part for me to solo through."

He went on: "The next night I watched the show and when it came time to play the song, I plugged into Adam's spare amp and he gave me the look – it was that musician-to-musician look of, 'Let's get fucking serious!' So I turned it on big time. We played some feedback together, which segued into some crazy dissonance thing that only Adam can do. Then we launched into the song. I said to Adam before the show that he could do all the sound colouring and I'd just take the part in the middle. When it came time for me to play I was so locked into the vibe that I started really quietly while building the solo. By the last third of the solo I turned on Adam's delay setting and played some really high notes that felt like the top of my head just shot off... It was incredible and I am the hugest Tool fan."

As the tour swung around the world, Tool avoided the temptation to rest on their laurels and instead tossed around ideas for their next project. Jones in particular was keen on the idea of a Tool-related film, a possibility that had been mentioned here and there for several years but now seemed like it might come to fruition at last. "It has to be a collective thing as far as the band members [are concerned]," he said. "Everyone has to be very happy, and it has to be done in a way where people would see integrity and hard work and not just something thrown together or home movies or some shitty filmed live show... It's a selfish thing. There's that selfish quality of what we want versus what everyone else wants. But I think at the end of the day if we get what we want, it's reflective in what other people see in that."

Adding that the right backer would have to be found for the project, he went on: "We all have ideas about it. If I had my way, it would be a narrative story in a surreal fashion, with as much money and special effects we could throw at it. I think some of the other guys would like to do pockets of all of that, or something that's live or we're playing. It's just talk right now."

Before any of that could happen, however, the band members had other, more pressing concerns. One of these was a lawsuit from their former associate Cam de Leon, the artist who had produced so much memorable imagery with them in the past. As Jones fumed, "He had done some artwork that we paid him to do in the past for our band, and he came with this ridiculous lawsuit saying he's the fifth member of the band, and a partner, and he was head of our art department. There *is* no art department. I just feel like it's total extortion. We've been fighting it and it's been really burning a hole in my stomach. It's just been very distracting."

Elsewhere, of course, Maynard had both Puscifer – which had now evolved into a merchandise brand as well as a musical force – and his wine business to think about. By the end of 2006, both concerns were making serious demands on his time and energy. Of the former, he said: "This is my 'catch-all, stream-of-consciousness, anything-goes' project. There is and will continue to be music associated with it, although it's not the main focus. There is no main focus, to be honest. I focus on Random. But currently I'm working on several tracks. All with different sets of musicians and engineers. Lustmord will be involved. Tim Alexander has expressed interest. Possibly Brad Wilk, Tim C. [Commerford] and Jonny Polonsky may want to be involved on a track. Joe Barresi, Matt Mitchell. Danny Lohner. The list keeps expanding. No label. No hassles. Just me and a few artists at a time having fun. One-off songs to be used wherever I choose… and lots of fun merchandise. I'm working on several designs ranging from the basic stuff like shirts and hoodies, to other items such as fuzzy purses, ballistic material backpacks, feminine hygiene wallets [and] cases, pet supplies, belt buckles, personalised targets, 'adult massage devices'…" He was serious about the personalised targets. Go to www.puscifer.com and you too can buy a paper target from a firing range, neatly shot through the middle by Keenan and signed for posterity.

He also explained that the Puscifer website would be auctioning items for charity ("Friends and relatives who donate an item for auction can pick where the proceeds will be donated. For example, my father will be donating a few of his platinum Tool albums"), and there would be more dedicated events for causes that were close to his heart. "Most likely we will be doing a co-presented charity auction with the Life Through Art Foundation," he said. "The Los Angeles Mission and the Humane Society will also be receiving funds. Prescott National Forest is right on the edge of my home in Arizona. [There are] huge fire risks in that area, with no adequate equipment to deal with any eventuality. So one of the accounts we will be setting up will be used to raise money for a fire suppression vehicle."

Meanwhile, there was a tour to finish – and the new boys on the progressive-metal scene, Mastodon, had been tipped to support Tool on their European tour in early 2007. "I love Tool," said Mastodon drummer Brann Dailor. "They're one of the only acts that's been able to be a gigantic rock band, selling millions of records [while keeping] their integrity 100 per cent… Right from the get-go they were able to call the shots. Label people will tell you, you have to be in the video, you have to do interviews, you have to be in the press. They kind of dropped out of that whole thing and created this whole mystique. Nobody knew what they looked like for ten years."

Keeping the pressure off was something that Tool were becoming good at. Although *10,000 Days* was only a matter of months old, people were already asking them about their next release, perhaps prompted by rumours that they were considering a live DVD as well as the full-length movie to which Jones had referred earlier. However, Chancellor dismissed this, reasoning: "If a band [puts out an album a year], how can you live any life? How can you evolve? How can you have anything new to say? Maybe you can, but I don't hear it. You win on one level and you lose on another level that way. With us, it sucks – you don't get any music for a long time, but when you do, it's something you can sink your teeth into. It lasts a little longer. Think of it like fast food – sure, it's instantly satisfying, but it doesn't really sort you out in the long run. I don't know which is better, but that's just how we roll, you could say."

Evolution, now as always, was the key theme of Tool's work – and where they would go next was impossible to predict.

Chapter 16

2007

The cult of *10,000 Days* grew exponentially, with fans linking up at social-networking websites to exchange theories about what the album really meant. Clearly the mystic elements that were perceived in Tool's latest songs hadn't been explained away by Keenan's insistence that it was all done in fun: if anything, their work was now among the most discussed of all modern rock bands, with theories both tenable and otherwise flying around the virtual and real worlds.

Keenan helped this along, deliberately or not, when he pontificated on the public record about the arcane philosophies he'd encountered over the years. "If you've ever taken tai-chi or chi-gong with an actual master," he ruminated, "you are putting yourself into these body positions. I have a friend who was taking chi-gong for years, and he would strike these poses every day with his sensei [teacher] in their dojo. Then one day he got into one of the positions and he apparently did the position perfectly correctly – he could feel the energy completely flowing through his body, like he was a battery. He just felt this change. And his sensei, from across the room, turned, looked at him and nodded. And that was it."

"Perhaps all this occult stuff is exactly that," he added. "It's years of practice, seeing a particular process to reach a particular result that, in the scheme of things, you're really not supposed to tell somebody about. You're just supposed to experience it. It's all about your own experience. So if you sit there in these strange positions, or you look through the *Book Of The Dead* and you practise this stuff, maybe there's an experience that you have alone that there's no way you could ever really describe it to anyone – so why bother? It's not really a secret, it's just impossible to translate."

He wasn't slow to mock those who thought the secrets of the universe lay within the grooves of *10,000 Days*, saying: "Isn't that great? They're playing it backwards, and they're like, 'You've got to get a Slurpee [Slush Puppie], but only half-full, and when you're drinking the Slurpee, right at that last slurp, the rhythm of the slurp coincides with...' My God. Are you kidding me?... We can barely decide whether we're going to do a baseball cap or a beanie. You know what I mean? Now, granted, if you subscribe to the whole spiritual, energetic level, when you get into that weird, meditative state... at some point, your body clicks out, and you have a weird out-of-body experience, and so you can tap into those things unconsciously. So if people are reading into those kinds of things that basically had nothing to do with us, that are just us clicking in a moment and being true to that whirling-dervish process of emoting with each other, some of that stuff just might naturally, accidentally come out. But it's not in any way a product of our design."

And so he denied that any occult content of Tool's music was deliberately put there. However, Keenan made it clear that he regarded the songs as useful vehicles for reaching a higher plane, explaining: "If you just want to look at the turbulence on the top of the water and stop there, [you can] – or you can go down in there and start to see that there's layers of silt, and you can go down deeper, and the deeper you go the more you discover, like layers of paint. A lot of the lyrics don't have anything to do with the song. They're a distraction. They're *meant* to be a distraction."

The songs, he emphasised, were the main focus, which makes sense if you've ever entered the trancelike state that deep music always offered listeners who are prepared to spend time on it. "The challenge for us," he said, "has always been to find that space where we all meet in the middle. When you're in a rehearsal space, like the one we've been in since day one, in 1990, [you think], 'OK… I'd love to go this way…' But you can't even let that enter your mind; you've just got to listen to what's happening and then react to what's happening from everybody. And whatever that result is, that's what ends up making it on the album. And in that way, since we're all four completely different individuals who are also growing in completely different ways [and] experiencing different things, that middle spot is going to be moving every time we get together. So in theory, the results should be different every time."

Whatever Keenan said about Tool, the band had built a huge fanbase after 17 years of performing and recording, and those within it were unlikely to stop inquiring about the musicians and their art. If Tool had made themselves available to every press request that came their way, perhaps this might have been rather different: we all love mystique, and Tool had built up plenty of it. Not deliberately, however, as Keenan said: "Initially, because we knew that we were going to be emerging in the wake of Nirvana and getting lost in the shuffle, we wanted to make sure that whatever that first impression [people had] of us was a lasting one. So we whispered instead of yelled; we said no instead of yes – and that worked for us in the beginning. And I think that initial impression was good for us, because you ended up seeing the things we wanted you to see, not something somebody else wanted you to see about us. Of course, the downside is that you have an equal amount of people that called themselves journalists who were denied access, and are still bitch-ing about it, saying that we're difficult and hard to reach… they didn't do their homework, and we basically shut them down."

Why people sought philosophical answers from Maynard at all con-tinued to mystify him. "I find [it] very interesting," he said, "seeing as I'm not a college graduate, or a doctor, lawyer or debate team captain. I have no degree whatsoever. I rarely ever had a job that was nine-to-five that I held for very long… Are you familiar with the movie *[Monty Python's] Life Of Brian*? I would hope that people wouldn't be standing there holding a sandal, thinking it's a sign. I would hope that they would just see us doing something, then go off on their own and do something. Be inspired by it. I love the idea of a kitchen full of cooks coming up with a new recipe, because they were listening to the album and doing their own thing. They're not worried about meeting us, or tripping on what we had for lunch or where we're going on vacation, or what we meant here or there. They were just inspired by the music and made an incredible dish."

A flurry of activity preceded Tool's 2007 touring schedule. A second single from *10,000 Days* – 'The Pot' – was released on February 11, and 'Jambi' was promo'ed to radio the following day: the former became the band's first number one on the *Billboard* Mainstream Rock Tracks chart. More importantly, Tool won a second Grammy the same month, this time for the spectacular (in both senses) artwork for the album. Jones said of the award, which he received personally as the band's art director, "We always try to think of something that's never been done before as far as album packaging, and I've been a fan of stereoscopic photography my whole life, [I] belong to the Southern California Stereoscopic Club. We thought if we could get this to work with our budget and put this out, it'd be really unique and reflecting a lot of the artwork that I appreciate from the Seventies."

With this recognition from the record industry that had come to disgust them, the band was often asked if they might find an innovative way to work within it while retaining their credibility. The business model that excited most attention in 2007 was the free download of Radiohead's latest album, *In Rainbows*, which the British band had placed online at a cost to be decided by the user. In the event, the band made their money back after the average revenue worked out at a few pounds per download, which surprised most observers and gave the exercise the aura of viability.

Maynard wasn't so sure. "I have no idea where that's going to go, but I think it's an incredible marketing plan," he said cautiously. "I don't necessarily agree with the idea of music being free. I know what goes into it, and I know how much it costs to produce it and make it and market it and duplicate the CDs and ship them – it's expensive. Of course, we're speaking in terms of physical items, but even if everything went digital, there's still a lot of expense involved. It's easy for me or Radiohead or Nine Inch Nails to be flippant about how we're going to go about it, because we have a little bit of a bank account and we have the luxury of touring and drawing lots of tickets.

"But I think who gets hurt are the guys in between – those guys who aren't just a local band, who are starting to get around a little bit, and people are saying, 'Well, the standard for paying for somebody's CD online is two bucks'. What? That thousand bucks is the difference between those guys going on the road or not going on the road, or being able to make the next record or the next song. That's huge. There's going to have to be a happy medium, because the misconception is that people can make music for free. You make a lot more money touring or selling shirts, yeah, but that's when you get to a certain level. That in-between spot is tough."

He also dismissed the common theory that the traditional record company was under threat: "I think the industry will figure it out. This is the X-factor that the industry is counting on: for the most part, generally speaking, musicians are kinda dumb. They're not really trained in business, they don't have a degree in marketing or law or any of that stuff. They're their own worst enemies. Just because they wrote a song that made this girl cry… that doesn't mean they're successful businessmen. They'll screw themselves or drink themselves to death, so the industry will always have a leg up. Most likely the reason that guy wrote that song is because he's damaged goods to begin with, and he needs someone to help him out on those levels."

As a record company owner of sorts himself, thanks to Puscifer, Keenan had strong opinions about the other new buzz-phrase of the day, the famed 360-degree deal in which an artist signs the rights to a record company not only for their albums, but for their merchandise, publishing, tours, legal services and everything else. "Some stupid band is going to come along," he sniggered, "and, like I said, they're dumb, for the most part… and their lawyer is going to be the guy who plays golf with the guy from the label, and the booking guy plays golf with the merchandise guy or the business affairs manager. They understand that the dummies come and go, and that they're the ones running the business. I think that's less relevant at the moment, but it will go back to being relevant at some point. When they figure out the new model, they'll trick these dummies into giving up huge percentages of their bread and butter by dangling this carrot in front – 'We're going to give you 20 million dollars'. Of course, they don't tell you that, by the way, it's standard for the lawyer to take five per cent of your life, and the lawyer will tell you it's standard for the manager to get 20 per cent of the gross, and of course the taxman takes half. All of a sudden, your 20 million dollars turns into 20 bucks and some fucking Starbucks coupons… the bands that fall victim to those kinds of things are going to realise, 'Shit, I only have this much left – and now every time I step out the door, it's going to be the same thing'. I had one friend who went on the road with a big tour in 2000 and was asking his manager, 'We want to do these big [stage productions], but this is going to be OK for expenses, right? We're not going to be screwing ourselves?' The manager says, 'No, it's all fine!' He comes to find out at the end of the tour that the manager got paid a bunch of money because he got paid on a gross percentage, so all those fun lights that went on the road came out of the band's pocket. So the manager made more than the band – like several million dollars, as opposed to being in the hole. Not only didn't [the artist] make any money, but he still owes money on the tour."

Talking of tours, the huge Tool outing for 2007 was put on hold for two months after Danny Carey tore a bicep during a wrestling match with his girlfriend's dog. The wound was severe enough to require surgery in late February, meaning that the band weren't able to start touring until April. Still, once they were rolling, it didn't take long to pick up the pace: the dates started auspiciously with a set at that year's Bonnaroo Festival in Tennessee, where Tom Morello of Rage Against The Machine (who had recently reformed) guested on 'Lateralus'. Rolling through five continents, Tool toured with only a couple of pauses for breath (and grape harvesting) until the end of the year. There was plenty of activity outside the confines of the tour bus, with Puscifer's first single, the Deep South-baiting 'Cuntry Boner', released in the autumn, although a viral video had been circulating some months before that. The song, the first deliberately comic release by a member of Tool, was a hoedown pastiche – originally written by Tom Morello in his school band, Electric Sheep – in which Keenan and the comedian Laura Milligan sang a list of country singers who they'd had sex with in amusing redneck accents. The single also included a cover of the Circle Jerks' 'World Up My Ass'.

The video, featuring Keenan dressed in a country singer's suit and cowboy hat with a prosthetic erection pressing out of his trousers, was interspersed with still shots of the various singers to which Keenan was referring in his lyrics, from Dolly Parton and The Judds to Elvis Presley and Johnny Cash. "This was filmed quite a while ago," wrote Maynard, "and I'm just now getting around to kicking it out of the nest. Feel free to pass it around. My gift to you. Laura [is] probably gonna kick my ass for leaking it."

On October 30 a full-length Puscifer album followed. *V Is For Vagina* – which could only have been titled by a member of Tool – was self-released by Keenan, although he'd agreed a mainstream distribution deal that meant that the record would be available in stores rather than merely through his website. "I'm basically paying for everything," he said. "I found printers and duplicators and all that stuff. I did a deal with a distribution company. So it's traditional in a way, but what's not traditional is that I'm actually doing it… having a little bit of a military background, I get off on order. Order within chaos. It's lots of chaos and it's very exciting and makes you feel alive. There's some payoff at the end of the day when you see that it all lined up, and everything went where it was supposed to go – almost not on time, but it got there all of a sudden."

Somewhat inevitably, major stockists refused to carry the album unless a sticker was placed over the supposedly offensive word in its title. Keenan sighed, "I've been having to deal with that this whole time. Once again, it's those corporate people, those guys that are scared about one person complaining. I had an ad for [satirical US magazine] *The Onion* and the ad department… rejected my ad because it had the word 'vagina' in it. *The Onion*, of all fucking magazines! So we had to start rattling cages with editors and writers and have them go, 'What the fuck are you guys doing? It's the fucking *Onion*!' So it all got sorted out, I think. But that's the world we live in nowadays. Your three- or four-year-old is allowed to say the word 'vagina', but God help us if you try to actually put it in print. It's the craziest thing.

"Honestly, I was being kind of flippant about the title," he added. "I didn't think it was going to get this much reaction. It was kind of a joke within a joke. I thought it would be received with a lot of groans – 'That's a very sophomoric, stupid title. Come on, dude, you can be more offensive than that'. Honestly! I thought it was going to be, 'That's just corny. Clearly you're from Ohio'. But it's been met with ridiculous reactions."

Life as an independent record company exec clearly suited Keenan, although he knew that he couldn't prevent incidents such as internet leaks, if any occurred. As he pointed out: "I'm sure that it's out there. The worst part about being on your own is that I don't have some big monster leaning over potential leaks and threatening to sue them… I hope it makes it. The only reason I'm really concerned is that I put a lot of money into this and put a lot of time into it, and I wouldn't have made CDs if it wasn't for the artwork that I got attached to them. I was having fun with a friend of mine with this idea for artwork, and if I didn't have the physical artwork in mind, I would have just done it all digitally. Of course, there's a similar issue there with theft, but it wouldn't have been such an output of money. I'm kind of relying on the sales to pay back what I've put into it."

Tellingly, Keenan wasn't aiming the music at Tool fans, and he was eager to have straightforward lyrics, the logical conclusion of the process he'd started with A Perfect Circle, which was itself several times more direct than the endlessly metaphorical Tool. "The music is very soundtrack-oriented, it's groovy," he said. "[I hope] people get their heads around the fact that it's not Tool, and why should it be? It's not A Perfect Circle, why should it be? We already have those things. This is just soundtrack music… it's meant to get under your skin and feel good. I made sure that the lyrics weren't puzzles. I didn't want puzzles. It's supposed to be a feeling. The music is where the complexity is – that's the part that gets under your skin and makes you feel good. So there is an intent to it, and there is a purpose."

The Puscifer album had attracted some major names, some of whom were longtime Tool and APC collaborators. Adam Jones had created some of the Puscifer clothing line (in particular a T-shirt with the slogan 'Your Mom's A Bitch'), and the fashion designer Paul Frank had worked with Keenan on a line of leather jackets.

Keenan was throwing a lot of effort into the project, lining up a song called 'Queen B' for release in September, pulling in Danny Lohner, Tim Alexander, actress Milla Jovovich, remixer Lustmord and even Tool's guitar tech Matt Mitchell to help and saying of the results, "This is absolutely just put-it-on-and-move-your-butt-and-get-completely-out-of-your-head music. This is purely body candy. It's meant to make you feel like I feel when I hear James Brown... music that makes you feel good. There's no math. Nothing wrong with math, but sometimes, it can be exhausting to be that forced, that focused. I'm a big King Crimson fan, but only when I have the energy to be. Sometimes I just want to hear Gnarls Barkley."

Short films, a regular podcast and newsletter at the Puscifer website and an active Myspace page with exclusive mixes and videos all added to the phenomenon, with Keenan and his collaborators clearly prepared to exploit all angles on the band even while the Tool tour was still in motion. Add to this Maynard's businesses in Arizona and his commitment to his young son, and his life must have been a constant blur of motion.

Another Keenan project that might or might not be permanently dead and buried, however, was A Perfect Circle. Keenan explained, "I think [APC] is over. ...We pushed this project as far as it could go, and I see ourselves playing again together in a few years to make one or two songs, nothing more." Billy Howerdel added, "[Maynard and I have] talked about it lightly. A few months ago, it was like, 'If we did A Perfect Circle again, I'd want to do this or that'. It was a benign conversation. I think we both entertain the fact that it could happen again, but for right now we don't have any plans to do it again. We're focusing on what we're doing now. A Perfect Circle is done for now."

Keenan expanded on this a little when he said, "The real problem with running Tool and A Perfect Circle at the same time was they both operate the same way. They're both live touring bands with a label, still working under the old contract mentality. So I thought it was time to let A Perfect Circle go for now and let Billy explore himself. It's tough for a guy who went from being a guitar tech [for Tool] to being in a band with a pretentious, famous singer and having to live in that shadow. It was important for Billy to go and do his own thing and really explore his own sound and let people hear what he has to say and how he would do it on his own, and then we'll get back and do some A Perfect Circle stuff." APC fans were thrilled by the optimistic nature of the last sentence.

The core of all this activity is simple to explain. Keenan obviously retains a love of working with different groups of people, resisting the temptation to stay within the same band. He cited a particular Australian rock phenomenon as an example: "I love AC/DC, but it's the same record. They do it very well, [but] they're an exception... That illustrates my point there's no growth; it's the one-trick pony. I like riding that pony, but it's still a one-trick pony. [People who are] not branching out and doing something with other people, they don't necessarily grow as individuals. You're not told this when you're out there doing your thing, and people are stroking your back and not telling you the truth. You think that the whole world is revolving around you, and this is the only world there is."

Tool, meanwhile, crashed to the end of their long world tour at the end of 2007: Danny, Adam and Justin promptly went into hiding. Only Keenan was left in the public eye, and he'd clearly had more than enough of the record industry for now. "There's a lot of stress involved when it comes to labels – especially nowadays," he sighed. "We've been able to maintain some kind of individuality in how we do things, but the way that labels consume each other, it's almost like watching *National Geographic* films of praying mantises devouring their young. Every time you go to do something, you have a whole new set of people who a) don't work for you – they have a paycheck from someone else who is afraid of their own shadow, and b) they don't really know what you're about. So they're not going to risk their job for your vision – especially for a band like Tool. We're not Britney Spears, we're not Metallica, we're not Pink Floyd's *The Wall*, we're none of those things. Somebody might think we're kind of that, but we're not that at all. We're never really going to appeal to a broad market. So when the businessmen really start crunching numbers, they go, 'You know, these guys aren't really worth all this hubbub,' and we end up getting the short end of the stick. It's a lot more difficult than you would imagine for us. The guys who have that Wal-Mart mentality don't really view us as a commodity."

Chancellor told the press that the band needed a break: "We'll definitely take some time off, I mean... some proper time off from each other. Whether it's six months or a year I don't know, but at that point then we'll decide what we'll do next. It's hard to plan stuff when you've got a year of stuff planned for you. That's enough to bite off and chew. We'll plan the future when we get to it." Of the next Tool release, he said: "We have loads of stuff that we didn't use on the last album and we write stuff pretty much every week... When you're out playing music every day, it comes naturally that you write new stuff. There's a big stockpile of things that we haven't really created into songs yet, so there's lots to do. I'm sure if everyone is still good at the end of this and we don't damage ourselves too much, then I'm sure there'll be another album, but I can't say when."

Perhaps Tool would finally jump off the album-tour-album-tour cycle and work on the film that Adam Jones had talked about before. "Pink Floyd are our heroes, and we'd totally love to do something on that level, but in our own way," he'd said. "We've been talking about that, and the people we've met with have the kind of pull to get it done... [but] it's so hard to find someone who's willing to invest in a project like this. So much of what we do is based on experimentation, and if you're trying to get money from people to make a film, they want to know exactly what it's going to look like, how many frames you're going to shoot, how many people you're going to work with and what the budget is going to be. And to me, it's not that concrete. [Making a film should be] more like jamming and writing music."

Keenan added: "Who knows, maybe the next Tool record will be a cool DVD with a whole film and soundtrack involved in it. That's a possibility. This whole project [Tool] has been about not limiting ourselves." He, of all people, knew the truth of that.

Chapter 17

2007-2008

When Tool's song 'The Pot' was nominated for the 50th Best Hard Rock Performance Grammy in February 2007, the band contributed to the ceremony by sending along none other than Maynard James Keenan, a man who rarely (if ever) deigns to grace such events with his presence. If you've been paying attention, you'll know why: few other occasions in the music-business calendar are as full of gurning sales executives and A&R palm-greasers than the Grammys, the antithesis of everything Keenan stands for.

Standing patiently beside his son, Devo, while the chaos reigned around him, Maynard shrugged: "Well, it's the 50th anniversary, and my son's never been to the Grammys, and I've never been to one, so I figured it's probably time. There are other things we could do, but this is very special, I think, and it will be the highlight of the year for him. I think he's pretty stoked about it. We're kind of easy-going." He added, when asked about his band: "We're going to start writing the new Tool record right away. The music always comes first. We all get in a room, shut out all the extra noises from the other people and what goes on outside the room, and just focus on the four of us, where we are that day. And then we just start making sounds."

'The Pot' lost out to the song 'Woman' by the rock band *du jour*, Wolfmother, to many critics' disgust. After all, 'Woman' is generic, catchy rock that wears its influences on its sleeve – a polite way of saying that it sounds exactly like Black Sabbath. However, Keenan kept his cool, remarking: "Of course that song won the Grammy! It's a great song… Wolfmother hit the nail on the head, and that's the feeling we're all looking for with music. For me, I've been listening to old Jackson Five, The Temptations and Motown stuff, because nothing is really presenting that [feeling] now… You and I both know exactly where that song came from. But never mind all that, because it was a catchy feel-good song, which is kind of what we all need right now. Forget the depth of it. If rock is dead, and nobody knows where to go and they're not moving forward, what else are they gonna do except go back and look at stuff that's been done? They want to rekindle that feeling you got when you first heard soul-inspiring rock."

In any case, Keenan had more important things on his plate: 2008 was set to be the year of Puscifer. Both the new band and the Caduceus/Merkin businesses had now got so big that they virtually commanded all of his attention. From the mere ten acres of land that Maynard had bought back in 2001, the wine business had expanded six-fold and was now occupying a rarefied position in the Arizona market. "I have about three vineyards," he said. "My partner and my mentor, winemaker Eric Glomski from Page Springs Vineyards and Cellars, whom I make all my wines through, has a similar amount of acreage. We bought about 60 to 65 acres together down in Tucson. We're the largest producer of wine grapes in Arizona at the moment… It gives us options. We actually supply all the other winemakers in the state with grapes. That way I can have a huge vineyard, we can cherry-pick the best grapes for our wines and then sell what's left over to anyone else in the state. We can really make great premium wines with a choice grape, rather than just being isolated with one small amount of grapes that one year might be good, one year might be bad. The average amount of cases [Eric] makes is between 4,000 and 5,000. I do about 1,200. The average winery makes hundreds of thousands of cases a year."

Glomski, it seemed, had been responsible for managing Keenan's transformation from eager amateur to winemaking professional. "I've been a fan of wines since the early Nineties," explained Maynard, "and it progressed to the point where I just decided to put a vineyard in my backyard, not really having any idea what I was doing or what I was going to be doing with the grapes. I met the right guy who had a plan of his own and I've been riding his coat-tails, learning as I go. We released our first wines about a year and a half ago and everything has sold out. Now we're just trying to get some more wine into bottles, so we can get it up for sale… it's a pretty grounding experience. The music industry and Hollywood tend to be very disconnected and not really about reality. Some of the activities that go on there don't have a lot of logic to [them]. You've got people from damaged childhoods that are emoting and running the business, when they have no idea what they're doing."

Although Keenan had brought in serious expertise to his venture, saying, "I had some guys come out from University of California Davis to check out the area, check out the elevation, make some suggestions on root stock and what varietals [vine types] would work in this climate… evaluation of temperature, soil content, elevation and all that stuff goes into them calculating what might or might not work here," he revealed that he himself is not a heavy consumer. "I don't normally drink a lot of wine," he added. "I'm not a huge drinker. I just really enjoy a good glass of wine with a meal and I know that I have an aptitude for it. It's like writing music, in a way. There are lots of levels and nuances to discover."

As for his other major concern, Puscifer, Keenan explained: "It was always a little project that I had going on. I used the name for *Mr. Show* because it just made sense to get it on the map. The original name of the band was Umlaut, a premier improvisational hardcore band: it lasted about a day. It was fun but it evolved quickly into Puscifer, [which] has basically been my little baby, and I kept working on it. I was inspired by all these tunes on the radio like oldies, Motown stuff and hip-hop. Stuff that feels good. I approached Puscifer like that. I'm just trying to [do] stuff that I don't have to think too much about. It's got a good groove. It makes you feel good and that's where I've been concentrating, because I have [Tool's] introspective, tortuous, painfully organised and arranged music that takes years to create and cuts really deep. But Puscifer does not do that. It's something that I want to have fun with and not worry about it being ground-breaking, or changing the world."

197

Tool fans might draw breath sharply at Keenan's dismissal of Tool's music, but in context, what he was saying was reasonable. Tool's difficult, challenging art, A Perfect Circle's political art-rock and Puscifer's lightweight groove merely represent equally important branches of the musical tree – and why should anyone be confined to only one of them? The major challenge for Keenan, he explained, was juggling all his concerns. "I try to wear one hat at a time," he said. "I find that's the best way to do it. When I'm doing tours I'm doing tours. If I'm doing A Perfect Circle then I'm doing that. But Puscifer has been a little different because it's not just music. It's actually as much a clothing line as it is a band. I've been talking with different manufacturers, so it's almost a brand at this point... I've been focusing most of my time on the vineyard and the winery. But because we [Tool] have quite a bit of a break, it's a perfect time to really start tracking some of these ideas I have in my head. Getting them on tape and developing some new merch ideas. I'll be going to Hong Kong in a couple of weeks to meet with some garment manufacturers and get some of the ideas together... With the internet the way it is, music is now a soundtrack to some other activity. You can make a living selling songs, but you make a better living playing them. If you're not going to play them, you've got to figure out what else to sell, and I guess that comes down to T-shirts and keychains."

Keenan stressed that the Puscifer brand was about fun, not work. "I pretty much rely on my fucking twisted sense of humour to put some of that stuff together and have fun with it, not take it too seriously," he said. "I don't want it to be a thing that gets so big that I have to worry about selling it. I've been doing really low-volume stuff. I may make only 500 copies of one shirt and never make another one. Some stuff is from collaborations with [design firm] Globe in Australia, and I'm doing a leather jacket with Paul Frank where there will just be a few of them."

While Keenan occupied centre stage, the rest of Tool had almost completely vanished off the radar, although new music could have been coming together behind the scenes, as Keenan had mentioned earlier in the year. Danny Carey had injured himself again, this time while swimming in the sea. According to the Tool website, he had been stung on one hand by "an unruly marine hazard, venomous and... dangerous... while vacationing in Hawaii. This aquatic critter was most likely a sea urchin or a scorpion fish." Two sets of surgery followed, which left his hand scarred, but he was as ebullient as ever, telling the press: "We truly are an alternative band. It's an alternative to what other people label as alternative, that actually all sounds the same. And I think people can identify that and they can relate to it, and they desire the real thing when it's available. You just gotta stick to your laurels and believe in what you're doing, and not do it for money – do it for the art of it, then you can't lose."

Adam Jones, always the least vocal of the band, was becoming deeply aware of the logistical ramifications of being in a huge touring band, and how this conflicts with artistic integrity. As he explained: "It's a business. And the bigger your business becomes, the more pressures you face – the more you need to become a better businessman. Most younger bands don't seem to care about these details. Hell, there are lots of bigger bands that don't care, and they're the ones who get ripped off and end up on VH-1. From the start, we've always tried to have our hands in our band's success. If we had done things the record company's way, I don't think we'd be together today. They would have chewed us up and spat us out. But you have to accept that it's going to be a slow climb. Maybe our [next] album's not going to come out and be number one, but two years from now we'll still be riding it, working it, touring behind it. We don't want to be a band that puts out an album a year: we'd become a cover band of ourselves. There'd be no room to grow."

He added: "I'm trying to expand my consciousness, and I'm not trying to take life for granted at all. Because I believe that this is it. You live, you die... that's it. Whatever else is out there is beyond our comprehension and it probably will be for a long time. I don't think the world needs answers... there's going to be questions that can't be answered, and it's OK not to know the answers."

Keenan was on a roll while the others avoided the limelight. Puscifer issued a second album, *V Is For Viagra: The Vagina Remixes*, in April – and when asked the obvious question, he said (truthfully or otherwise): "I, personally, have only done Viagra once. I took a half a tab and it did nothing. Later that night I took the other half and it did nothing. By the time it actually kicked in, I was actually at the airport going through security. Not a fun situation." The album, which contained tweaked versions of the *V Is For Vagina* songs by artists such as Paul Barker of Ministry, Aaron Turner of Isis and Dave Ogilvie of Skinny Puppy, as well as longtime collaborators such as Lustmord and Danny Lohner, was revealing of Keenan's endlessly restless state of mind. As he put it, "We're getting into an age where this whole 'conquer the world with consumerism' thing falls apart at some point. So the idea is just to create a few fun things, and that way I don't have to worry about storing it anywhere. There are a couple of them, you sell them, they're gone, then there are the next couple other ideas and you get rid of those. I can make a living but not have to have some crazy overhead and infrastructure, or some building where I'm paying rent and utilities with staff that have to put food on the table. It's small enough that I can latch on to independents and just have fun with it."

The Puscifer organisation, such as it was, was smaller than most people might imagine, he explained: "It's basically two or three of us. Of course I have people that I [use] to manufacture the shirts, those are companies in and of themselves. But it is pretty much me mailing off artwork, designing shirts or jackets. I've also been selling targets I shoot at the range [and] then autograph… If [the company] got bigger I would license it to somebody else and then it becomes their headache. If they can't move them, it's their problem. But I'm making things in low quantities so we won't end up with a huge warehouse of stuff I can't get rid of… I think that when it gets to be as big as this corporation known as Tool is, some of this business stuff ends up making it more difficult to enjoy the process. That's why I end up doing all these little things, because I'm trying to make sure I'm enjoying [it]. I really enjoy making and recording music, but I don't really enjoy the business end of it. It ends up putting a knot in your stomach."

Retaining the fun side of Puscifer was crucial to Keenan, whose usual sense of humour came to the fore when he was told that a model from the popular Suicide Girls website had had a tattoo of his face inked onto her back. Describing this as "real creepy", he joked: "I usually make them sign a waiver so they can't sue me when they can't get a job. 'I couldn't get a job at a bank and it's your fault.' 'Fuck you buddy, you signed the waiver'… My guess is that she passed out at a party and somebody did it when she wasn't looking. She probably doesn't look at her back in a mirror very often, so she didn't notice. It was probably supposed to be a portrait of Christina Aguilera, but whoever did it made it so ugly that they pretended it was me." He also kept his hand in comedy, he revealed, but with some help from the professionals: "I'm one of the guys that has 16 ideas every minute and then tries to scratch them all down. I write down characters and little scenarios and then I hand them off to... a guy who's actually funny and can write. He finishes them up until they're up to the 90 per cent margin, then I nudge them that final few per cent that really gives them their shape."

By now, Keenan had become a genuine celebrity, with fan pages all over networking websites such as Facebook. He used this fact cannily, making occasional appearances to sign bottles of his wine. One such event took place at a Whole Foods supermarket in Chandler, Arizona, in April, where he and Glomski fielded questions from a small number of wine enthusiasts (and the occasional Tool fan) about their work. "Generally speaking, the people that are into wine are adults and respect people's space, and it's not about the person who made it, it's about the wine," he told one reporter. "So there's definitely a calmer admiration that goes on in those circles."

Maynard also signed up for a couple of appearances on his friend Tom Morello's Axis Of Justice tour that spring, as part of the philanthropic work he had in progress more or less constantly. Each date of the tour, on which Morello appeared as his solo acoustic act The Nightwatchman (a far cry from the shred-heavy antics of his main band, Rage Against The Machine), featured, as the press release said: "A day of activism to focus on a sphere of social justice in America: homelessness (Los Angeles), safe, secure and affordable housing (New Orleans), a living wage (Asheville), peace and veterans care (Washington, DC), affordable healthcare (Boston) and labour organising (Chicago)". Ben Harper, Slash, Perry Farrell, Sen Dog of Cypress Hill and MC5 founder Wayne Kramer were set to appear, with Keenan among the biggest names on the bill.

All this heavyweight activity reflected Keenan's status in the wider rock community. He was constantly quizzed at this point about his personal life, although the furthest he would go was usually about his tastes in TV. Clearly an Anglophile, he explained: "*Extras* is just off the hook. I like *My Name is Earl*, *Reno 911* and that kind of stuff. Also Borat and all the stuff involving Sacha Baron Cohen is true genius… Like everybody else, I was one of those purists, because I had watched all the seasons of *The Office* in the UK. So when the American *Office* started they were trying to fit the formula and do exactly what the UK version had done. Now I'm so glad they've abandoned that formula and gone down their own path. It's an incredible show… it's painful. It's like watching *Curb Your Enthusiasm* where you almost have to watch it from across the room… The problem with me being involved in comedy is that I'm not funny. So if I'm in a comedy I have to be in a scene or a sketch with somebody that's actually funny, and then I can play the straight man. But without anybody actually funny in the scene, then I'm just a dork trying to be funny and not doing it. Having said that, I'm working on some short films with a friend of mine who's a writer, which we would show on a Puscifer tour… [like] Tom Waits when he did his live album, *Big Time*."

If only comedy was the only thing he had to worry about. He hinted darkly that the interpersonal relationships within Tool had not always been without friction, saying: "There are times you just have to get through things. Like any marriage, there are rough spots… [because] we never left. You never leave any of it. You're married to these people. It's a relationship. Everyone that you come across in your life that you had intimate relations with, [is] still part of you. You don't really leave them [even though] you might not be standing in the same room with them all the time… If there was no money involved it would be easy to do this, but as soon as the money comes into play, everybody gets weird. It has an affect on everybody… people get fucking goofy. When you don't have money to lose, you don't have to worry about somebody taking the money. All that bullshit aside, I'm trying to prove that I can just make music and make my living doing that and selling shirts for fun." No easy task…

Chapter 18

2008

Things were changing for Maynard James Keenan. His two bands were drifting further and further apart, for one thing. Note the dividing line that he drew between Tool and Puscifer when he said: "[Puscifer is] just two guys hanging out, making some stuff, and because it doesn't have anything to do with dead relatives or child molestation or hating or wanting to shoot somebody or whatever, it's viewed by many of my fans of other projects as being lesser. But actually it's not, it's just a different experiment. I tried to see if I could make cupcakes with syrup instead of sugar. Whatever. It tastes good, shut up... I'm really picking my experiments. The lead track that we just released, 'Queen B', was an experiment. It was me and Tim Alexander in his new-built studio on two-inch tape, going, 'Let's see if we can do a song that's just drums and vocals'. And who gives a shit about the lyrics? It's not about that. It's about, 'Let's just see if we can come up with some catchy groove, and let's see if I can riff over it and layer it and see what we come up with as fun'."

As if two hibernating bands (Tool and A Perfect Circle), a fully operational one (Puscifer), a wine business and guest appearances with the Axis Of Justice wasn't enough, Maynard also sang guest vocals at this time on a single released by Jubilee, the new band featuring Aaron North of Nine Inch Nails. Jubilee were a supergroup of sorts, and their album also included contributions by members of Queens Of The Stone Age, Foo Fighters and other luminaries of the once-alternative, now-mainstream rock set. Other developments for Keenan came thick and fast in the summer: no doubt to the local Arizonans' surprise, he opened a Puscifer shop in Jerome, the town near his home and vineyards, where the band's merchandise was placed on sale as well as locally manufactured coffee, artworks and other items.

While Keenan performed his guest appearances and managed his various businesses, Justin Chancellor was doing the occasional bit of press. Asked why *10,000 Days* had taken so long to appear, he pondered: "We were on the road almost two years, and by the end of that time we wanted to give each other some space. Maynard wanted to do another album with A Perfect Circle, and everybody else was interested in pursuing other musical things. So we took a year off from each other. After that, it wasn't hard for us to get to the point where we all wanted to get back together and make music again… I think it's important to interact with other people and explore different ideas. Then when you come back together, you've got things to offer each other, different ideas to bounce around. It is a really positive thing to do… Any idea we bring in pretty much gets ripped apart and changed to something completely different. That's the fun thing about this band – the other guys really push you by exploring your ideas and tearing them apart. Before you know it, you've come up with something that hadn't existed before."

Notably, Chancellor appeared not to have reached the point of exhaustion that Keenan had arrived at some time before. Asked why Tool still excited him after so many years, he said: "I just love music. It's something that doesn't go away. Aside from playing in front of thousands of people and sharing that moment, you're on the edge, you're trying to play well, you're trying to express yourself emotionally. That's an awesome experience, and the draw to do that is always there, because it's very fulfilling. But also, I listen to music all the time; I'm a huge music lover, and to be able to create it as well is a great privilege. I don't think I'll ever stop wanting to make sounds, explore melodies, rhythms… it's just an enjoyable way to express yourself."

It would be too much to suggest that Keenan had become disillusioned with Tool. It's apparent, though, that the pressures that come along with being in a huge band had come to nauseate him, and that his drive to perform other kinds of music had been strong since A Perfect Circle first formed nine years before. He still had much to say on the subject of the record industry and how it eats its own young, too. As he pointed out: "One thing that I see the musicians wanting is more independence and more control over their destiny. The one downside to it is that for the most part, the reason they make music is because they're damaged goods, and they're generally not that bright when it comes to making business decisions. So eventually the vampires that survive the aftermath of the industry collapse will figure out a way to get their fingers back into these guys."

Money, the root of all evil in the record industry as everywhere else, lay at the heart of his ruminations about the music business – and specifically how free downloading wouldn't work, given that artists need to be paid for their work. "I keep going around in circles over it with my friends," he sighed. "I can't do this for free. It's ridiculous and insulting… [There are] so many costs involved in recording and making it right. The goal of every musician is to achieve the pantheon of writing songs – and that requires skills, tools, focus. And all that requires financing. I acknowledge I am one of the winners of the lottery. Around the time Nirvana came out, labels were out there looking for something different. Tool got lucky, we got a record deal – but we were also smart and planned to do as much as we could to take advantage of it… kids out there need to understand that if they dig a band's music, then they have to find some way to get compensation to that band for their art, so that they can ensure the band can keep making it."

Keenan had once been quoted in *Rolling Stone* as saying that "heavy rock is sinking". Asked about this, he explained: "It has stagnated, it's no longer moving anywhere. Part of it is large labels signing stuff they think is easy and a quick buck, but I also think it's the bands that aren't evolving their ideas or stretching their legs musically. And the ones that are, you don't hear about… they're overlooked because they're not moving units. The independent stuff is out there, bubbling underneath, but no one's giving it a chance because they're all scrabbling for the next Linkin

Park or Backstreet Boys-style band… I just think it's one-dimensional, I'm sorry. Or maybe that really is the best that they can do."

Perhaps Maynard felt misunderstood. He often spoke of the disappointment he felt about the actions of others. This could be the press, who didn't understand Puscifer: "This whole project started in the comedy arena, onstage in a comedy club with a variety show. So all the things that went into that show over the last ten years is what this project is about. Not just music… all the press that I'm doing at the moment is specifically music press. And they are all looking at just the music. But really, there are so many facets to this project. And the title of it draws on those facets which haven't even been looked at yet… there's a lot of discovery in it. I'm inspired by writers like Shakespeare who have an equal amount of comedy and tragedy within their work. It's very complex and there's all this … stuff wrapped up into it. There's a lot of the comic and the tragic in this project, and you just have to discover it."

On the other hand, his disillusionment might also apply to the starstruck fans who shadowed his every move. As he complained: "I think I expect a lot from people. I expect them to be adults, and some of that creepy fan stuff really gets under my skin. It doesn't make any sense. It would be like if you really liked tomatoes, and so you went looking for the guy who grew the tomatoes and were staring at him from behind a fence, and then showed him the tattoo of the tomato you got on your arm. It's just weird!"

Of course, his disillusionment could also stem from the political situation and the way that people had reacted to 9/11. Of an Indiana gig that had almost been cancelled in the wake of that tragedy, he said: "Terrorists are not targeting this barn in the middle of Indianapolis. This is not a target for terrorists. The World Trade Center [has the people] who run things. If you just sit down for a second and walk yourself through it, the Punch Bowl in Boise is not a target. It just isn't… I think [9/11] affected everyone deeply. It was definitely a shift in, 'Oh, shit, we can be gotten, too'. I don't want to get into the politics of it, but I was, personally… I was the guy fighting, 'Fuck it, let's play the show'. What else are these people going to do? My brain works in a very strange, logical manner in those instances."

More seriously, he felt that Bush's government was stripping America of its rights. Much as he tried to avoid the subject, he couldn't: "We're getting into politics and I don't want to go down that path, but with the Patriot Act being shoved through... The whole way we set up our government to begin with, was so that if things went weird we could pull the plug on those guys and set up a new system. Right now, if you wanted to do that, you couldn't. And if you tried to do it by force, you couldn't, because you're standing there in your bare feet at the airport, having your butt X-rayed. There's no way to retaliate, they've taken away all your weapons. It's gotten pretty ridiculous... as an individual I feel a little more frustrated. When it comes around to it, you've explained all you can explain as far as the way things are working. You try and show people, historically, what happens when these kinds of events come around [and] when a particular government is set up, or a culture of people, their evolution in time comes to a head, then deteriorates. We're way beyond the point where if we were Rome, we'd be over by now."

And then there is the classic American belligerent mentality, which had of course been the subject of Tool's lyrical ire for a decade and a half. "I see a lot of patterns in our behaviour as a nation that parallel a lot of other historical processes," he remarked. "The fall of Rome, the fall of Germany – the fall of the ruling country, the people who think they can do whatever they want without anybody else's consent. I've seen this story before. I think people in general have neglected to learn about history. But then it hasn't really been a focus of our government to make us an educated people. Just in general, any government throughout history hasn't really wanted its people to be educated, because then they couldn't control them as easily. If the education of our kids comes from radio, television, newspapers – if that's where they get most of their knowledge from, and not from the schools, then the powers that be are definitely in charge, because they own all those outlets."

He went on: "If we just had better school systems, and people just studied history properly, they could prepare for what's coming – just by having an idea of where we've been and where we're heading, and using other people as examples. The thing that most people don't understand is, you don't fully learn by experience. As an intelligent person, you have to learn by other people's experiences, otherwise you have to keep trying shit. Well, I don't need to put a gun to my head and pull the trigger to know that it's going to blow my head off. Somebody else did that. I've learned, as an intelligent person, from somebody else's experience. There's historical precedent set about the way things go, the way men in power struggle for more power, and what they'll do to keep it. You can read about it. We've done our best in the past 20 to 30 years to make sure that the schools can't teach anything."

And don't mention the state of popular music. Although he had some respected musical idols with roots in Seventies punk ("People like Mike Patton and Josh Homme are a major source of inspiration to me, the way they can wear many hats and do all these things. Both of them were a huge nudge for me to get this thing going, for sure"), Maynard didn't support the pop-punk movement kick-started by Green Day some years before and still going strong today. "I can't listen to the radio," he said. "It bummed me out heavily when all that punk shit started happening again. The same fucking guitar, bass and drums I've heard a million times from back in '79. Maybe they don't consider themselves artists, but I think they should have a little more responsibility to try and do something more than cash in on a trend. I think that shit drags humanity down… I hope we can provide an alternative to all of the lowest-common-denominator shit going on right now. I just wish people were doing something weirder than we [Tool] are."

Still, he retained his sense of humour in the face of it. "I'm on a mission," he said. "I've been assigned to be the guardian of a highly classified, highly effective Sonic Weapon of Mass Disruption. This sonic technology when 'unleashed', if you will, causes parts of the anatomy to vibrate uncontrollably. Not unlike when someone yawns, everyone in the surrounding area will be affected. If executed properly, the subjects will be temporarily distracted from their duties. Their bodies will appear to be abducted by the Soul Train, as if J-Lo were auditioning for the 'Thriller' video. Awe-inspiring. Don't speak a word of it." He added of Puscifer's female alien mascot: "She hatched out of an egg-shaped space pod that emerged from a seventh-dimensional vaginal portal just north of my third eyehole. My guess is she is the reincarnation/hybrid of a long overdue Magdalene/Venus De Milo/fertility goddess. A powerful fifth-element superbeing with an infinite energy source not unlike bio-diesel, and hips to match. I wouldn't be surprised if she runs for public office and wins."

Looking back, it seems that Puscifer had come together remarkably smoothly. Keenan had been surrounded by the right people at the right time, he said: "Sometimes it's a case of looking in your backyard, quite literally. Tim Alexander is a neighbour of mine and he's got a studio set up. Sometimes it's just a convenience. This person is there, you get along with them, and all of a sudden all this music starts coming out, and you're like, 'Wow, this is fun!' Also, seeing as I'm on the road with Matt Mitchell [Tool's guitar tech], on our days off we were able to slowly put this thing together. It's been a very rewarding process, and I'm really happy to be doing it."

Typically, Keenan wanted to do something rather different with Puscifer. Touring it was an obvious option, but he said: "There's a lot of ideas I'd like to present first. Taking it on the road with a whole bunch of musicians interpreting it would put it too much in the band realm, and I don't want that. If I did do it, then I [would] want to do it in a small theatre for a week of shows, with different musicians each night, and have it involve film, cabaret and dinner. Something totally out of the ordinary."

This extended as far as the very elaborate packaging of the two Puscifer albums to date, one of which folded out into 'emergency instructions' for use on 'Vagina Airlines'... "I made sure I went to this really amazing printer in Los Angeles that has this advanced press that no one else has," Keenan said. "You always have to go the extra effort to have something that you want to hold in your hand." As for the sound of the album, he'd made a point of experimenting with a digital studio (recording to a computer drive) and an analogue counterpart (recording to tape). "Hands down, the analogue sounded and felt the best," he said. "I think, eventually people are going to rediscover that. I mean, I don't want to sound like the guy trying to bring back Betamax, but I really think analogue and vinyl sound great, and that's something I can see myself doing with Puscifer by putting it out on vinyl."

Of the project's target audience, he explained: "It's a much looser recording process, focusing on more techniques, art and experiments rather than it being this ferocious octagon-style piece of work that's designed to knock people out. It's not that. It's more like inviting you in and serving cocktails at your party... having found that kind of quieter space in yourself [and knowing] that your life is not dependent on it taking over the world, that very American perspective of world domination in some way [with] whatever product you're pimping. In a way, I am trying to pimp it and make it survive in its own space."

It's interesting to note that despite Keenan's willingness to name and shame those around him that he felt made the world a worse place, his character had mellowed over the years. For one thing, he knew how fortunate he was to have found success at a relatively late stage in life: "One of the worst things that can happen to an individual, not necessarily for somebody listening to the art or watching the spectacle, is to have your ego stroked between the ages of 18 to 23. If you become famous as a rock band during that time, just plan on being fucked by the time you're 30, because that's a difficult time to be able to process that much attention and that much focus. If you can make it out of that and not be an asshole, wow. Cos most of the guys I've seen that got popular during that period of time, it just really consumes them; all their worst characteristics come out. It's just bad for your body and your psyche and your emotions. You have to be a really special person, have some kind of special armour – ethereal, emotional, spiritual armour – to make it through that period of time at that age. It's a tough thing to navigate, and most people don't navigate it that well."

For those fans who missed the old, enraged Keenan, he merely said: "You can go out and buy the records. There's *Opiate*, there's *Undertow*. The whole idea is to get it out: write the song about it, spout off about it and get over it. I suppose I could repeat myself over and over again, but what's the point of that? The idea is, if I can't heal from my art, then how can [I] heal? So I've worked some things out and moved on."

The interplay between the Tool members was still there, they all insisted. Keenan felt that he had become less difficult as a person, explaining: "I think the biggest problem working with me would be that I'm an only child, and so I have an internal dialogue that goes on that I just assume you can hear. Because as an only child, you have your own little world. Then you go into a situation where you're working with other people, and unless you actually vocalise what you're thinking, the other people will go through hell trying to figure out what's going on. I'm a lot easier to work with now than I have been in the past, for sure." Danny Carey added: "The hardest part about putting a band together is to find three, four or five people with a similar vision. The chemistry has to be right so you can reach that higher ground. In some bands, it happens all the time. In other bands, it never happens. It can't be forced and we were lucky to find each other. Five years from now, who knows if we will be Tool? I think we have a couple of good albums left in us. It's hard to judge beyond that. We will know when it's time to move on. The band wasn't always the centre of our lives and it won't always be the centre of our lives."

And what is more, Tool still had a place in the modern rock scene, side projects and pop-punk revolutions or not. "You have to at least stay here to represent your ideas, otherwise the mediocre stuff will just march in and take your place," said Maynard. "There are so many magazine covers, so many spots on MTV, so many spots on the rack at Wal-Mart, and they're going to fill a hole. So if nobody is representing some higher ideals, or is trying to push the art to a new level, then somebody else is going to fill in the space and it'll be mediocre.

"You have to figure," he added, "if people like us weren't doing it, who would be?"

Chapter 19

2008-2009

As Keenan worked on his various projects from out in the Arizona
desert, the other three members of Tool slowly came out into the
public view once again. *10,000 Days* had made such an impact – selling
many more copies in its first week on sale than *Lateralus* had, and out-
doing the number two album in the week of its release by two to one –
that shock waves from the record were still reverberating.

One consequence of the album's success was that the people associated with it, even outside the band, became stars. One of these was Alex
Grey, whose profile as an artist was already huge but who gained a whole
new fanbase – the intelligent heavy rock crowd – thanks to his work
with Tool. A visionary who, like the members of the band, often admitted to using psychedelic drugs to achieve heightened perspective, Grey
knew that Tool's music was a perfectly complementary vehicle for his
work. "Because of [Tool's] mass audience, it reaches people that con-
temporary painting rarely does," he said. "If you don't get to see a painting in the flesh, then how are you going to get to see it? Maybe you'd
see it in a magazine. Maybe you'd see it in a book. But if you see it associated with powerful music and you love that music, maybe it even
engenders a love [of] the artwork."

Adam Jones recalled the moment when he first saw Grey's picture of a cosmic network – the one that was adapted for the cover of *10,000 Days*. "He just rifled through his sketchbook and opened to a page," he remembered. "He said, 'What do you think of this? It was the *Net Of Being* drawn out with a pencil. You could see that Alex was working out the math of getting the grid right for it. I was like, 'Oh my God'… I could just see myself in there… I think it's really important that you work as hard as you can on something. You have to do that nowadays because you can just download [an album] off the internet or you can just get it from your friend and tape it. I'd rather always be about giving people more than their money's worth… After we're all gone and in 300 years or 500 years, Alex will be a master. He, right now, is a modern master to me."

Jones, always slightly in the more loquacious Keenan's shadow when it came to discussing matters philosophical, explained about the album's recording that it had brought him to tears at times. "This is going to sound really pretentious, but it's emotional," he said. "For us, writing music is very therapeutic. You get to these different states, and it's almost like you're entertaining yourself. You're leading someone by the hand, but the hand you're leading is your own. I don't get choked up when I hear other people's music, except in a few rare instances. The Melvins did something that I thought was absolutely fuckin' beautiful. But if we write something I really like, I get teary-eyed. I'm the kind of guy who can cry really easily. The really long song on the record that starts very classically and builds up ['10,000 Days (Wings, Pt. 2)'] is my favourite song that we have ever done. I get really choked up whenever we play it. I was really worried where Maynard was going to go with it, but he nailed the lyrics on that one… I never bought a record and thought, 'Oh, this song is long'. I never thought 'Stairway To Heaven' was a long song. I loved how there was this part and then there was another part that was completely different. If you're making music for all the right reasons, people are going to be receptive to that and appreciate it the same way you did when your were writing it."

Surprisingly, Jones was relaxed about the fate of Tool's material once it was out of their hands – even if mainstream radio planned to hack it down for airplay purposes: "We'll pick a single that we think will do well on radio and we give it to them in its entirety. A band we knew told us that they'd edit their songs for radio, but even if they edited a song down to four minutes, radio stations would edit it down to three minutes. So we just give it to radio as it is. We can't control it anyway. It's their world, and if the song does good, great." A refreshing change from the usual control-freak rock star, you'll agree – and he also knew exactly what the relative dynamics within the members of Tool were, saying: "It's a lot of subtle things: like Justin's from England and I'm from here. We have similar interests in comedy, music and art and similar views on life, but at the same time we often disagree about certain types of music, art and philosophies. The main thing I like about us is that there's a friendship and understanding of communication, compromising and working together. Basically, we've been married since 1990. It's those normal things you'd have with any of your close friends. Sometimes we fight and disagree, but we're big enough to go, 'Well, what did you want out of that?' 'I wanted this.' 'Let's meet halfway.' There's a lot of negotiating going on. It's not always structured like that; it's something that we feel. It's like asking me what I like and don't like about my mom… If you sat each of us down and asked, 'What are your views on politics? What kind of music do you like?' you'd find we all have very different answers. What the four of us do is what Tool is, and that's where that magic happens."

The guitarist also spoke openly about the band members' belief in the fundamental structure of the universe, and how it applies to their music. "All of the members of Tool agree on sacred geometry," he said, "which is a study of taking everything that's complicated about the world, and everything that's concentrative of *our* world, and breaking it down to the simplest things: simple patterns, shapes, colours, vibrations… all that kind of stuff. To me that is what Tool is, because everyone in my band gets that. I hate it when art is forced, when you look at something and go, 'God, give me a break!' because you can tell that person was trying to be artistic and show themselves off as being some weird, arty guy. It's not from the heart. Life is short, and it's so rewarding to try to get to a certain point. Is writing songs for Tool fun? No. It sucks. It's hard; it's a long process; it can be gruelling; but it's fucking rewarding. When we're doing a video, throughout the whole process I'm going, 'I'm never doing this again. This sucks. Everyone is against me. I'm just trying to get some-

215

thing done'. But as soon as we're done I'm like, 'Let's make another one!'"

Danny agreed with this, adding: "I think it's more about finding a personal harmony, where you can be comfortable with the resonations between your body and finding that place where it fits with your surroundings and trying to be as aware of that as possible. It's such a subjective thing that I don't think there are cut-and-dried rules as such. You have to find your niche and figure out how hard you want to push that dissonance, or what resonates with you and feels natural. I think it can be different for each person, but I've always found what feels right for me and then you become aware of the more subtle vibrations. You have to pay attention to them, but even then I'm still not certain if it will make any difference at all. Maybe subliminally, though."

This had manifested itself on *10,000 Days* in unusual ways for a drummer. As he recalled, "I would have played a different instrument if I'd had to play like a metronome... I've developed more on the last record by being more involved texturally and even harmonically, and just being more sensitive to all that was going on musically and really having a conversation with my bandmates, rather being there just to keep a beat. But most drummers are quite content, I guess, to be a metronome, even though I know a lot of music doesn't call for much more. It's lucky for me that I can express myself however I want, and it's a healthy position for me to be in."

He listed his key influences: "In the prog world, Bill Bruford [of King Crimson]. He was always really free-thinking about electronic drums and things like that, and I always appreciated that a lot, especially at one point when all of a sudden it became so uncool to use electronic drums, but I just thought, 'Ah, man, everyone should do what pleases themselves'. So yes, he was a big influence in that way. Other than him I drew my influences from some of the jazzier guys like Billy Cobham – and I loved Steve Gadd's playing too. He made a lot of great records with Chick Corea and Steely Dan. I just loved his drumming."

Adam and Danny had forged an important musical relationship within Tool, with the guitarist becoming aware of the beat and the drummer becoming involved with the harmonics of the songs. As Jones said, "I got into studying polyrhythms and experimental math,

216

seeing what different kinds of math worked together. If they didn't work, I'd try to figure out why and determine what I had to throw in to make them work. I listened to a lot of classical and electronic music as well as a lot of metal, especially the heavier stuff. I tried to get into as many paths as I could... I like soundtracks and I like film. I try to think in those terms, but it's more emotional. How can you describe something without telling the person what it is? If you wanted to explain the yellow colour... without showing the person yellow, how would you do that? You might be able to do it by saying, 'You know when you fell like this, or when this has happened, or you're sitting under a tree?... There's always the influence of music, film, art and the other things that drive me. I'm usually inspired by my environment and whatever is making me happy or mad. By the time we decide to get together again and start jamming, Justin and I have a huge amount of material. We bring it in and everybody rips it apart like wolves. We explore every avenue and path of it and then choose the paths that work best with one another."

Informed that he played his guitar like a percussion instrument, he laughed and replied: "I've always been interested in rhythm. I wrote the main riff to 'Ænema' based on Danny showing me how to play three-on-four [three-four and four-four time signatures played simultaneously]. One hand is doing three and the other is doing four. And he taught me this rhythm that goes 'Pass the goddamn butter'. That made me wonder what other rhythms I could explore. My nephew Joe was in this Arizona drum corps, and his teacher really liked our music and Danny's drumming. They played Tool arrangements. Joe sent me a tape of it, and we loved it. When we played in their town, we had them open for us. I hit up Joe to show me some rhythms, and he showed me weird beats you can play with one hand while you play straight four with the other hand. That really comes in handy."

"I think we've got a bit better at our craft," said Danny, "and have learnt to get a bit more concise and to weed out extraneous things. It's weird but I thought that this album didn't quite fit together as a larger picture, but that each song was a lot better defined and with more personality to it, so in the end the whole record has a heavier vibe because of it being a collection of all those pieces."

He revealed: "I've always been a bit of a frustrated guitar player, but I've never really said that to anyone before! I might be a little bit more frustrated if I didn't keep going out and buying guitars and hoping that their vibrations would rub off on me. It was always something that I was fascinated with… string instruments. When I was going through school, it was all about percussion instruments there, and I played the vibes and the timpani, so now I'm beginning to get into things with just a little more strings. So far I've bought about 15 of them… I really liked [Adam's] Gibson Les Pauls, so I went out and bought a couple that were like his, then I just started buying my heroes' instruments such as [Yes'] Steve Howe's and one like the guy [Geordie Walker] in Killing Joke. I've been going for different basses too, as I used to play a little more bass."

Both men looked back on the making of the album as a positive – if exhausting – experience, with the bigger budget afforded Tool this time around exploited to the full. "We had a little more time to experiment," said Adam. "We had everything written before we went into the studio. Maybe only five per cent wasn't ready, and we always have at least one song that we build in the studio. That's been a rewarding process. I talk to people who are in bands and who write their whole record in the studio. They don't know what they're doing, and they have a producer come in to help them write songs. We didn't have a producer this time. Joe Barresi just recorded the record and mixed it, although he did have some input in the process."

Carey was appreciative of Keenan's development into a more relaxed individual than the uptight frontman he'd been for so many years previously. "He was there throughout the whole process," he recalled. "It was really good. Much more so than when we made *Lateralus*. He had a bit more time, as people had been a bit more excited about the first A Perfect Circle record, so he was able to put a lot more time into *10,000 Days*. Even back when *Lateralus* came out, he saw the value of Tool compared to his other project, so each time he came to work on this one, he was full-on into it, heart and soul… [On stage] he's been coming out a little more, even though he's still set up back in my area, but the main point of that is that we really don't want people to focus on one thing. The human voice is such a powerful thing, and everybody wants to look at that, but we always wanted to keep him just a little bit darker, so people will have to look at the whole show and what's going on with everything that we bring to it."

Interestingly, Carey revealed that the band had almost fallen out over one particular song. As he sighed, "With ['Wings For Marie' and '10,000 Days'], I know [Maynard] had to go through the fire a bit more. It was definitely a very heavy personal thing for him, but each of us had particular songs that were the most cathartic to us. As a band, I suppose that one came together a little easier for us than some of the others. We didn't nearly break up over that one like we did for 'The Pot'. A lot heavier battle ensued over that tune than any other… it's just that our work ethics differ, I suppose. Maynard's definitely a person who relies on a flash of inspiration. No one ever wants to second-guess him because he convicts right away, whereas Adam just wants to try every possibility over and over again. With 'The Pot', Adam knew that the very first thing we tried really was a flash of inspiration, but he was not going to let it go until he'd tried every conceivable way of doing things, so by the end of it we really were ready to kill him. But when we're really ready to try something out, then we want to kill Maynard because he gets frustrated and doesn't want to keep working. And of course, we think Maynard's lazy and we think Adam's a slave driver and we all get close to death. It all falls somewhere in the middle ground where it all makes sense, but it's just so difficult at times. These little idiosyncrasies of our different personalities come out, and they drive you crazy, especially after 15 or 16 years!"

Still, the band saw their future together evolving in many different ways – and in better ways. As Carey put it, "I think we've gotten better at what we do. Our songs have become more concise vehicles for emotional travelling. We always have different conversations with each other as we grow and learn about ourselves, and the intention's still pretty much the same. As long as our intentions are pure, we're hopefully inspiring people to go in a good direction instead of a bad one. You never know, though – some people could hear a Beatles song and go wipe out a family. It's not up to us. We just have to do our job and then cast it out… I don't think our motives have ever really changed as far as that goes."

Musical diversity would still be key to the Tool sound, of course.

"[There are] places on the new record," Carey went on, "where maybe it's mellow and leads toward a kind of mellower emotion, but [there are] also places that are heavier than anything we've ever done. Hopefully, our palette is being expanded in every direction possible. I hope we're still getting heavier, but we're also able to maybe provoke emotions that we haven't before. That's the goal… We just try to use the words in our songs and the artwork – which we all contribute to, and the music also – as a whole. We try to do the best that we can, so it can be interpreted on a lot of different levels. That's what good art usually does, where there's something in it for everyone. It doesn't really matter to us who gets it and who doesn't, as long as we're doing the best we can."

The live show, too, lay at the heart of the Tool experience, just as it does with all the best bands. Asked what he thought concertgoers would take away from the average Tool gig, Carey echoed Maynard's sentiments when he said: "Inspiration, one way or another. We hope that they learn something. We hope they get inspired to do something themselves. Everybody looks to get something different out of a rock concert, I think. We hope we provide the vehicle. Like any other artwork, we want to take people onward and upward… I think the word's kind of getting around about the show. We try to put a lot into it. I think it's paid off now. People are getting really good shows now, that's for sure. The word has gotten around that the tickets are worth it. Our crew's been really good. We've had the same guys out for the whole year, so now they really know the songs well and it's all really locked together – all the lighting, video and everything… we try to keep certain areas during our set where we get to improvise and keep changing things, and we keep trying to add new songs along the way too as much as possible. It keeps it fresh for us, though. That's all we need on stage. As long the cylinders are firing, it just becomes contagious in the crowd."

Fans hoped that at some point soon Tool would commit to a new album release date. However, like his bandmates Carey couldn't or wouldn't do so, although he did drop some hints about a possible Tool movie. "We talked about it for a long time. There's no definite plan yet," he said. "We probably won't do one until we do another record, I'm thinking, so it'll be a while down the line when we pull that off. We're doing really well just doing our albums and doing the live shows, so there's no reason to interrupt that process now. To take on something like a movie would mean probably at least three years in the making, so it'll be a big vacation in the public's eye. I don't think we're ready to go that route yet. Somewhere down the line we may. We'll see how it works out... [It might be] like a fictional animation. We'd probably do it all stop-frame animation and go that route. Like a *Pan's Labyrinth* sort of thing..."

A more realistic short-term prospect might be an in-concert DVD, he said: "We really planned on making [one], but we just ran out of time. At the end of the *Lateralus* tour we made a big effort, and even video-recorded the last ten shows and audio-recorded the last 15, so we have all this material. There is a chance, if we have time, that we are going to start going through it and editing for a live DVD, so I'm hoping that we will have one out." However, he knew that Tool had the luxury of leaving some years between albums – a privilege that few other bands enjoy. He explained: "We're lucky that we're accepted, that we can take five years between records, where most bands can't get away from that. It's not like we aren't conscious of it. But we really don't want to come out and repeat ourselves. I think that's what it takes. You kind of have to grow as people and have time to have a sabbatical and learn something new on your instrument before you can make another record and not repeat yourself. We try to be more conscious about the quality of the product, rather than how long it takes to put it out."

Tool's modus operandi when it comes to songwriting remains the same as it always has been. As Carey said, "We do long, freak-out jams when we first get back together after our breaks, and maybe do that for a few months – just have these long crazy jams and keep the tape machine rolling. Then we find the really cool parts of them that pop up along the way and find ways to piece it all together and make songs... we usually aren't very good at writing while we're on the road. Occasionally, we'll have a little jam at a soundcheck or something like that. But most of the songs we've written, we just do in our space when just the four of us are there alone. We work much better when no one else is around. You have to get into your creative zone, you know, when you have control over the environment a little bit more... Some of [the songs] fit together really quickly and some of them take a lot of work.

Some tunes we can write in a couple of days, but they're pretty rare. Some of the other ones, we work on for up to two months before we can get the arrangement right. It's a lot of hard work and all four of us are in the room together banging it out. I think it's worth it that way, even though it's a little more painstaking, because you hear a lot more of the personality of the band that way when it's a more organic process."

Freak-out jams? Sounds like a new progressive-rock wave is on its way – and many other musicians agree, including Mastodon drummer Brann Dailor, who said: "I hope we can start a prog revolution, because the timing's right. You've got [*10,000 Days*], an Isis record that's coming out, a Mars Volta record that's coming out, a Mastodon record that's coming out, and I hope that converges into something really awesome for music, where it doesn't become pop, but there's a little more sharing of the pie. It would be cool if you had kids in their bedrooms not trying to learn Linkin Park songs, but they're trying to learn Mastodon songs. It's cool music that's honest and from the heart, and it's technically challenging."

Music to Tool's ears, of course. As Carey said: "We grew up on [prog] bands. I did, for sure, so I think it's a compliment. We put a lot into our artwork on the albums and our artwork that goes down for the live show, and [we] create a whole new reality, if you will, for people. In that way, I guess we are. We try to pick up where, say, Pink Floyd, or some of the bands who are really into presenting a whole new reality, left off."

With the phrase "a new reality", Danny summed up what Tool are all about in the most succinct manner yet.

Chapter 20

2009 And Beyond

At the time of writing, live dates and recording a new album in the near future are on the cards for Tool, but nothing is set in stone. They've never been the most prolific of bands, and the music scene has changed its spots several times over the last couple of years while we've been waiting for them to reconvene – but the mark that they've left on music in general and progressive heavy rock in particular is indelible.

This is largely due to the extraordinary combination of personalities within the band. Maynard James Keenan, of course, has outgrown the status of mere rock singer to become a figurehead in multiple branches of the entertainment world – and doesn't feel the need to confine himself to any one of them. As he put it: "Music is about listening: the more you play, the more the magic spreads. For me, life is writing and I can do it anywhere. It doesn't matter where I am. I listen. I write. I live. And if you don't live, you have nothing to write about."

The future of Tool as a live act seems assured, as it's both their creative forte and their major source of revenue. Keenan expressed it perfectly when he said, "Shows are really strange. Sometimes you really don't know what to expect. Sometimes you're playing in the sunshine... [or there's] something that just doesn't seem to go with our sound. It isn't worse, it's just different, absolutely different. Then there are some days when we really don't want to go on stage at all, when we feel terrible and think we really shouldn't play. And pretty often those shows turn out to be absolute highlights… So much plays into it. There are so many factors and so many things that all play a part in shows, that you really never know what makes a good show. Sometimes we wonder if we – the musicians – do really play a big part in it, or if we can hardly influence it."

As for the necessary evil of money, the band's business grasp became apparent when Maynard recalled a negotiation with their record company about the artwork budget for *10,000 Days*: "We had to [go to] the record company and show them, 'See, this is [how much money] we make when we tour. This is what we make on album sales. We don't need to make albums. You want us to make an album, dinosaur? How's that tar pit doing for you?' If they want to survive into the next millennium, they have to figure out a way [for us] to have fun with our album artwork, because they understand that it's something they have to do to be relevant in this new world order."

When Keenan looked back over Tool's career, he picked out certain live shows as a highlight, in particular the King Crimson dates from a few years previously. "It was an honour for us," he said. "For our fans, it was something like an education. A lot of our fans weren't really aware where we were coming from, what inspired us. I find it a bit sad. I think to share one stage with King Crimson was important. It showed where our roots are, where we are coming from. After all, in today's music scene every band seems to steal from other bands. They're all stealing from each other and they all claim to be the originals. I think it's limiting – limiting for the bands and for the listener." He certainly didn't identify Tool's Grammy awards and nominations as in any way important, saying with his usual scathing tone: "The Grammys are nothing more than some gigantic promotional machine for the music industry. They cater to a low intellect and they feed the masses. They don't honour the arts or the artist for what he created. It's the music business celebrating itself. That's basically what it's all about… [but] why should we refuse it? First of all, that would just gain a lot of attention, and we are certainly not attention-seekers. And if our record company and the music business want to have a party, why should we spoil it for them? Just because we're not interested? Just because we don't like it, why ruin it for them...?

"I don't care at all," he went on. "We're just four guys and we're enjoying what we're doing with Tool. We are eager to learn – to learn about ourselves and to learn about music, about life, about everything. And, of course, we always hope that we can change something for the better through our music, give someone else some inspiration. I believe that music is a force in itself. It is there and it needs an outlet, a medium. In a way, we are just the medium... Nothing ever happens smoothly or perfectly fine, but it all makes sense. I believe everything happens for a reason, no matter if it's good or bad. There is no point in trying to change the past, because if something would have happened differently, we wouldn't be here now; we wouldn't be talking. You never know what would be or what would change, if you could go back in time and just change one single thing."

Keenan was, at this stage in his career, firmly against the idea of dealing with either press or fans on an intimate level – and for valid reasons. Of the many music journalists who plagued him, he complained: "Sometimes interviewers are almost insulting, especially when it comes down to video or TV interviews. Pretty often they've got such an ego that we sometimes wonder how we fit on the same screen. They're clowns, goofballs and they think they're so funny – full of energy and personality. Do you know what I mean? They're just full of themselves and they don't have a clue and they're not interested in anything else but themselves. They don't even listen. They got a bunch of questions and you don't even get the chance to have something that remotely resembles a conversation. I really can't respect them – and if they'd take a minute and realise what they're doing and how ridiculous they are, they wouldn't be able to respect themselves."

And of the fans who tried to follow his every move, he explained that spending time with them wouldn't be best for the band's music. It sounds pretentious, but his words made sense: "We really don't like it. It's not arrogance at all. We just consider it slightly unnatural. It's not that we're looking down on our fans and that's why we don't want any contact. It's just if we would mix with our fans, they'd most likely feel that they have to tell us how much they like our music, and that can easily get to your head. Look at the other bands out there – with a lot of them, I always get the feeling their success has gone to their heads. If you start taking yourself too seriously it's not good for the creative process. I always believed that music should speak for itself, that people shouldn't see us as heroes, that our fans shouldn't concentrate on us, that they shouldn't try to feed our egos. Once your ego gets in the way, it is much more difficult to feel music."

"I get great emails from our fans," laughed Adam Jones. "My favourite was from this girl who wrote to me on MySpace. She said, 'I finally figured it out – *Lateralus* was written to the [movie] *The Passion Of The Christ*. It's so amazing how it links up. I want to thank you for doing that'."

Jones, like the others, is more interested in improving his performing and songwriting than hanging out with fans, saying of his influences on the guitar: "In Seventies rock there were leads in every song. I used to like Frank Zappa, but I thought that when he played a lead he would go on for way too long. In the Eighties everyone had a gimmick. Michael Angelo Batio had four necks, so the other guy would have to have six necks. Tom Morello is a friend of mine, and he comes from that school where it's got to have a crazy sound and he'll do wacky things. He really gets off on that... but I was always bored with three-hour solos. I think Joe Satriani is amazing, but after three songs he puts me to sleep. I used to play no solos. I've come out of my shell a little bit. If it's tasteful and it's what the song needs, it's OK. There's a big difference between talent and gimmick.

"I'm really lucky that the three other guys I work with are so incredible," he added. "It's not perfect; we don't all see eye to eye. We fight, not with fists, but we disagree or get into arguments when one person wants to go in a certain direction and the others don't. But we all respect each other and try to work it out. It's a four-way arrangement. We split everything four ways. I think that's why we've been together as long as we have."

By now the band had mastered the art of working in a studio, as was demonstrated by the absence of an outside producer on *10,000 Days*. "Every time we've made a record, our songs were already worked out by the time we started recording," he explained. "But every time we've

226

worked with someone they've wanted a production credit. We'd say, 'OK, why not?' But to me a producer is someone who comes in when you don't have your songs worked out, or you want to be a certain kind of band, and you need someone to come in and make you into that type of band. It reminds me of *American Idol...*

"People ask us to explain what we do, and I can't!" he laughed. "The only thing I can explain is that it's completely experimental and based on the most concentrated aspects of what we like. After it's done, we connect the dots... You've got to try new things, but we didn't want to go into the studio and turn on every [software] plug-in and try every new pedal. It was a matter of figuring out what the songs needed. It's also about experimentation. That's the process with us."

Like Keenan, Jones didn't feel the need to spend much time thinking about other people's perception of his band – whether fans or critics. He sniggered: "Maynard and I [once] read this review where we were compared to one type of music and the review bagged on us. That happens a lot. When we started out, metal was moving away from glam and getting harder, thanks to bands like Corrosion Of Conformity. Critics compared us to that. Then Nirvana hit and we started getting compared to grunge. Then Nine Inch Nails got big, and suddenly critics thought we were an industrial band. Whatever group we were being compared to, that group would go, 'Fuck Tool. They're not like that'. Maynard put it perfectly. He said, 'We fell in the cracks'. That's what we are: we're the band that fell in the cracks... I've done interviews where I was asked, 'Don't you think music is worse than it's ever been?' It's exactly the same. When I was a kid, there was always pop shit being played on the radio; there was always *American Idol* kind of shit going on. But there was always something that was against the mainstream, and it was kind of popular and underground. If anything is different today, it's that corporations are involved in the business; there are no handshake deals any more."

Jones also proposed a theory that few others had considered before him, which was that Tool's interaction with their fans, especially in the live environment, is more intimate that you might think. "The relationship with an audience is almost like a sexual one," he mused, before clarifying: "It's not sex, there's no nudity, but it's this intimate thing where you have to let these people be what they are. Our last record was very healing, very 'Think for yourself'. The attitude on this record is more about putting people in their place, but without controlling them. We're saying, 'You have an opinion on this, but this person who went through that whole thing may have a different perspective. You should think about that before you say something. You're not bad for thinking what you thought, but you need to consider the perspectives'. There's a lot of that on this record... Maynard writes all his lyrics and he'll pull in subject matter from our mutual ideas. It might be something that happened to him, but it's always something that we can all relate to, like telling a friend to back up for a second and try to see things from a different perspective. Maynard can explain these things better, but suffice to say, it's all positive. At the end of the day, there's a lot of love from our band. I'm not kidding."

A band as uncompromising as Tool, spreading the love and encouraging people to find their independence, sounds a little hard to justify on paper. But think about what Jones said, and then look at one of the major driving forces behind Maynard's wine business, which you might understandably think is nothing more than a rich man's indulgence. Keenan's stated aim is to revive a certain section of Arizona with his industry, rather like an American version of *A Town Like Alice*. Like Adam, I'm not kidding either – witness his words on the subject: "We're up against a teetotalling, Republican-community perception of what this is all about, so there are lots of hurdles – but I think we'll be able to navigate them, because at the end of the day, it's going to foster exactly what these people are claiming to want to foster, which is family values, small community [and] self-sufficient farmers surviving... if we can make this work, then it's not just busloads of blue-haired geriatrics on a budget [visiting] there to buy a rubber tomahawk and a glass of tea. It's going to be people that want to come through and do a bed and breakfast, buy some local wine and go to a nice restaurant, which there are very few of. But as time goes on, there'll be more competition, and therefore better chefs, better restaurants, people trying a little harder."

He went on: "The winery's going to be a far more family, community-based, nurturing kind of thing that fosters those kinds of feelings. And Puscifer's going to be everything that your mother warned you about. It'll be all that crazy, sacrilegious, push-the-envelope, question-authority stuff. The dark side. It'll be my little angel and my little devil. Puscifer is the little devil on my shoulder and my angel is the wine. Coexisting… There will be some crossover, but I'm not sure that the wine community is necessarily a rock community. Not the fine wine community. So I've made an effort to separate Puscifer from the winery. At the moment the winery is looking to be a very small production. We're very hands-on, maybe just three or four blends. If I do anything on a larger scale, it winds up being an investment in somebody else's company. It won't be my brand, then: just something I'm investing in."

Asked if he was trying to build a secure refuge for himself, which his childhood had so sorely lacked, he pondered: "I think that's what I've found in Arizona. I finally got up there, got into the traffic, met some people who — as right-wing as they are — are still more grounded than anybody you meet at a fucking opening in LA. And so it's a little refreshing — although, you know, you'd like to think they would be OK with your brother's gay marriage… I kind of refer to Arizona as the evil anti-California. You know how there'll be these superheroes whose egos got split in half, and they're kind of fighting each other, but they're actually mirror images of each other and completely integral? That's basically Arizona and California."

Note that Keenan's disgust with Los Angeles was now complete. "It's just a bad place," he said. "It's the kind of place that fosters drug-addicted kids by the time they're 17. There's just too much ego stimulus here at too early an age, and all of a sudden, that novelty wears off a little, and the attention they get — you know, because attention is not recognition; attention is attention — starts to wear off when they get into those early teens, so they start turning to another stimulus. And pretty soon, they're fucked up. You know, not everybody can bounce back like Drew Barrymore… I think it's really important for people who have some kind of access to this industry, or some kind of success, to understand that this is not the real world. If you really want your children to grow up in a stable environment that's going to foster actual skills that will translate globally, you can't do it here. Either that, or you have to put them in a situation where they're going to grow up in a different way."

Occasionally Maynard talked about his personal tastes in culture when a rare connection was formed with the right interviewer, as with the *Vulture Droppings* webzine. Discussing films and their soundtracks, he hinted towards possible future endeavours in those areas when he said: "There's all this subtle stuff you can do now with ProTools and all the other behind-the-scenes music programs. They create tension through imperceptible sounds – beds of sound and white noise – things like that. Soundtracks nowadays really know how to hone that feeling, how to direct the way you're going to react to something. And then there's the dead quiet, the absence of sound. That's the build-up, right before they hit you with something. And then you pee your pants."

Horror films, he said, had played a particularly large part in the formation of his cultural awareness – not a fact that would surprise anyone who has seen Tool's videos. As he said: "I can remember watching horror films in my early days visiting my grandmother's house in Ohio, the Saturday-morning monster movies. I would watch these movies, borrow my aunt's Black Sabbath albums and play them in the background, because I never felt the movie soundtracks were good enough. Then, as the movie played, I would eat all kinds of sugary snacks and get all jacked up and run around the house... my particular flavour of horror film is one that almost has a little bit of camp to it. Some of the stuff almost makes you giggle as much as it startles you. I like lower-budget stuff, like some of the old Ed Wood movies. Then there's the psychological stuff, which is what really got me as a kid. Watching *The Exorcist* really put the zap on me. I grew up in a fundamentalist Southern Baptist household: to go see *The Exorcist* when it first came out, at that age [he was nine when it was first released]... I was way too little to be seeing that movie."

Modern horror appealed to him in parts, he said: "I like *Ringu*, the Japanese version of *The Ring*. Or *Ju-On*, the Japanese version of *The Grudge*. Get a big wide screen, and make sure your bladder's full of urine. I also like Klaus Kinski's *Nosferatu*, the one with Bruno Ganz. Creepy, so creepy. I also like *Manhunter*, the Michael Mann film. No special effects or clever modern digital lighting tricks. To me, Brian Cox is a far, far scarier Dr. Lecter than Anthony Hopkins. He's far scarier, because he's a believably creepy guy who could have been a college professor. A kind of guy [when] you look at him, you're not threatened by him at all. He's not scary, not so in-your-face as Hopkins. He's just this creepy dude, and then when he actually does speak and turn to look, you go, 'This guy is really creepy'. Hopkins, on the other hand, is like right up in your face. He's pressed up on the Plexiglas spouting crazy poetry. You're like, 'Who wouldn't know that this guy's a serial killer? Why'd it take so long to catch this creep?' I mean, come on!"

However, any potential Tool or Puscifer film seems more likely to require more investment on the part of the viewer than the usual modern horror flick – a situation analogous to Tool's albums and their distance from so much current music. As Keenan noted: "A lot of films, and art in general for that matter, are only relevant to a particular historical period. *The Exorcist* will never feel the same way as it did on its initial release, because the special effects don't have the same impact. Or take *The Deer Hunter*. It's so hard to get somebody to sit through a film like that now, to understand why there's 45 minutes of really boring shit. Nobody understands that it's necessary to set up the next scene when they're passing the gun around, playing Russian roulette. You need 45 minutes of mediocre high-school graduation stuff to set up the mood. My favourite movies might not translate nowadays, unless you really have patience… We're so numb these days that it's really difficult to startle people any more. They don't really believe in ghosts as much as they used to. So the only way you can really startle them is to offend them. *South Park* and *Family Guy*, that's the stuff that's really shaking people up, because you're like: 'Ooh, I can't believe he said that'. To me, that would be the new era of shock-value horror film, one with more political stuff. The guy jumping out of the closet is pretty played out. There's a ghost in the house! There are snakes on the plane! Uh, who cares?"

Back to Puscifer, and as 2009 dawned it became clear that some live activity on that front would be seen before too long. Keenan said: "Some day… it's not really going to be a tour. It'll be more of a cabaret, an installation in one town for four or five nights. Once again, with different players each night. That way it's fun. It's fresh. More people get to be involved. It's non-committal, so you don't have to be too precious about it. You can just really have fun and be in the moment with it… We all write together, depending on where it's going to be. I write lyrics on my own, but generally speaking, we come up with the music first. Always music first, except there's some songs with Puscifer that I've kind of explored key lines first and built rhythms around them. Mostly with Puscifer, it's kind of a rhythm-based project to begin with. That way, if the melody's relatively secondary, that allows other people − other remixers, or other people who interpret the music − to give them a lot more free range."

By now a third *V Is For Vagina*-themed album had appeared, this time a set of Lustmord remixes called *D Is For Dubby*. Along with the existing *V Is For Viagra* remix album, Puscifer now had three sets of material in the public domain thanks to Keenan's large network of studio contacts. As he explained: "I put feelers out to see who's available. That's part of the charm of Puscifer: the randomness and random availability of friends who are around doing stuff. It's definitely inspiring to have a core of ideas. A lot of bands get caught up in the whole solidarity − the 'us against the world' kind of mentality where there's a complete disconnect between who they are and who the rest of the world is. 'You can't touch me. We're this solid entity, untouchable.' I think it's kind of limiting. With something like this, it can spiral off in infinite directions. It can inspire far more of a community-based experience, like when the old jazz guys used to travel around the country playing with different players. They're the same thing... other projects are always in the works. There's always something going on. So nothing's changed. Just as before, every time I go out with A Perfect Circle, people ask me what's going on with Tool. I go back to Tool, people ask me what's going on with A Perfect Circle. They're still alive."

Maynard had alluded before to his military background and how it had made him an efficient organiser. This came to the fore in his obvious business sense, which many years in several successful bands had given him. "Money is getting a little tighter nowadays," he said. "But when budgets are strict, that actually improves a lot of music and film and art in general. When you really have to rely on pure ideas to drive a project rather than new technology, that's when the good stuff starts to surface. The bulk of any creative industry doesn't care at all about quality. To them, it's just another project. Who cares how good it is? Just sell it enough to get the budget, to get working, so the carpenters are working, the routers are working, the directors are getting paid, the catering service is there. There is this whole infrastructure [of people] who make

232

their living off of shit [projects] that are so safe they're boring. When all that money disappears and people have to work for something other than money, that's when we're going to see some decent [art]… there's this whole new world of music where it's no longer about putting out albums and being this band 'personality', and going on tour and having managers and lawyers and people fighting over this and that and lawsuits. In this new MySpace, iTunes world it's just 'make a song'. Make a song that's appropriate to whatever you're making it for. Express yourself in a focused manner. Don't worry about a bigger-picture project like a whole album or CD."

The idea for making wine had come to him at least partly thanks to increased business awareness, he explained: "Being a small-town guy on the road, all of a sudden you're watching your accountants and agents and managers walking around with these glasses of red juice that look pretty appealing, and they're oohing and aahing over it while you're, like, stuck with a bag of chips, sniffing your fucking bandmate's ass and feet all the way to fucking Boise. And you're going, 'What the fuck's in that glass, and who paid for that?' And, of course, I did!" he laughed. "So we just started taking their bottle when they weren't looking, and I was indulging a bit and realised, 'Hey, there's something to this'. As time went on, I discovered more, and had that kind of epiphany when you actually have that one bottle with the right meal that really makes sense. And then I headed off into my decadent wine-collecting stage, which segued into me looking outside my door in Arizona and looking at the land, going, 'Man, this is definitely vineyard property; this could happen'. So we started breaking soil… It's great – we're up about 5,000 feet, 4,000 feet in some spots, and Dick Erath, the guy who pretty much pioneered *pinot noir* in Oregon, sold his winery and his label just recently, and bought land next to some land that I'm buying down in the Wilcox area, in Arizona. So he sees what I see in Arizona, that there's potential for amazing, intense, sun-driven wine… I think of it as planning for the future. I have the energy for it now, and when I don't have the energy for it, I'll back off on what I need to back off on. Right now, I'm doing OK juggling, but it's definitely something you have to pay attention to. With all the little irons in the fire, some of them fly, some of them don't, but the only way any of them are going to fly is if you're passionate about them and you actually get involved in them and do them. Some people are OK with just putting their name on something and letting it sell. But the proof is in the pudding – especially with wine. They can talk all they want, but if you drink – you open a bottle, and you know."

And so the picture of Keenan, the face of Tool, is almost complete. He has his intimidating side, but that too only extends to a certain point, as he joked when discussing his martial arts skills. "You realise that, when you're a guy my size, you're going to get your ass kicked no matter what," he laughed. "I have some skills that I can use, but I'm just a small guy – and it really taught me that when it comes to males and their testosterone levels, and what happens in a situation where those testosterone levels are elevated, there's no amount of reasoning and discipline in the world that can take a middle-skilled or lower-skilled guy and make him realise that it's not OK to hurt somebody. It's kind of like the Stanford Prison Experiment mentality – when it gets to a certain point, it's just pitbulls fighting. I learned that the hard way: you're in there just trying to train, trying to learn, trying to develop your thing, and then all of a sudden, there's this 190-pound guy who just cannot control himself; he does not realise that every day, he bench-presses 300 pounds, and I only weigh 150, dude. So when you push on me, you've got to remember that. They don't remember that."

He even apologised for one unforgettable moment during a Tool gig when a fan jumped on the stage and ran to him with his arms outstretched, presumably offering Keenan an embrace. The singer watched him for a second, still singing into his microphone, then grabbed the intruder, flipped him over his shoulder onto the floor of the stage and sat on him for a while, continuing to sing. Search for it on YouTube, it's amazing. Keenan laughed in some embarrassment when reminded of the incident, saying: "Yeah, that was a gig where some dickhead got onstage – and it had already been one of those nights where, you know, a lot of things went wrong, and people were testing my patience, and then some kid got on my stage. Sorry!

"Let's face it," he said, "we're entertainers; we're not philosophers in any way – we're just basically clowns. That's what we are. So you dress up like a clown, and it makes it easier to be a clown. It allows you to express yourself freely, to step out of your own body and just have fun with the character. Hopefully, somebody gets something out of it. I know I get something out of it. I have fun… you either get it or you don't. If you read up, and you're a person who has enough of a knowledge base and a frame of reference, then you're probably going to get some of [my] jokes. In the big picture, it doesn't really matter; there's plenty of jokes and humour out there for other people. My big thing is, for Christmas, I always buy people subscriptions to *The Onion* – that's my big present every year. And for the most part, my friends get it. But I love having that newspaper sitting out in places where somebody picks it up and doesn't know what it is, and just starts to get fucking pissed off: 'How can they say this?' In a similar way… *The Phil Hendrie Show* [is] the most entertaining two hours of driving you'll ever have, just listening to people get worked up: 'You can't say Thomas Jefferson was a rapist! You can't teach that in school!' 'Yes, I have to teach the kids; it's the truth…' People just freaking the fuck out!"

He signed off, saying that those who are prepared to listen will understand and those who are not, will not – the essence, if you like, of the 'think for yourself' message that Tool had been propagating (for people who were able and willing to see beyond the superficial *Sturm und Drang*) for years. "[Puscifer] is my own little catch-all bin of dumb ideas that that don't fit with the band projects," he said. "I can cut loose, make my political statements, make my sacrilegious jokes and just have fun with it. Just make fun, retarded merch. I've always been a fan of Gucci, and all the retarded stuff that they sell in their store. You know, frisbees and nunchakus and dog tags. It's so retarded. I have to buy it, just to support the lie. It's such a house of cards, and such an emperor's new clothes kind of thing… Puscifer is going to be small batches of stuff. If we get complaints, it'll be like 'Oh, you don't like [it]? OK, we won't sell that one any more'. And I'll just wait until you go away. Then I'll sell a different one. Once again, I'm not looking to take any of this global – I'm already making a living in other areas. I'm just looking to just have fun and to sell enough of it to support the project. So it'll just be my sense of humour. People that get it will buy it, and the ones that don't aren't invited."

Danny Carey, as much a driving force behind Tool as Maynard, and more vocally forward than Jones or Chancellor, draws a line under the band, emphasising that they will always do what they do best despite outside pressure to change. "I've always liked bands who sound like bands," he said. "I just don't think bands can have a longevity when there's one kingpin or one driver telling everyone what to do… There's always that thing where it's not quite as multifaceted or it doesn't have as many connections to it, because you can mainly hear Mr Dictator, whoever he is, and you don't get that crossover. You don't hear all the sacrifices between different personalities being made that can take it to a higher level. When we do our rehearsals and we have an idea for a song, it's devastating sometimes when you see it being drawn and quartered to end up so far away from where you'd envisioned it. It's just thrown to the wind sometimes, but just by our experience we've learnt that the sacrifices we make always seem to pay off, and the song seems to grow and get bigger than you ever expected. The band is like any other relationship I suppose, and with the sacrifices there is a payoff; having stayed together this long, there is a trust that has developed over the years."

At last, it should be noted, Tool had chosen to expose themselves a little more to the public – thanks to the portraits of the band within the artwork of *10,000 Days*. "We thought it would be neat to be a bit more revealing this time," explained Carey, "as we felt as though we'd got to the point where the music was understood as itself. We had never wanted to be in a position where we were selling ourselves through our artwork, more than the music… we all set up our own photographs and we had the chance to take them in whichever direction we wanted, and to have fun with them. Some of my things are Buddhist emblems and from the occult, [because] I've always been interested in that area and I collect books on it. It was my way of expressing my head-space… we wanted to treat the images like that and for them to have a timeless feel, as though they were really 100 years old or more. Adam became really fascinated with stereoscopic photography. He's even joined a club here in California where they meet once a month. He took a couple of those cameras out with him when we were on the Lateralus tour and became more and more engrossed, so when the time came to do the artwork, he was very happy to do the art direction."

You may be wondering if Tool has a grand plan that will take them to a specific goal. Well, as Carey says: "There's never really any focus or plan other than exposing ourselves to the chemistry where we all four are. After [a] record's done, it does tend to take on quite a character, and we try to embellish the vibe and feelings [which] get brought out as we work through the whole process on stage, including the lighting, the projections and everything to bring out the dramatics… We never really have any preconceived ideas."

Tool's grand plan is already in place: as a vehicle for expressing the concept of independence to those who will listen, there is no better musical force. And yet the band themselves are, as always, firmly attached to reality. "I don't think we're writing anything that's timeless," laughed Keenan. "In the big picture, I think that in ten years nobody is gonna care. Twenty years, definitely not. Even if 15 million people bought our record, and you gathered them together and tried to see them from the Moon… It's nothing!"

The last words come from Adam Jones, who first formed Tool and invited the others to join him in this crazy, essential venture. "Our music has to inspire us and make us think – and it has to inspire everyone who hears it. It must make them think too. If it doesn't do that, then what was the point of making it in the first place?"

Discographies

TOOL

Albums	Released	Label
Undertow	1993	Zoo
Ænima	1996	Zoo
Salival	2000	Tool Dissectional
Lateralus	2001	Tool Dissectional
10,000 Days	2006	Tool Dissectional

EP		
Opiate	1992	Zoo

Singles		
Sober	1993	Zoo
Prison Sex	1994	Zoo
Stinkfist	1996	Zoo
H	1996	Zoo
Ænema	1996	Zoo
Forty Six & 2	1996	Zoo
Schism	2001	Tool Dissectional
Parabola	2002	Tool Dissectional
Lateralus	2002	Tool Dissectional
Vicarious	2006	Tool Dissectional
The Pot	2006	Tool Dissectional
Jambi	2007	Tool Dissectional

A PERFECT CIRCLE

Albums	Date	Label
Mer De Noms	2000	Virgin
Thirteenth Step	2003	Virgin
Emotive	2004	Virgin

Singles		
Judith	2000	Virgin
3 Libras	2000	Virgin
The Hollow	2001	Virgin
Weak And Powerless	2003	Virgin
The Outsider	2003	Virgin
Blue	2004	Virgin
Imagine	2004	Virgin
Passive	2005	Virgin

DVDs		
aMotion	2006	Virgin

PUSCIFER

Albums	Date	Label
V Is For Vagina	2007	Puscifer Entertainment
V Is For Viagra	2008	Puscifer Entertainment
D is For Dubby	2008	Puscifer Entertainment

EP		
Don't Shoot The Messenger	2007	Puscifer Entertainment

Singles		
Cuntry Boner	2007	Puscifer Entertainment
Queen B	2008	Puscifer Entertainment
DoZo	2008	Puscifer Entertainment

Sources

(1993) Metal CD, Musiqueplus, Rip; (1994) Axcess, San Francisco Chronicle, Guitar World, M.E.A.T., Metal Hammer, Hit Parader, Raygun, The Music Paper, Hot Metal, BAM, Winnipeg Sun; (1995) Faces, Time Off, Chart; (1996) Eye, JJJ Radio, Kerrang, NY Rock, Rip, San Bernardino County Sun, Strobe, University Reporter, Access; (1997) Austin Chronicle, Bass Player, Circus, Defacto, Hit Parader, Juice, LA Times, Livewire, Rage, Terrorizer, Time Off; (1998) Metal Edge, Alternative Press; (1999) MTV; (2000) Billboard, Guitar One, NY Rock, Tape Op, Revolver, Wall Of Sound; (2001) Aggro Active, Australian Musician, Bass Player, Blunt, Buzz, CD Now, Circus, Classic Rock, Drum Media, Esky, Farmclub.com, Guitar Magazine, Guitar Player, Guitar World, Hit Parader, Ice, Juice, Kerrang, Mean Street, Metal Hammer, Modern Drummer, MTV, MTV Online, Muchmusic Spotlight, News Tribune, Ontarion, Penthouse, Q, Rip It Up, Rock Sound, Rollingstone.com, Sain, San Antonio Express-News, San Diego Union Tribune, Spin, Tearaway, Terrorizer, The Record Warp; (2002) Drum Scene, Guitar One; (2003) Dallas Music Guide; (2004) Knac.com; (2005) Spin; (2006) AOL Music, Guitar World, IGN, Kerrang, Maximum Ink, Mix, The AV Club, Vulture Droppings; (2007) Artistdirect, Launch, Revolver, NWLA News; (2008) Bass Player, Beat, Drowned In Sound, IGN, Live Daily, MTV News, New Times, Suicide Girls. Visit www.toolshed.down.net for a great source of information on Tool and related projects.

Index

246